THE BROWNINGS

By

OSBERT BURDETT

BOSTON · AND · NEW YORK

HOUGHTON MIFFLIN COMPANY

1929

Republished 1971
Scholarly Press, Inc., 22929 Industrial Drive East
St. Clair Shores, Michigan 48080

Library of Congress Catalog Card Number: 78-144919
ISBN 0-403-00882-4

PREFACE

THE aim of this book, as the title is intended to explain, is not to combine studies, biographical and critical, of two poets into one volume, but to tell the story in which each took part, and to consider the writings of both mainly in so far as they contribute to it. There have been numerous lives of both poets, and numerous studies of their separate works, but I have not found a joint study of the pair, as a unity, and such a plan has involved certain modifications of procedure. To tell their story at all, we have to follow each life from its beginning; and to pursue his through the long years of widowerhood which succeeded her death. When we come to their writings, certain difficulties have to be met. The value of her poetry has diminished for us to that part of it which is accepted as her best, a verdict that I have no desire to challenge. On the other hand, her letters have a lively interest still, both as a revelation of personality and for the delightful prose in which they were written. His letters are much less fascinating than his poems, so that we linger over her prose but touch on his lightly. When we come to consider his poetry, another difficulty occurs. His noblest poem was written after her death, and the second half of his life was no less productive than the first. Consequently, the treatment of the later half of his work has had to be drastically foreshortened.

Two reasons may reconcile us to this. A renewed study of his writings confirms the impression that the poetry of Browning is more remarkable for quantity than for development. He multiplied examples, but his manner and his method did not change.   Consequently a general discussion, passing rapidly over the many poems that he composed after Mrs. Browning's death, seems permissible, as it would not be, for example, with a poet whose development was less simple and sure.   The second consideration is this.   No examination of Browning's poetry can be entirely satisfactory which does not have something to say of almost every poem, because almost every poem has a story or an argument on which information, or the clearing up of some difficulty, may be welcome.   Between a general survey and a detailed primer a choice has to be made.   The primers are easily accessible, and to compete with them, beside, would over-weight one half of the subject of this book.   I only wish to guard against the inference that the long poems of the later half of Browning's life should be considered unworthy of attention.   True, we baulk at the immense literature that he bequeathed, but merits in the later work are as conspicuous as the defects, defects our weariness tends to magnify.   It is a question of amount rather than of quality; for in the later volumes beautiful and even famous lyrics abound.   If nothing had survived earlier than *The Ring and the Book*, the culminating poem of his middle period, Browning would still be recognised for the great poet that he was.

The short bibliography at the end of these pages gives a very inadequate idea of my indebtedness to others. From that list I should like to refer to four.   Mrs. Orr's *Life and Letters of Robert Browning* could hardly be bettered from the materials that were available when she wrote it, almost immediately after the poet's death.   With much more than these at his disposal, Edward Dowden produced in *Robert Browning* a combined biographical and critical study that is extraordinarily thorough and comprehensive both as to the facts and to the poems, though naturally Mrs. Browning took a very minor place in it. Mr. Arthur Symons' *Introduction to the Study of Robert Browning* is indispensable, a criticism and a primer in one. Lastly, I should mention an American work with the same title as mine by Lilian Whiting. She had the advantage of personal information from Mr. Barrett Browning, the poet's son, and tells the joint story in detail. Her wild admiration for both poets, however, left next to no room for criticism, and consequently the present volume scarcely trespasses upon her ground except in title. Mrs. Browning has not attracted recent critics, and has written her own life in her letters so delightfully that her biographer has little to do. What is scarcely to be found in the Lives of either poet is the vivid contrast presented by the Barrett and the Browning families. Every glimpse of Mr. Barrett is a precious glimpse of a very queer man, and Mr. Browning, senior, offers the liveliest contrast to him.

There is, in short, a common story rich in contrast to be told, of which either half gives only an inadequate picture. Even in the matter of literary criticism a certain lopsidedness appears. In the lifetime of the Brownings he was called "the husband of the poet." To-day perhaps we are more inclined to think of her as "the wife of Robert Browning," but such an impression is corrected when we consider her letters as well as her verse, and place her prose beside her famous Sonnets. The popularity of dead poets has so little to do with the changing attitudes of literary criticism toward their work that it is hard to tell how far Browning is now alive or dead among our classics, how far he is under a passing cloud of reaction, or how far his genius as a great man of letters has survived the eclipse of his vogue as a teacher with a lesson for his day. In the hope of seeming platitudinous, I can only say that a fresh study of his vast literature has left the conviction that he is one of our greatest men of letters. His opportunities were equal to his powers, and his life has the interest of a rich nature developed unimpeded. Thus he becomes the measure of what a great poet in modern times is capable, of what a man of genius can be whose nature was too healthy to succumb to the eccentric or abnormal. His great qualities were tested not only by the strange circumstances of his marriage, but by the long years, with and without his wife, that lay beyond. In the best of her work, as in her life, she was his complement, but unlike some women of genius she was wholly feminine. The story of a man and a woman, the contrast of a masculine and a feminine poet, combine to give us a little picture of ripe humanity in the Brownings. Human beings are capable of so much and no more, and among the human pairs open to observation Robert and Elizabeth Browning were not far from reaching the limit of their tether. If Ann Hathaway had been a poet, we should still miss such a picture, for two divided halves do not make a whole.

The extracts from *The Browning Love Letters*, *Poems*, etc., are reproduced by kind permission of Mr. John Murray, the owner of the Browning copyrights.

O. B.

CONTENTS

" In the arithmetic of life
The smallest unit is a pair."

THE BROWNINGS

CHAPTER ONE

"A BIRD IN A CAGE"

—E.B.B. ON HERSELF

I

IT was a stroke of malice that several of the notabilities of the nineteenth century should have been the children of slave-owners. The Barrett and the Gladstone families are two examples, and between legal slavery in the West Indian plantations and industrial slavery in Lancashire there was not much to choose. The system, in either of its forms, which these rich men were loath to abandon or to modify, sometimes affected their personal outlook on social and domestic life. Repentance did not come until the children of the slave-owners grew up. One sign of this was " The Cry of the Children " by which Mr. Moulton-Barrett's daughter shamed the public conscience more successfully than the official report from which the poem grew.

It is strange to think that Mr. Barrett should have been the father of this authoress, and that this frail being, whose body seemed hardly more than a transparent lamp, should have owed her preservation and her educational advantages to the Plantations. Her blessings, such as they were, sprang from principles exactly the reverse of all she was or had been taught to know of love and sym-

B

pathy.   The flower is nourished by manure, and mush-rooms are cultivated best on dunghills.   Yet we are never more alive to the contrast than when a being sensitive enough to be a poet is thrown up by such conditions.   How should it be that the flowers of civilization ungratefully revolt against the conditions upon which they have thriven ?   That such a question would have seemed profane to Mr. Barrett, and torment-ing to his daughter, is a measure of the difference between them.

Like his contemporaries, Elizabeth Barrett's father was untroubled by the source of his wealth, but much troubled by emancipation, from which he suffered first in pocket and then in mind.   Possibly his tranquil acceptance of slavery confirmed the obstinate indifference to the claims of others which has made his character a target for attack. We can forgive him for resembling his contemporaries in his attitude to a public controversy in which his own interests were involved.   It is not so easy to be generous over his private behaviour in the family circle.   Not that Edward Barrett Moulton-Barrett was an unaffectionate man.   His wife accepted and his eldest daughter loved him.   All that he gave was given on the assumption that he must not be crossed in any way.   He thought himself, and probably every father, to be the Owner of his children.   He understood the Bible to impose " passive obedience, especially in the matter of the affections," upon them, and he was fond of quoting passages from Scripture in support of this convenient view.   He dwelt with gloomy pleasure upon thoughts of another world.   In his home and outside it, he had the common habit of dividing the world into two classes : those using authority, and those subject to it.   In other words, he had no sense of human fellowship.   As a slave-owner, a rich man, and a parent, he possessed a triple right to domineer, and we can neglect no clue to explain his unbending rigidity. From whatever cause, he was an abject authoritarian. As such, he would probably have made an excellent slave himself.

The accident of fortune had placed Mr. Barrett early in a position of authority. When, therefore, hardly yet a man, he succeeded to his maternal grandfather's estates in Jamaica, he simply added a second and final Barrett to his names, and accepted the divine blessing complacently. He was a man of principles, of sombre and fervid religion, a nonconformist by practice, prepared to suffer for his cherished rights, and to make a duty of exacting them. Parental authority was one of these. Even his children thought that he did suffer for the authority he deemed it impious to yield. It is a pity that we do not know more of him, though his type is not very uncommon, and his point of view survives in many to-day who cannot now maintain their dominance as he did. We all know some people to whom a sign of independent action in their neighbourhood causes positive pain, who believe that their duty in this world is to cultivate an unsleeping instinct for keeping others in their proper place. Independence is rarely valued in children or in dogs, whose helplessness is a perpetual temptation to exact obedience. People are sometimes ashamed of yielding to it, but they are rarely ashamed of suppressing other human beings when they themselves are made that way. These have one thing in common. They are not happy people. Their instinct tyrannises over them as they over their victims. Mr. Barrett was no exception. He is remembered as a domestic monster because his famous daughter has unavoidably dragged him to light, and because the contrast between them is glaring.

Was her customary submissiveness to him the reverse side of his own despotic nature, or did she owe it to her mother, who could " never resist," and, exhausted by child-bearing and by Mr. Barrett, thinned away before the youngest of her eleven children was very old? If the mothers of famous men are usually remarkable, from which parent did Elizabeth Barrett derive? I think she was a mixture of Mrs. Barrett's gentleness and her father's determination. A touch of his wilfulness she had, and it did not fail her when the choice came, at last, between love and continued submission.

A young man already rich, Mr. Barrett had had the prerogative of choosing, and in 1805 he married, when scarcely twenty, a Miss Mary Clarke, who was several years older than himself. She was the daughter of Mr. J. Graham Clarke of Fenham Hall, Newcastle-upon-Tyne. According to Mr. Percy Lubbock, the uncertainty over the date and place of Elizabeth Barrett's birth was at last set at rest " by the discovery of the entry in the parish register." The future poetess was born on March 6, 1806, at Coxhoe Hall, Durham, the home of one of her uncles. Elizabeth, the eldest of the eleven children, was not baptized till two years later. Then she was taken with Edward, her favourite brother, to the font.

The family had been moving about while her new home was being built to the plans of her father. When it was ready, in 1809, the Barretts took possession of Hope End, near Ledbury, in Herefordshire. The estate that her father had recently purchased was on the fringe of the Malvern Hills. " Nearly surrounded by small eminences," Hope End nestled in the woods, and its deer park, shrubs, and adjacent water made up in charm for the absence of a wider view. The original house was too modern for its new owner, and Mr. Barrett pulled it down in order to make room for a semi-Oriental mansion, garnished with minarets and " turkish windows," more suited to the tastes of a wealthy West Indian proprietor.

Like all autocrats, Mr. Barrett had his favourites, and it was Elizabeth whom he singled out for his regard.

She was his eldest child, and was very early to appeal to his parental pride as well. She loved him, for she was very affectionate by nature, and loved the setting of her home. Indeed, her poetry is only less full of memories of her early surroundings than of gratitude, amounting almost to worship, of her father. In this leafy corner of England she lived and grew, and the recollections of its countryside survived the contrast, no less dear to her, of Italian hills, olives, and vineyards, among which the final third of her life was passed. In *Aurora Leigh*, written when she was fifty, she gives to her heroine the same childish background, and this part of that fictitious autobiography is obviously true to her own life. Even in middle age Elizabeth had only to shut her eyes to :

> view the ground's most gentle dimplement
> (As if God's finger touched but did not press
> In making England), such an up and down
> Of verdure,—nothing too much up or down,
> A ripple of land; such little hills, the sky
> Can stoop to tenderly and the wheat-fields climb;
> Such nooks of valleys lined with orchises,
> Fed full of noises by invisible streams;
> And open pastures where you scarcely tell
> White daisies from white dew,—at intervals
> The mythic oaks and elm-trees standing out
> Self-poised upon their prodigy of shade.

The memory never left her, and there are few poets who have put more of their visual memories into words than Elizabeth Barrett Browning. She was an eager, fluent writer. Most of her poems have something of the rush of an impulsive letter. Indeed, her own letters are not unlike prose versions of her verse. Of the feelings and thoughts which filled this ardent spirit, we have a record almost embarrassingly full. She has told practically everything herself; and to read her poems and her correspondence is like listening to the voluble familiar news of a vivacious invalid, poured out with much

fluttering of the hands. She has left us a picture of one
of the inner corners of Hope End, the small room
occupied by herself :

> I had a little chamber in the house,
> As green as any privet-hedge a bird
> Might choose to build in, though the nest itself
> Could show but dead brown sticks and straws ; the walls
> Were green, the carpet was pure green, the straight
> Small bed was curtained greenly, and the folds
> Hung green about the window which let in
> The outdoor world with all its greenery.
> You could not push your head out and escape
> A dash of dawn-dew from the honeysuckle.

There is a hint of studied uniformity here, in this unbroken
scheme of colour, and the occupants were expected to
conform, with the same precision, to the tastes and
requirements of Mr. Barrett. The precocious little girl
at his heels seems sometimes to have felt the need for a
breath of freedom, since we also read, in *Aurora Leigh*,
how she

> Used to get up early, just to sit
> And watch the morning quicken in the grey,
> And hear the silence open like a flower
> Leaf after leaf, and stroke with listless hand
> The woodbine through the window.

Then the temptation would come sometimes

> To slip downstairs through all the sleepy house,
> As mute as any dream there, and escape
> As a soul from the body out of doors,
> Glide through the shrubberies, drop into the lane,
> And wander on the hills an hour or two,
> Then back again before the house should stir.

This was an adventure, because she was a knowing little
girl who sucked in a learned education greedily, and
found most of the wild honey that her imagination loved
in her father's library. On one side of it she was allowed
to browse at will, but there was the shadow of sur-

veillance over all her pleasures, and it is charming to catch a glimpse of her in the early mornings asserting a child's privilege to do sometimes as she liked, alone. Pope's translation of Homer was the first verse to stir her imagination, and books and study must have been the chief occupations of her girlhood. Though she had brothers and sisters to play with and a pony to ride, something was denied to her, and no doubt her excursions into stolen freedom were the most spontaneous moments of her early life. At nine, she tells us, she was already scholar enough to make the Greek gods and heroes the companions of her games; to sacrifice flowers to Minerva, because she was the goddess of Athens; and to cut out of the turf a giant figure of Hector. This last she would lay prone in the garden, and fill out his features with flowers. We can turn to " Hector in the Garden " for part of her description of it :

> And the sun and I together
> Went a-rushing out of doors !
> We our tender spirits drew
> Over hill and dale in view,
> Glimmering hither, glimmering thither,
> In the footsteps of the showers.
>
> In the garden lay supinely
> A huge giant wrought of spade !
> Arms and legs were stretched at length
> In a passive giant strength,—
> The fine meadow turf, cut finely,
> Round them laid and interlaid.
>
> Oh, the birds, the tree, the ruddy
> And white blossoms, sleek with rain !
> Oh, my garden, rich with pansies !
> Oh, my childhood's bright romances !
> All revive, like Hector's body,
> And I see them stir again !

If her pleasures were these, it is not hard to guess how Elizabeth spent her lessons. She would seem never to

have found them dry, were it not for one line, which
declares something " as dull as grammar on an eve of
holiday." Having gained from Pope a zest for classical
subjects, she determined to make herself acquainted
with the original authors, and set to work with almost
feverish energy. In English poetry she soaked herself
in Pope, Byron, and Coleridge, together with the books
on the one side of the library that she was allowed to read.
On the forbidden wall were Gibbon and *Tom Jones*, but
her father forgot that she might be drawn to Paine,
Voltaire, and Hume, which she found upon the other.
There was a sense of strain as well, or she would not
afterwards have written :

> My sympathies drooped towards the ground like an un-
> trained honey-suckle—and but for one in my own house
> (her brother Edward)—but of this I cannot speak. . . .
> Books and dreams were what I lived in—and domestic life
> only seemed to buzz gently round, like the bees about the
> grass.

It was Edward's studies that Ba, as he led her intimates
to follow him in calling her, desired to share; and when
a tutor arrived to coach him for Charterhouse the chance
came. She clung to him in work, as in play, because he
was the only one with whom unfettered companionship
was possible. She worked hard enough at Greek, and
then at Latin as ' an aid ' to Greek, to be able to read, if
not with grammatic nicety, her cherished authors.

II

Such a voracious appetite for reading was naturally
accompanied by a desire to write, and in a letter, written
long afterwards to Robert Browning, she recalled her
abounding endeavours :

> I was precocious too, and used to make rhymes over my
> bread and milk when I was nearly a baby. . . . Only really it

was mere echo-verse, that of mine, and had nothing of mark or indication, such as I do not doubt yours had. I used to write of virtue with a large V, and Oh Muse with a harp, and things of that sort. At nine years old I wrote what I called ' an epic '—and at ten, various tragedies, French and English, which we used to act in the nursery. There was a French ' hexameter ' tragedy on the subject of Regulus. . . . And these were my ' maturer works,' you are to understand.

Such eager productivity could not but be observed by her father, and when, at the age of thirteen, Elizabeth brought to him an epic in four cantos on " The Battle of Marathon," the steel spring of his proud emotion was released, and he had fifty copies printed (1820). Here clearly was a little girl of whom he could be proud, and he was further rewarded by a dedication. This is of more import to us now than the poem itself. If her style indeed was not doctored, its imitation of formal prose was precise enough.

To him to whom " I owe the most," and whose admonitions have guided my youthful muse, even from her earliest infancy, to the Father, whose never-failing kindness, whose unwearied affection, I can never repay, I offer these pages as a small testimony of the gratitude of his affectionate child, Elizabeth B. Barrett.

There is a long preface which begins : " That poetry is the first, and most celebrated of all the fine arts, has not been denied in any age, or by any philosopher. . . . It is alone the elevation of the soul, not the form of the body, which constitutes the proud distinction." So the young writer held to the end of her life, warning us thus to expect in her rather the feeling of the poet than the form of the artist. Except in a few sonnets and lyrics, her poetry is like a spray of honey-suckle, drooping and untrained, because it relies almost entirely upon its wayward impulse toward the light. Thus, it is rather the effect of Pope than of the battle of Marathon upon her imagination which the immature verse reveals. We are tempted to say that nothing can be less like poetry or more like Pope. Elizabeth has the mannerisms of the great man to perfection, and probably admired the single alexandrine in her poem, but so little of his mastery that the very likeness of her mimicry becomes a fault. Her own later criticism of the poem was : " Pope's Homer done over again, or rather undone; for, although a curious production for a child, it gives evidence only of an imitative faculty and an ear, and a good deal of reading in a peculiar direction." Yet the poem cannot be dismissed without remark, for it is remarkable that a girl of thirteen should have written it, and surprising that such a young blue-stocking should not have been in the least a pedant or a prig. Indeed, it is a tribute to this poetess that we have almost forgotten that she was a learned woman. Even thus early she is more inclined to fret against her knowledge than to display it. She quotes an alarming list of authorities, because her thoughts are quotations themselves.

All this encouraged her father to give to her a tutor of her own, in the person of H. S. Boyd, the blind scholar, who was almost the Barretts' neighbour in Malvern. As a scholar who was blind, Boyd made a double appeal to her warm heart. She wrote three sonnets about her tutor, and, in the one composed after his death in 1848, she says :

> Three gifts the Dying left me—Aeschylus
>   And Gregory Nazianzen, and a clock,
>   Chiming the gradual hours like a flock
> Of stars whose motion is melodious.
> The books were those I used to read from, thus
>   Assisting my dear teacher's soul to unlock
>   The darkness of his eyes.

III

We must not, however, entirely lose sight of her outdoor pleasures, or of the black pony that she used to ride. He was called Moses, and though, she says, "I dreamt more of Agamemnon" than of him, she was as eager as any spirited child to clamber on his back. Here too she paid a sad penalty for her impatience. "One day," writes Anne Ritchie, "when Elizabeth was about fifteen, the young girl, impatient for her ride, tried to saddle her pony alone, in a field, and fell with the saddle upon her, in some way injuring her spine so seriously that she was for years upon her back." There is some doubt how far this fall precipitated the illness that made her an invalid for many years. She herself, while declaring that she nearly died when she was fifteen, said that "a common cough, striking on an insubstantial frame, began my bodily troubles." A very human glimpse of Elizabeth's grandmother occurs about this time. She would sometimes pay a visit to Hope End, where, according to the same writer, "the old lady did not approve of these readings and writings, and used to say she would rather see Elizabeth's hemming more carefully finished off than hear of all this Greek." As her father encouraged it and her mother was too weak to interfere, perhaps it was this grandmother who suggested some of the traits of the aunt in *Aurora Leigh*.

Books, however, are the customary indulgence of the invalid, and are an occupation less tiring than sewing to one forced to spend much time upon her back. Though the dates are a trifle vague, there is no reason to suppose that her studies with Mr. Boyd were interrupted, and he led her such a dance through the Greek authors of different ages that even she could not have followed him in any short time. In his own fashion he was as wayward as herself, and Greek to him was always a living literature whether in Christian or classical times. He and his pupil scoured the centuries together, and in "The Wine of Cyprus" and in her subsequent review of "The Greek Christian Poets," by Boyd, we meet most of the authors from the Greek dramatists down to Gregory Nazianzen. Even his blindness, no doubt, became a Homeric touch to her. They often studied out of doors, and there is a pleasant picture of these readings in "The Wine of Cyprus." Elizabeth would pause to listen to the sheep-bells; and the voices of the animals, the sound of the trees, the movement of the clouds, would blend themselves with the rhythm of the verses :

> Then, what golden hours were for us !—
>   While we sate together there,
> How the white vests of the chorus
>   Seemed to wave up a live air !
> How the cothurns trod majestic
>   Down the deep iambic lines,
> And the rolling anapaestic
>   Curled like vapour over shrines.
>
> Ah, my gossip ! you were older,
>   And more learned, and a man !—
> Yet that shadow, the enfolder
>   Of your quiet eyelids, ran
> Both our spirits to one level,
>   And I turned from hill and lea
> And the summer-sun's green revel
>   To your eyes that could not see.

The pleasure that she found in her studies is infectious, and any immediate experience she had the power of passing into verse, but it is curious that she gained no tinge of the Greek spirit, that she never shared the Greek passion for perfection of form. Greek literature was never more to her than a romantic pasture from which colour and allusions could be plucked, like flowers. She addressed "The Wine of Cyprus" to Mr. Boyd,

who probably did not complain if she read the Greek
Fathers and the classical writers with equal and undis-
criminating appetite. His " Select Passages from the
Greek Fathers " was blended with the wine that she is
praising here. Two other lines in this poem are worth
notice for a reminder of one greater than themselves,
and this shall be the only comparison that we will make
between the poetry of the Brownings. Is it possible
that her couplet, which he quoted in his works :

> Our Euripides, the human,
> With his droppings of warm tears,

suggested the famous apostrophe of Robert Browning :

> And last—wide stream of tears—Euripides !

He alludes to this poem in the Epilogue to the *Pacchiarotto* volume, and the two quotations happen to be an
admirable example of the difference between feminine
and masculine verse.

To suppose that she confined herself to reading Greek
and Latin, however variously, would be a laughable
mistake. After the poets, the philosophers ! Here
again there was little discrimination, and no pause. Her
appetite for philosophy gave its customary record in
An Essay on Mind and other poems, published as early as
1826. The *Essay* proves, if it needed proving, that she
had swallowed them all, from Plato to Berkeley, at a
draught. In her preface to this ambitious work, the
title of which again suggests Pope by implication, she
makes the dangerous assertion that " ideas arising from
an elevated subject are themselves elevated." In her
previous volume she had declared " elevation of soul "
to be the proud distinction of poetry, and therefore it
followed that a profound subject should be enough to
produce a philosophical poem. Since she had a spark-
ling sense of humour, she might have asked herself

whether the history of the pulpit was not sufficient for
our doubts; but books were her world, and she was still
at the age when the sight of a famous book was an
intellectual surrender. The *Essay on Mind* marks the
next step in her development, the step in which she
wanted to echo not so much the poetic form of others as
their thoughts.

It seemed so easy to that fluent pen of hers: the pen
which was always running ahead, and which she had only
to trust in the manner or matter of her masters. She
had still to learn that the matter of an author is not his
materials but such portion of them as has become
intertissued with himself. Thales, Bacon, Plato, New-
ton, Locke, Boileau, Quintilian; History, Physics,
Metaphysics! These are the proud leaves that flutter
down her verses, and the pen off which they trip is
unconscious that allusion is not understanding, for she
forgot that the only proof we can give of our knowledge
of a subject is to add something of our own. The
elaborate preface does not contain an idea beyond
its quotations, and yet it is disarming because of the
ardent young mind that it reveals. Even the rhetoric
of the concluding sentences, introduced successively by
the phrase ' I wish,' is not in the blue-stocking style.
Elizabeth Barrett writes of the great authors as naturally
and affectionately as another girl might of her dolls.
She may be impulsive, but she is appealing; and it is
easy to imagine the sensitive face framed in its long curls.

The poem itself reproduces in waxen couplets the
leading ideas which she has learned to associate with the
subjects named. The style is equally borrowed and
conventional. We are tempted to ask what a formal
education is worth when it produces no more from an
apt and willing pupil. Did her classical attainments do
more than provide her, even later, with a garden of
make-believe allusion, with a bouquet from which to

weave a daisy-chain of romantic flowers ? From this
necklace of stolen blossoms, her face peeps out, it is true,
in the shorter poems, now appended to the *Essay*.
They appeared originally in company with her translation
of the *Prometheus Bound*, in the volume of 1833. Her
own voice begins to be heard in these shorter pieces,
once more to remind us how warm a place her father and
her brother, Edward, held in her heart.

IV

Her deepest need was for human affection, and she
was of those who need, even for this affection, to look
up and to admire. There was her father to revere, her
brother to work beside, Mr. Boyd to tend and under-
study : all men, and, therefore, senior to herself. For the
rest she lived " in a retirement scarcely broken to me
except by books and my own thoughts; and it is a
beautiful country, and was a retirement happy in many
ways." In many ways ! She felt, one fancies, like a
bird in a pretty cage, or rather, with wings clipped so that
she scarcely knew whether or no it was only her ill-
health which confined her, and placed such rigid, if
mysterious, bounds. There was nothing in her outward
life to correspond with the wayward freedom of her
private reveries. She lacked companionship, the careless
freedom of contrast and change. She noticed this, by
implication, from the formal calls which represented the
polite society of the place. They fretted her, because
society without companionship made the missing element
clear. So little could she bear this social circle that it is
one of the few recollections of Hope End which she
recalls bitterly :

> Do you know what English country life is (she wrote in
> 1845), which the English praise so, and 'moralise upon in a
> thousand similes,' as that one greatest, purest, noblest thing ?

It is to my mind simply and purely abominable, and I would rather live in a street than be forced to live it out,—that English country life; for I don't mean life in the country. The social exigencies—why, nothing *can* be so bad, nothing! That is the way by which Englishmen grow up to top the world in their peculiar line of respectable absurdities.

Men we expect to be roamers, but most of us know a woman or two who can live only abroad, who freeze, not in the English winter, but on the rectory lawn, or the tennis court, or at those garden parties where the visitors are bedded out like flowers for display rather than for human intercourse. Elizabeth was one of these restive ones. She hated the chill formality of it all.

In October 1828 Mrs. Barrett died, in her forty-ninth year, and in one of her daughter's letters we have a brief but vivid glimpse of this anxious, overborne woman :

Scarcely was I a woman when I lost my mother (Elizabeth wrote in 1846); dearest as she was, and very tender, and of a nature harrowed up into some furrows by the pressure of some circumstances : for we lost more in her than she lost in life, my dear, dearest mother. A sweet gentle nature, which the thunder a little turned from its sweetness—as when it turns milk. One of those women who can never resist; but in submitting and bowing themselves, make a mark, a plait, within,—a sign of suffering. Too womanly she was—it was her only fault.

Was ' the thunder ' Mr. Barrett, and need anything be added to the phrase, " we lost more in her than she lost in life " ? It is one of those epitaphs that contain the soul of a biography. The final sentence of the passage, " too womanly she was—it was her only fault," may be applied to the poetess also. The verse of Elizabeth was too womanly to be the verse of a great poet. Her mother's death made her, Mr. Barrett's eldest daughter and favourite child, indispensable to him. He looked to her to take her mother's place in the strange economy of his heart. He needed consolation, for he too had 'lost more' than Mrs. Barrett by their parting, and he bore his losses with the resignation that is not repose. Whether he leant in authority or in need, he leant heavily. He could not live without making claims upon others.

A favourite child who is not indulgent would be a monster, and Elizabeth was hardly yet aware of these claims. Her mother's example of submissiveness had been more revealing than her father's exigence; and now that example was removed. Of course she responded to the human need beside her. Impulse, love, and duty were at one. There was still nothing to modify the sentiment in the lines " To my Father on his Birthday," which she had probably written two years before her mother's death :

> Amidst the days of pleasant mirth,
> That throw their halo round our earth;
> Amidst the tender thoughts that rise
> To call bright tears to happy eyes;
> Amidst the silken words that move
> To syllable the names we love;
> There glides no day of gentle bliss
> More soothing to the heart than this !
>
> For parted Joy, like Echo kind,
> Will leave her dulcet voice behind
> To tell, amidst the magic air,
> How oft she smiled and lingered there.

In the " Verses to my Brother " she celebrates an almost ecstatic affection; and if the heart of a poet, as she declared later in her best-known lyric, " A Musical Instrument," written to the reed of Pan, must be plucked from him, then she was predestined to this fate. The two tragic experiences of her otherwise happy life were bound to the loss of this very brother and father. For the rest, these early lyrics have a certain charm. In one

c

of them she says truly : " Mine is a wayward lay," and adds :

> Unfashioned by the cunning hand of Art,
> But coming from my heart.

That heart has the trick of engaging us, but we like the verses for the sake of their author rather than for themselves. If there is no originality in the song which tells us that :

> Joy, most changeful of all things,
> Flits away on rainbow wings;
> And when they look the gayest, know,
> It is that they are spread to go !

there is the attraction of a pretty piece of Chelsea. The young poetess is in the stage when an aptitude for verse is trying to lyricise morsels of thought, most of which are not her own. She has hardly yet learned, save perchance in such familiar ideas as that just quoted, to think lyrically. Her feelings are sensitive enough, and her feelings run readily into metre. But she is still setting her thoughts to song. Only her affections come to her singing. She broods, as a youthful spectator, on death, on fame, on natural beauty, on the exquisite ' minstrelsy ' of the poets, above all on the heart and its affections, but she is still writing about these objects, not giving to us, through her poetry, the spirit of the objects themselves.

V

With the publication of the *Essay on Mind* in 1826, and with the death of her mother two years later, the dreamy days at Hope End were drawing to a close. She said good-bye to the house in 1832, when Mr. Barrett was forced to part with his minarets through a loss of fortune consequent upon the emancipation of the negroes.

> Of course you know (wrote Elizabeth in 1833) that the late Bill has ruined the West Indians. That is settled. The consternation here is very great. Nevertheless I am glad, and always shall be, that the negroes are—virtually—free.

This letter was written from Sidmouth, whither Mr. Barrett, still rich, but no longer very rich, had carried his family until a new permanent home for them could be found.

> What we shall do ultimately (his daughter confessed) I do not even dream; and if I know Papa, *he* does not. My visions of the future are confined to What I shall write or read next ? and When shall we next go out in the boat ?

Her idea of the future was more than a continuance of these favourite occupations. It was the finding of a vocation. Elizabeth had now determined to become a poet, and to devote her whole life to poetry. Of her vocation she felt no doubt, though she did not exaggerate her powers. Indeed, she was aware of the possibility that they might fail her, and so lead to the shipwreck of her hopes.

It was in this mood that she issued her translation of the *Prometheus Bound* in 1833. Since she condemned it herself afterwards, and even made a fresh translation ten years later, we need not linger on it now. It remains a proof of vitality, if not of the vitality of verse. The Greek and Latin literatures remained to her a romantic pasture from which the classical spirit had disappeared.

She was twenty-eight years old when she left Hope End, and with her maturity her life passes into the shadow. She was saying an unconscious farewell to the country, to fair health, to peace of mind; but to her the future held no promise beyond the promise which poetry insistently held out to her.

The three years at Sidmouth, for their temporary stay prolonged itself, possibly from Mr. Barrett's constitutional difficulty in finding a house precisely to his mind, must have been otherwise happy in Elizabeth's life. She had broken with the past; her present was unsettled; but her precarious health was sufficient to allow her to join her family boating and on donkey-rides, as we learn from the published letters, which begin shortly before her mother's death. It was also, as we have seen, in the year after her arrival at Sidmouth that the volume containing her translation of Aeschylus and a handful of short lyrics appeared.

Now it so happened that, in this same year, 1833, there was also published anonymously a poem called *Pauline*. It attracted such slight attention that even Elizabeth Barrett missed it, but we must note its appearance before returning to her days in Sidmouth and in London, days which, unknown to them, were to bring the translator of Aeschylus and the author of *Pauline* together.

She had fond memories of Sidmouth, and in " A Seaside Meditation," included in this volume of 1833, she is perhaps describing a familiar view from her Sidmouth window :

> Thou shalt behold
> Only the pathless sky, and houseless sward;
> O'er which anon are spied innumerous sails
> Of fisher vessels like the wings o' the hill,
> And white as gulls above them,

in contrast to the " winds, and leaves, and birds " which she had left behind in Herefordshire. Another of these short poems, called " To Victoire, on her Marriage," seems to refer to a visit to France, but, if so, it has otherwise left even a scantier record than the Sidmouth interlude. Elizabeth sends her blessing to Victoire in a wish very characteristic of her own heart :

> May he who calls thy love his own,
> So call thine happiness !

The husband whom she had had the longest opportunity

of observing had not so understood his love for Mrs. Barrett, and the inference that Elizabeth had drawn, perhaps subconsciously, from her parents' one-sided relationship gives weight to these apparently but graceful words. They are a kind of thumbnail sketch of their author, for part of the charm that her friends found in her mobile face was the blend of depth and light in the eyes, of tenderness and vivacity in the expression. These lines can be read playfully, but they can be read also very gravely indeed. Human affection has, sometimes, a voice in her verse which is not quite the voice of pure art because it is warm with her particular tenderness. In making this personal appeal she wins or chills, even at her best, according to the more or less friendly attitude of her reader. For the same reason, at or below her average, she is the more or less exasperating according to the degree in which she arouses the critical spirit. This, as such, she had not the detachment to satisfy. If you do not ask her for pure poetry, she will sometimes give it to you by the accident of finding a very idiom for her limited, impulsive self. As a rule, the form is faulty; but the faults are often the mirror of herself.

The most noteworthy event of her three years at Sidmouth had been the publication of her version of the Aeschylean tragedy, for it was this which bruited the notion that she was a learned woman. Anything else that she wrote in later life was read with the awe that belonged to a young woman who had first come before the world, not only as the authoress of philosophical poems, but also as a Greek scholar. In the public eye she was less adorned with gifts than upholstered with erudition.

VI

While Mr. Barrett was unable to make up his mind upon a suitable home, his family, or rather his sons, for

the daughters were never allowed to come of age, were
growing. He therefore determined to migrate with his
family to London, and, in order to do nothing hastily,
he took a furnished house in Gloucester Place. Writing
soon after their arrival there, in 1835, Elizabeth explains
the situation :

> Papa's object in settling here refers to my brothers. George
> will probably enter as a barrister student at the Inner Temple
> . . . and he will have the advantage of his home by our
> remaining where we are. Another advantage of London is,
> that we shall see here those whom we might see nowhere else.

In what curious circumstances visitors were admitted
to the house of Mr. Barrett we shall shortly learn.
Elizabeth's first impressions of her London home are
worth recalling. She calls it ' a dungeon,' not altogether
in play, and probably but half-conscious where the real
captivity resided. It was the sunlight and the free air
that she missed most at first :

> You see we are in London after all, and poor Sidmouth
> left afar. I am almost inclined to say ' poor us ' instead of
> ' poor Sidmouth.' But I daresay I shall soon be able to see
> in my dungeon, and begin to be amused with the spiders.
> Half of my soul, in the meantime, seems to have stayed behind
> on the sea-shore, which I love more than ever now that I
> cannot walk on it in the body.
>
> London is wrapped up like a mummy, in a yellow mist, so
> closely that I have scarcely had a glimpse of its countenance
> since we came. Well, I am trying to like it all very much,
> and I daresay that in time I may change my taste and my
> senses—and succeed. We are in a house large enough to
> hold us, for four months, at the end of which time, if the
> experiment of our being able to live in London succeed, I
> *believe* that papa's intention is to take an unfurnished house
> and have his furniture from Ledbury.

This first experience of a London fog after the clear
sunlight of Sidmouth produced in *Aurora Leigh* its
smudge of memory :

> I saw
> Fog only, the great tawny weltering fog,
> Involve the passive city, strangle it
> Alive, and draw it off into the void,
> Spires, bridges, streets, and squares, as if a sponge
> Had wiped out London.

She goes on to say :

> Your city poets see such things
> Not despicable.   Mountains of the south,
> When drunk and mad with elemental wines
> They rend the seamless mist and stand up bare,
> Make fewer singers haply.
> (Book III.)

And, doubtless, her own attitude to poetry is also represented by the thoughts that she has put into the head of her young heroine at the opening of Book II :

> Times followed one another.   Came a morn
> I stood upon the brink of twenty years,
> And looked before and after, as I stood
> Woman and artist,—either incomplete,
> Both credulous of completion.   There I held
> The whole creation in my little cup . . .
>
> I felt so young, so strong, so sure of God !
> So glad, I could not choose be very wise !

And of what, precisely, was she too thinking in the exclamation :

> The lion in me felt the keeper's voice ?

She was not imprisoned, but surrounded, and, as usual, there were many excellent family reasons for such care. Meantime, however, she had become a published author. This, the one independent activity that was not denied to her by her health, her queer home, her father, was suggesting vaguely some freer existence : a freedom indeed that should not be confined to lying on a sofa with pad and pencil, materials to be promptly slipped out of sight as soon as anyone opened the door.

She had said that the family would probably " see here those whom we might see nowhere else," but it would be a mistake to suppose that she was hungry for society. Hope End had taught her to be suspicious of it. She shrank from bustle, invariably preferred private conversations, and was only less shy of being visited than of making calls. She wanted intercourse and companionship, and some friends with literary tastes, but she wanted them, apparently, upon impossible conditions. Besides, even were the right people willing to come, and she to receive them, the condition of the household, for which she was not responsible, was peculiar.

The circumstances seemed convenient for visitors : her brothers were at work all day; Elizabeth had her private room; her sisters were occupied with their own pursuits; there was no mother to fuss or to interfere, and Mr. Barrett now mysteriously vanished every day into the City, where he was understood to be husbanding his remaining wealth. If the sons were never permitted to ask a friend to dine at home, doubtless for the greater repose of Mr. Barrett's daughters, the girls were allowed to receive friends, an indulgence to their natural helplessness. The only condition attached was, that no friend of his daughter's must consider himself or herself a friend of Mr. Barrett's. Friends had the entry to the daughter's room, but not, of course, to the house, nor must they expect the father to seem aware of their existence. Young men, we may fear, would generally have embraced this condition with alacrity, for a father of likeable daughters must be enchanting if raw youth prefers his society to his girls'. Evidently, then, whoever might come must also be a person capable of receiving tactfully " an explanation," a few words more embarrassing to give than to receive. This rather limited the field of prospective visitors. Plainly the only folk immediately eligible were kinsmen, who would have heard

something about Mr. Barrett, and could smile at his
regulations without offence, should these be applicable
to blood-relations.

VII

Everything, then, depended on such kinsmen as were
at hand and upon the kind of people that they were.
Suppose that they were all like Mr. Barrett ?

As fortune would have it, a very fine specimen of the
clan was now in London. This was John Kenyon, a
stately and genial gentleman of fifty-one in this year 1835.
In circumstances he was as like, in character as remote
from, Mr. Barrett as a distant cousin could well be.
Kenyon also was a rich West Indian, and his parents
had been sugar-planters on both sides. Born in Jamaica,
he was sent to school at Bristol—where the future
banker, a certain Mr. R. Browning, was a schoolfellow
of his—and, again like Mr. Barrett, Kenyon had lost his
parents at an early age. He too thus became a gentleman
of leisure, with the world for his oyster, almost before
he was grown. From the first he became an amateur
of the arts and sciences, and, after passing through
Charterhouse, and leaving Peterhouse College, Cambridge, without taking a degree, in 1808, he made an
early marriage and settled with his wife in the West of
England. Mr. and Mrs. Kenyon made their home not
far from Nether Stowey, in Somerset, and Kenyon soon
became acquainted with Coleridge and his circle. Almost
at once, therefore, Kenyon's native generosity was
called into play, and among the earliest to benefit by him
were Coleridge's dependants.

Kenyon was a delightful person. He was not old;
he was without ambition; he was generous and he was
rich: he seemed to be without a flaw. A man of
cultivated taste, he had a kind of genius for friendship

and hospitality. He delighted in travel, conversation, the arts; he was a connoisseur of wine and food, and is said to have been one of the first to introduce a brace of canvas-backed ducks to an English table. This was a moment that meant much in his life, and he begged his guests, with easy reverence, " not to talk, but to eat and think " while the duck was being served. His weakness was: timidity before public opinion. He was hesitant. He was undecided. He loved to give; he loved to draw out the best of others; his genial, dignified face inspired the kindest thoughts of caricature. One of his friends compared his mazard to an idealised version of Seymour's representation of Mr. Pickwick. Another, Crabb Robinson, said that he had the " face of a Benedictine monk and the joyous talk of a good fellow." There was nothing but his resources to betray the slave-owner. He had a keen sense of the value of property, to others; but he remained, in spite of some endeavour, an embarrassed favourite of good fortune to the last. Soon becoming a widower, he married again, in 1823, a certain Caroline Curteis, the sister of a wealthy bachelor. When this brother-in-law died in 1849, Kenyon, being again a widower, inherited £100,000. The bulk of this he immediately handed to the remote kinsmen of the Curteis family. His minor gifts were numerous enough for Sisters of Charity to be regularly employed dispensing them, and, when Kenyon himself died, he divided his property between his friends.

His largest bequest was a legacy of £11,000 to the Brownings.

The question of money should not be slurred in the lives of disinterested artists, in which it often plays the part of a secret ogre, but it would be an injustice to John Kenyon to associate him with those who think of generosity in terms of cheques. Any fool can send a cheque, if few, who are fools, do; but it requires a generous man to do the work that Kenyon did in order, for example, to ensure the success of the distracted Southey's trip abroad. A bevy of friends conducted that author with the object of sparing him the smallest trouble. To lend a graceful air to their responsibilities, they transformed themselves into the poet's suite. Kenyon took charge of the tiresome posting arrangements, under the style of Master of the Horse. It is one of the few incidents of his good nature to others beside the Brownings that has survived, but they must have been as regular as his own meals, and as little considered (except imaginatively).

He was also something of an author, incidentally and by the way. We do not now read his heroic couplets on the joint theme of Charity and Zeal, or his volume of occasional verse, though it might yield something to an anthology of the minors, nor do we visit Tivoli with his poem in our hands; but we do well to think of him as a rare specimen of an increasingly rare clan, a patron of the arts—in England, in the nineteenth century! How beautifully inconspicuous in the age of successful philanthropists! Blake had already observed that " generosity had become a trade that men get rich by." Kenyon was spared the ugliness of monumental statuary, but he still lives for us, in honour and affection, as the good friend of many men of letters.

Since he knew everyone, and charmingly insisted that all his friends should meet each other, to know him was to know any man that one cared to see. He was an excellent instance of a man who without children had the real thing, which is fellow-feeling, and there could be no richer contrast than between the ripe humanity of the habitual diner-out and the narrow prison of the English home in Gloucester Place. Possibly disguised as a kinsman, but anyway irresistible in himself, Mr. Kenyon soon crossed the dark portals of number 74. He must

already have heard something of that young authoress
Miss Elizabeth Barrett. The arts were his honey-pot,
and few more stately or more stingless wasps have ever
yielded to their craving.

This " feeder of lions," as he was jokingly called,
though actually never asked to dinner, adopted Elizabeth
from among the Barretts. He must have enjoyed a
chuckle over the one house to which he was admitted
but at which it was impossible for this famous diner-out
to dine. He was Elizabeth's property, and that was
enough. We can picture him, delighted with her, and
nursing two desires : to draw her into the pleasant paths
beside him, and to coax some manuscripts from her into
the pockets of his editor-friends. He was as successful
as he deserved to be, for Elizabeth was shy, easily tired,
easily alarmed, and (by now) a little uncomfortable in the
strange atmosphere of liberty. Socially she had lived in
a hot-house from her birth.

The by-streets of literary London offer a tempting
saunter in any age, and, in the retrospect, there is some
charm in the amateurs that began to throng them so
soon as art and letters were considered respectable
pursuits. In the eighteen-forties there were great,
small, and indeterminate fry; and, with John Kenyon
or Crabb Robinson or Samuel Rogers for centre, we can
beguile ourselves too easily with a genial swarm. Among
them were the explosive R. H. Horne, the forgotten
' tragic writer ' Miss Mitford, Serjeant Talfourd, author
of the Copyright Bill and Charles Lamb's executor,
Miss Martineau, Mr. Chorley, a writer for the *Athenæum*,
Mr. Dilke, its proprietor. These, apart from Wordsworth and Landor, came Miss Barrett's way, though she
preferred to hold most of them at pillar-box length. Her
letters are so accessible, if less well conned than they were,
that we need not quote again her descriptions of Wordsworth and Landor, or the little, if illuminating, excursion

into such society that, with Kenyon's gentle encouragement, she made.   Suffice it to say that she had become,
however innocently, herself a person to meet, that it was
her second nature now to decline invitations, and that,
after two uninterrupted years in town, she was surprising
one friend by saying :

> The truth is that I have almost none at all in this place ; and,
> except our relative, Mr. Kenyon, not one in a literary sense.
> Dear Miss Mitford, one of the very kindest of human beings,
> lies buried in geraniums, thirty miles away, [at Reading]. . . .
> Indeed, dearest Mrs. Martin, it is almost surprising how we
> contrive to be as dull in London as in Devonshire. . . . No
> house yet !   And you will scarce have patience to read that
> papa has seen and likes another house in Devonshire Place,
> and that he *may* take it, and we *may* be settled in it, before the
> year closes.   I myself think of the whole business indifferently.
> My thoughts have turned so long on the subject of houses,
> that the pivot is broken—and now they won't turn any more.
> All that remains is, a sort of consciousness that we should be
> more comfortable in a house with cleaner carpets, and taken
> for rather longer than a week at a time.

Mr. Barrett, who was not easily suited in the matter
of houses, kept himself rigidly aloof.   He seems to have
entertained no one, and was content that his children
should devote their lives to him.   His ideal was that they
should grow old without growing up.   To imagine an
alternative would be treason.   He had become, in the
Greek sense of the word, an idiot in this matter.

Miss Barrett's activities, then, were limited to visits
from Kenyon and from one or two more, such as Miss
Mitford, who penetrated her room and were allowed to
return ; to fairly copious correspondence with friends
known and unknown, such as with Mr. Boyd, now living
at St. John's Wood, with Horne about the verses and
articles that, through Kenyon, she was beginning to
contribute to various periodicals ; and lastly to her own
writing.   It was Kenyon who had introduced Miss
Mitford to the dim chamber, which he brightened with

gifts of primroses and flowers; and it was Miss Mitford
who preserved in her *Recollections of a Literary Life* that
familiar pen-picture of the " slight, delicate figure, with
a shower of dark curls falling on either side of a most
expressive face, large tender eyes, richly fringed by dark
eyelashes, a smile like a sunbeam, and such a look of
youthfulness that she scarcely seemed ' out.' "   It was
Miss Mitford too who called Elizabeth's letters " just
what letters ought to be—her own talk put upon
paper."

This correspondence was much concerned with the
criticisms of obscurity that her friends found in Elizabeth's
published poems, and of such assonantal rhymes as
" islands " with " silence " (which, surely, is innocent
enough).   Many were unhappy, and there were certainly
graver defects.   These criticisms are recalled, however,
because she met them very naturally, with the real
detachment that is rare.   As Percy Lubbock has con-
cisely put it, " To answer criticisms naturally, without
embarrassment, without nervous effusion, is one of the
last graces given to an inexperienced writer. . . . She
can speak of her writing as simply as she might have
spoken of her needlework, if she had had any. . . . Not
many enthusiastic writers have avoided both these
maladies of inexperience as did Miss Barrett.   It is
agreeable to notice that Robert Browning was another."

Tied to the house, as the family was to London, for
Mr. Barrett during the summer would only tantalise
them with talk of stirring, the excitements were provided by her brothers.   With a rashness that is strange
in this home of resignation, they would sometimes go
abroad—abroad !   This was a sign of natural independence as awful as an unpredicted eclipse.   The family
quaked at things like these.   Papa did not approve, and
yet they happened.   It was as if a law of nature had
been broken.   That Elizabeth was growing weaker,

apparently shrivelling away under his eyes, was beginning to be noticed. It was very sad, no doubt, but it was not unbecoming. Her mother had withered away too. In an atmosphere of care, this almost seemed to be the destined end of gentlewomen. Fortunately, it did not interfere with an important step on which Mr. Barrett had now decided.

He had found at last a house to suit him, and the family was told to move to 50 Wimpole Street without delay. They further learned that it was to be their permanent home, and that they were once more to have their own belongings about them. The illusion of personal possession was to be theirs again. Mr. Barrett's decision, as much the mainspring of their lives as the twitch of hand that jerks marionettes into activity, was the event of this year, 1838. It placed Elizabeth's mysterious decline in the perspective of a detail, and makes hardly worth mentioning that she published a new volume, *The Seraphim*, during the same year. In truth, while she remained under her father's roof, his figure, character, and influence were immediately more important to her than any act of her own, though, being what she was, she was shaping the unimagined future. It is easy now to forget how this move to Wimpole Street then dwarfed every other event. Her death would have seemed an incident beside it. There could be no change in the lives of these grown children. As for prisoners, their greatest change was to be moved to a different cell. Elizabeth's room was becoming a sick-room, and it was from her dungeon, as she called it with playful pathos, that these new poems had sprung.

VIII

This volume of 1838, besides possessing several minor points of interest, is the first collection of Elizabeth's

poems that can be called properly her own. The faculty
that she had exercised by imitation, by translation, by
running her reading of varied poets and thinkers into
verse, issues here with direct utterance. She had always
been sincere; indeed, nothing is more sincere in intention
than the imitativeness of a young writer; but now she
had a better ground for the statement in her preface:
" while my poems are full of faults . . . they have my
heart and life in them: they are not empty shells." It
is the quality of that heart and life, rather than the
interests on which it had fed, which the new collection
reveals. She had romanticised Greek themes and
philosophy in her previous attempts. She now tries to
invent a romantic subject to suit her tendency, but still
with an eye upon the classics. She justifies the choice
of subject in *The Seraphim* with these words:

> I thought that, had Aeschylus lived after the incarnation and
> crucifixion of our Lord Jesus Christ, he might have turned,
> if not in moral and intellectual yet in poetic faith, from the
> solitude of the Caucasus to the deeper desertness of that
> crowded Jerusalem where none had any pity;

—from the Titan's " I can revenge " to the Victim's " I
can forgive." She thus attempts to portray the feelings
of two Seraphim upon Calvary. It is, manifestly, an
impossible theme, and one of the signs of a limited gift
is to conceive impossible subjects. Perhaps by an
instinctive sense of weakness, a diffident imagination will
pursue exalted subjects under the delusion that stolen
strength, instead of actual weakness, is thence to be won.
Miss Barrett had a facile imagination, a diffusive, not a
concentrative, mind. It was natural to her to be beguiled
by abstract themes. It is difficult to discern any virtue
that she had gained from her wide reading, except the
relief of satisfying her appetite for books. The philosophy that she had read left no impression, Greek
literature no impression. Such observations of life and

reflections upon them as are remarkable in her work owe everything to eyes and heart, nothing to study. It was her heart, not her books, that encouraged her to think.

She needed concentration, and her problem was to find an experience that should force both heart and mind into activity. As a rule, she is at her best in her poems of the affections, yet she is not good, as we should expect her to be, in the verses upon her dog, Flush, a companion so close that he preferred her bedroom even to a walk, and to whom she was devoted. There was a radical weakness, an incurable facility, in her imagination, from which only love was to enable her to escape in the future. She had no sense of narrative, not much of construction, but the drive of her facility tempted her, when she ceased to be abstract, with ballads, stories, and an epic at last. The lyric was her real field, and here she wrote unevenly. It was in the strict form of the sonnet that she wrote best. To this she had not come in the poems collected in the volume of 1838.

We must not make the old error of asking a poet for the virtue that he lacks, of decrying the rambler because it is not a standard rose. We must realise that her imagination belonged to the order of climbing plants, watch the tendrils feeling for their attachments, look for a certain disorder that, when not extravagant, is indeed part of their proper charm. To cling is another, and when her verses cloy it is often because she conveys the human emotion without making poetry of it. In this conveyance she hardly ever fails, and the moment when we compare her with worse instead of with better writers, her degree of talent becomes more clear. There was a level of feeling and insight, but not of faculty, which was naturally hers. Again, unlike the typical minor poet, she could also write to order. Several of the poems in this volume were so written: the two upon Queen

D

Victoria's accession, which appeared punctually in the *Athenæum*, " The Dream " and " The Romaunt of the Page," to fit illustrations in *Finden's Tableaux*, which Miss Mitford was editing, for example. The qualities of human feeling, facility, professional readiness, to which disorder bordering upon melodrama in her ballads and narrative verses must be added, explain her growing popularity. Not till Italy had cured her of insularity did she conflict with her public; even the later " Cry of the Children " gave words to a protest already aroused. If time is inevitably more critical than most of her contemporaries, it still regards " Cowper's Grave," " The Deserted Garden," " The Lost Bower," " The House of Clouds." " Lady Geraldine's Courtship " contains a direct allusion to Robert Browning, whose " Bells and Pomegranates " had won Miss Barrett's praise on its appearance in 1841, and we may include it here because her miscellaneous poems between 1838 and 1850 can be considered most conveniently together.

It might sound harsh to say that almost all her verses are " psalms of life " in the manner of Longfellow, though with a lighter touch than he could generally attain. She did not realise, however, that the art consisted in the grace, not in the psalmody, for, like most of her contemporaries, she confused poetry too much with moral ideas. The ideal life of that day seems to have been passed upon a rectory lawn, with a wistful sense that much in the world falls short of this ideal standard. None of her poems, not even the beautiful " A Musical Instrument," is complete without its moral, and there is something, even in her Christianity, which suggests that she is nursing the emotions. More or less, we feel this sentiment, this softness of the mind, in the poets of that day, Poe excepted. The energy that they put into their blameless ideas he spent upon his art. He is a poet or nothing.   Judged by any intellectual test, they are mostly moralists in verse.

Indeed, is it not evidence of some dis-ease to poetise ' about ' beliefs ?   In proportion as they are profound, are beliefs not unintrusive ?   From the intellectual twilight of her time Miss Barrett was not free, but the best of her nocturnes have the spell of twilight.   They affect us as evensong in a candle-lit country church. The feelings overbrim, but is it with a wholesome benediction ?

" The House of Clouds " was one of the poems that appealed to Poe;   and perhaps the difference is that he enjoyed blowing bubbles, whereas she wished to live in them :

> I would build a cloudy House
>   For my thoughts to live in,
> When for earth too fancy-loose,
>   And too low for heaven. . . .
>
> Build the entrance high and proud,
>   Darkening and then brightening,
> Of a riven thunder-cloud,
>   Veinèd by the lightning :
>
> Use one with an iris-stain
>   For the door within,
> Turning to a sound like rain
>   As I enter in.

The mood throughout is diffident, and her cloudy house has none of the glad confidence for its builder that Poe had in creating his nebulous but magnificent " city in the sea."   His own poetry is finely untroubled by the trouble that it describes.   Hers, whatever its subject, remains wistful.   Being in the air of her day, this was an unconscious pleasure to her readers, and sweetened for them the facile accomplishment of her verse: as in

" The Lost Bower," where she lingers over the description with a love of detail not unlike Poe's in the poem named above :

> Rose-trees either side the door were
> Growing lithe and growing tall,
> Each one set a summer warder
> For the keeping of the hall,—
> With a red rose and a white rose, leaning, nodding at the wall.

Perhaps the best epithet to describe the charm, accomplishment, delicacy of feeling, and unaustere art is feminine. " The Poet's Vow," to separate himself entirely from his kind, is another extravagant subject, and " Lady Geraldine's Courtship " is not the better for reminding us of " Locksley Hall." The " poor poet " who loves Lady Geraldine is hardly more convincing than the Lord of Burleigh in the converse plight of Tennyson's poem of that name. It is curious that, while the beggar maid and the king, Cinderella and the prince, are the oldest of romantic subjects, the Victorian versions of them somehow contrive to reduce the romance to the level of social blunders. They make us more conscious of the class-distinctions of the lovers than of the love. With an uneasy feeling that the subject really praised in these poems is gentility, we gladly turn the page. There is the graceful " Catarina to Camoens," though the same line at the close of each of its nineteen verses becomes rather a strain. " The Dead Pan " exults (oddly, for a scholar) in the eclipse of the Greek Muses, and here many of the rhymes that shocked her contemporaries are to be found; " A Man's Requirements " may be contrasted with Robert Browning's " A Woman's Last Word "; and in the following lines, the opening of " The Soul's Travelling," Miss Barrett renders the poetry of religious feeling, not, as often, some religious sentiment put into verse :

I dwell amid the city ever.
The great humanity which beats
Its life along the stony streets,
Like a strong and unsunned river
In a self-made course,
I sit and hearken while it rolls.
Very sad and very hoarse,
Certes, is the flow of souls :
Infinitest tendencies
By the finite pressed and pent,
In the finite, turbulent;
How we tremble in surprise,
When sometimes, with an awful sound,
God's great plummet strikes the ground !

For the most part her imagination is the embroidery, not the foundation, of these poems, which can be sweet, tender, Christian at their best. The desire to impress some lesson in otherworldliness, however, will sometimes seize upon a theme beyond the reach of her gifts, beyond all poetry indeed except a tragedy in which the ordinary bounds of human feeling have been broken by inhuman grief. " Isobel's Child," for example, tries to convince our imaginations that the mother of an infant would pray for its death were the child miraculously endowed with speech to remind her that earth compares sadly with Paradise. One of her best passages, however, shows that her imagination could create, not human subjects indeed, but pictures of wild life and nature. It comes from " A Drama of Exile," which describes the first experience of Adam and Eve after the Fall, and is Lucifer's recollection of the curse :

Dost thou remember, Adam, when the curse
Took us in Eden ? On a mountain-peak
Half-sheathed in primal woods and glittering
In spasms of awful sunshine at that hour,
A lion couched, part raised upon his paws,
With his calm, massive face turned full on thine,
And his mane listening. When the ended curse
Left silence in the world, right suddenly

> He sprang up rampant and stood straight and stiff,
> As if the new reality of death
> Were dashed against his eyes, and roared so fierce
> (Such thick carnivorous passion in his throat
> Tearing a passage through the wrath and fear)
> And roared so wild, and smote from all the hills
> Such fast, keen echoes crumbling down the vales
> Precipitately,—that the forest beasts,
> One after one, did mutter a response
> Of savage and of sorrowful complaint
> Which trailed along the gorges.   Then, at once,
> He fell back, and rolled crashing from the height
> Into the dusk of pines.

There is more vigour of imagination here than she was wont to command, and we must remember that it was not published till 1844, six years after the removal of the family from Gloucester Place to Wimpole Street.

IX

In the summer of that year, 1838, her health seemed definitely to fail, and she has left an alarming picture of her condition :

> One lung is very slightly affected, but the nervous system absolutely shattered, as the state of the pulse proves.   I am in the habit of taking forty drops of laudanum a day, and cannot do with less, that is the medical man told me that I could not do with less, saying so with his hand on the pulse. The cold weather, they say, acts on the lungs, and produces the weakness indirectly, whereas *the necessary shutting up* acts on the nerves and prevents them from having a chance of recovering their tone.   And thus, without any mortal disease, or any disease of equivalent seriousness, I am thrown out of life, out of the ordinary sphere of its enjoyment, and made a burden to myself and to others.

The words in italics, here added, suggest that her treatment was part of her disease, if not its cause, and the responsibility must rest upon her blameless doctor, and on her father.   She is not the first to have nearly died of family life, and her eventual recovery dates from her escape from home.

All that Mr. Barrett could see at present, however, was that his daughter could not risk another winter in London, so she was dispatched with her brother Edward to Torquay, where she found rooms at the foot of Brecon Terrace. They had a fine view of the bay, and the thought that the " Bellerophon " had lain upon that water led to the writing of " Crowned and Buried." The poem celebrates the return of Napoleon's ashes to Paris, and declares that England should blush for having sent him to St. Helena. For the next eighteen months Miss Barrett was better, if not well. She continued to write, to publish verses in the reviews, to correspond with Horne, Miss Mitford, and her literary circle. She received occasional visits from her family, the most momentous of which was from her father. Their extraordinary relations, deemed satisfactory by them both, are revealed in one of her letters :

> My beloved father has gone away; he was obliged to go two days ago, and took away with him, I fear, almost as saddened spirits as he left with me. The degree of amendment does not, of course, keep up with the haste of his anxieties. It is not that I am not better, but that he loves me too well; *there* was the cause of his grief in going. . . . His tears fell almost as fast as mine did when we parted. . . . Well ! but I do trust that I shall not be ill again in his absence, and that it may not last longer than a fortnight.

Their love was mutual and sincere, but love is conditioned by the nature that feels it. Thus love can never be its own justification. It rouses a nature into action. It does not hallow the appetites aroused. In its name all crimes, as well as all sacrifices, have been committed. It is as ready to devour its objects as to die for them. The word means a dozen different things because no nature is transformed by it. Love is not to be trusted, except to reveal each of us as we really are.   It is not surprising therefore to see Miss Barrett's warm-heartedness glow, and Mr. Barrett's possessive instincts deepen, under the same influence.   His ownership of her was threatened by her ill-health : her sympathy was quickened by his anxiety.

Her condition seemed, indeed, precarious.   In the spring of 1840, in spite of the sea air and sunshine of Torquay, she had not dressed throughout the past winter, but, says Miss Mitford, had been " lifted from her bed to the sofa, and for the last month not even taken out of bed to have it made."   This was written in March, and is so hard to reconcile with her mental activity (she had composed and published a long poem on the Queen's marriage the month before) that we suspect domestic solicitude to have formed part of her feebleness.   She appears to be suffering from the continual disuse of her limbs.   Otherwise, how can we explain her physical power to survive the shock that she now suffered ?

It was July, and her brother Edward had gone for a sail with two young men with whom he had become friendly in the place.   Their boat, the *Belle Sauvage*, was a yacht that had won several prizes for speed in local regattas.   The young men, who were accompanied by a capable pilot, intended to run across the water of the bay, a trip easily within the possibility of a Saturday afternoon.   But twilight came, and they did not return. On Sunday there was still no news, and anxiety became despair when a report arrived that a boat with four men on board had been seen to sink in Babbacombe Bay. It was not till a week had passed that the first of the bodies was recovered.   Edward Barrett's was not found until August 4th, when his father, who had offered a large reward to the searchers, identified the victim, who was found to have been " accidentally drowned."

In the bitterness of her grief, for Edward had been the

closest of her family, Elizabeth reproached herself.   But
for her, she argued, he would never have been at Torquay,
and the ingenious torment that grief invents wove itself
into the sound of the waves below her window.   They
" rang in her ears like the moans of one dying."   Among
her " Last Poems," issued the year after her death, is one
called *De Profundis*.   The last line of each of its verses
records the mood of her return to daily life after this loss :

> The face which, duly as the sun,
> Rose up for me with life begun,
> To mark all bright hours of the day
> With hourly love, is dimmed away,—
> And yet my days go on, go on.
>
> The tongue which, like a stream, could run
> Smooth music from the roughest stone,
> And every morning with ' Good day '
> Make each day good, is hushed away,—
> And yet my days go on, go on.
>
> The heart which, like a staff, was one
> For mine to lean and rest upon,
> The strongest on the longest day
> With steadfast love, is caught away,—
> And yet my days go on, go on.

For months she was prostrated.   Her family feared
for her life, and she for her reason.   If grief could kill,
it would have killed Miss Barrett, but only animals seem
to die of broken hearts occasionally, and so one of the
stings of such sorrow is the recoil of the human imagination from the body's survival of an emotion which the
imagination likes to think supreme.   If we nurse grief,
it is because our grief needs nursing.   If we " make
ourselves ill," it is because sorrow is survived, despite
our tears.   It was a shock for her to discover a reserve
of strength in one whom everyone declared to be hover-
ing on the brink of death, and barely kept alive when
spared the smallest exertion.   Her survival during the

summer must have made her existence a nightmare. It was not till the winter of 1840 was well on its way that she could force herself to re-gather the threads and lose herself in work once more. At the end of March 1841, she wrote to Mrs. Martin :

> My faculties seem to hang heavily now, like flappers when the spring is broken. My spring is broken, and a separate exertion is necessary for the lifting up of each—and then it falls down again. I never felt so before : there is no wonder that I should feel so now. Nevertheless, I don't give up much to the pernicious languor—the tendency to lie down to sleep among the snows of a weary journey—I don't give up much to it. Only I find it sometimes at the root of certain negligencies . . . Perhaps it is hard for you to fancy even how I shrink away from the very thought of seeing a human face, except those immediately belonging to me in love or relationship.

Moreover, she could not escape from the scene of her tragedy, was not thought strong enough to be moved from the hateful sound of the sea. The only exit from her prison was by death, and even that door was locked against her. All that was romantic in her imagination rebelled against this tedious mockery of existence. A winged creature, who could neither fly nor run, her plight was pitiable. Tedium is the modern form of tragedy, because nothing happens, and the consequent blankness does not destroy. To accept the prosaic for the inevitable was the bitter lesson that this romantic was being forced to learn.

Luckily she was wanted by her friends, who were always eager to coax her into discussing, or even sharing, their literary projects. Thus R. H. Horne interested her in an absurd project for writing a lyrical drama, in Greek form, on the birth of the human soul. This, luckily, came to nothing; instead she contributed " Queen Annelida and the false Arcite " to a collection of modernised renderings from Chaucer which her friend was preparing.

To escape from Torquay was her one desire, and her courageous attempt, during the summer of 1841, to resume her work was rewarded with a return of strength so that escape at last seemed to be possible. By the time when the summer had grown dusty, the great day in August came, and she was helped into an invalid's carriage, brought specially from town, before moving by the gentlest of stages to her home in London.

X

If it is rare to die of grief, it is less rare to die of domesticity, and, once the family had Elizabeth upon her sofa in the dim room at Wimpole Street, they assumed that she was their invalid for life. Every disability of hers was taken for granted; she received no encouragement except to rest; she was indirectly reminded every day that she was a spinster, one, the very sound of the word implies it, who must subsist altogether upon her past. When the duke in *Twelfth Night* commends the antique dirge: " Come away, come away, death, and in sad cypress let me be laid," he commends it for being " old and plain," and he adds: " The spinsters and the knitters in the sun do use to chant it." We know a little better now the power of suggestion: how, that is, such an attitude has a way of fulfilling its forebodings. Elizabeth was expected to be resigned. She was now thirty-five, the appropriate age for the uncomplaining; and when a frail person of this age is not testy or selfish, she can become a cherished ornament in a household, to be treasured, to be with due precaution displayed, to be even, with a smile, admired. The most lively face, and companionable head, in the family had been the brother whom she had lost. It is no wonder that Elizabeth's ardent emotions suggested that the lamp of her quiet life had flickered out with him.

She lay on the sofa. She looked at Mr. Kenyon's yellow flowers. When the door opened, it was usually to admit a brother or a sister. She lived, as it were, to listen, and she listened for the postman's knock. The budding instinct of authorship often finds an exquisite apprenticeship in letter-writing. When young people show a precocious passion for books and yet are condemned by acid aunts or heavy uncles for 'producing nothing,' someone should always ask : What about the postman ? It is to immense letters and to replies by return of post that the sprouting literary instinct turns for exercise. Now, though she had become that object of reproach, a maiden lady in her thirties, Elizabeth Barrett remained, in this aspect of her talent, a letter-writing girl to the last. To her shy nature it was more natural to write than to converse. She conversed, by preference, upon paper. It is a vice as insidious, and as pleasant, as tea-drinking : letter after letter, or cup after cup. It is an indulgence that never needs an excuse, for who does not enjoy receiving a friendly letter ? The habit wastes, in fact, a great deal of imaginative energy, and this, no doubt, will explain the preference of correspondencious celebrities for postcards. Mr. Gladstone was famous for them once. Mr. Bernard Shaw is famous for them now. Nor is it only to the good nature of these ready writers that the postcard habit is due. They dare not trust the pen with a larger scrap of paper. Such a pen feels the clear field beneath it with the same thrill as an Arabian stallion feels the turf. But the postcard was not invented in England until 1870, so Miss Barrett had no way of curbing her temulence to a dram of postcard-size. She had now a new excuse for her weakness, for she was becoming a professional author : a being who lives upon the post, which wafts his work away, and brings an unwanted number of letters. The editors were skirmishing for her. She was being found out.

The following picture of her room makes us wonder
if any of her verses, except the sonnets not yet born, can
rival the prose that she dedicated to letter-writing :

> You would certainly never recognize my prison if you were
> to see it. The bed, like a sofa and no bed; the large table
> placed out in the room, towards the wardrobe end of it; the
> sofa rolled where a sofa should be rolled—opposite the
> armchair : the drawers crowned with a coronal of shelves
> fashioned by Sette and Co. (of papered deal and crimson
> merino) to carry my books; the washing table opposite turned
> into a cabinet with another coronal of shelves; and Chaucer's
> and Homer's busts in guard over these two departments of
> English and Greek poetry; three more busts consecrating the
> wardrobe which there was no annihilating; and the window—
> oh, I must take a new paragraph for the window : I am out of
> breath.
>
> In the window is fixed a deep box full of soil, where are
> *springing up* my scarlet runners, nasturtiums, and convolvuluses,
> although they were disturbed a few days ago by the revolu-
> tionary insertion among them of a great ivy root with trailing
> branches so long and wide that the top tendrils are fastened to
> Henrietta's window of the higher storey, while the lower ones
> cover all my panes. It is Mr. Kenyon's gift. He makes the
> like to flourish out of mere flower-pots, and embower his
> balconies and windows, and why shouldn't this flourish with
> me ?

Her father figures in these letters, and every glimpse
of this strange man is welcome. " Well," Elizabeth
tells Mrs. Martin :

> Papa came back from Cornwall just as I came back to my
> own room, and he was as pleased with his quarry as I was to
> have a sight again of his face. During his absence, Henrietta
> had a little polka (which did not bring the house down on its
> knees), and I had a transparent blind put up in my open
> window. There is a castle in the blind, and a castle-gateway,
> and two walks, and several peasants, and groves of trees which
> rise in excellent harmony with the fall of my green damask
> curtains—new, since you saw me last. Papa insults me with
> the analogy of a back window in a confectioner's shop, but is
> obviously moved when the sunshine lights up the castle,
> notwithstanding. . . . Well, and then Mr. Kenyon has given

me a new table, with a rail round it to consecrate it from Flush's paws, and large enough to hold all my varieties of vanities.

Sometimes she will bring the whole family before us, and all was liveliness and content when they were busy doing honour to one of Mr. Barrett's acquisitions :

> Our ' event ' just now is a new purchase of a Holy Family, supposed to be by Andrea del Sarto. It has displaced the Glover over the chimney-piece in the drawing-room, and dear Stormie and Alfred nearly broke their backs in carrying it upstairs for me to see before placing. There is also a new very pretty landscape piece, and you may imagine the local politics of the arrangement and hanging, with their talk and consultation; while *I*, on the storey higher, have my arranging to manage of my pretty new books and my three hyacinths, and . a pot of primroses which dear Mr. Kenyon had the good nature to carry himself through the streets to our door. But all the flowers forswear me, and die either suddenly or gradually as soon as they become aware of the want of fresh air and light in my room.

As readers of Dickens will remember, it was the age of the four-poster, the heavy curtain, the shut window, the night-cap. The *Pickwick Papers* had lately appeared, and the world was full of Twist, Nickleby, and Martin Chuzzlewit. People fled from fresh air as if from the kiss of Judas, and a superstitious dread of " night air " survives to this day. In fifteen years or so from the date of this letter, that is to say in 1859, Florence Nightingale was to scandalise affectionate parents, carefully wrapping their declining offspring in warm rooms, by asking, " What other air can we breathe at night but night air ? The choice is between pure night air from without, and foul night air from within. Most people prefer the latter. An unaccountable choice ! " In the house in Wimpole Street no one, not even Mr. Kenyon, thought of measuring the salubrity of Elizabeth's room by the mortality of the flowers with which he filled it. Dr.

George Boddington had begun to advocate the open air treatment in 1835, and was thought to be a dangerous man in consequence.   Harley Street was too circumspect to welcome an innovation so revolutionary as an open window, and if Elizabeth did not follow her flowers to an early grave it was not the doctor's fault, much as she liked him.   In the same letter she writes of " the exquisite weather.   What a summer in winter ! . . . Nay, yester-day I had the door thrown open for above an hour, and was warm still ! "   The door open, and warm still—it was unbelievable.

Beside the flowers that she received from Mr. Kenyon were presents of wine from Mr. Boyd, the wine of Cyprus mentioned in her verses.   She acknowledges the bottles in an amusing letter to the donor :

> The Cyprus wine in the second vial I certainly *did* receive; and was grateful to you with the whole force of the aroma of it.   And now I will tell you an anecdote.
>
> In the excess of my filial tenderness, I poured out a glass for Papa, and offered it to him with my right hand.
>
> *What is this ?* said he.
>
> *Taste it*, said I as laconically, but with more emphasis. He raised it to his lips; and, after a moment, recoiled, with such a face as sinned against Adam's image, and with a shudder of deep disgust.
>
> Why, he said, what most beastly and nauseous thing is this ?   Oh, he said, what detestable drug is this ?   Oh, oh, he said, I shall never, never get this horrible taste out of my mouth.   I explained with the proper degree of dignity, that it was Greek wine, Cyprus wine, and of very great value . . . the taste reminded one of oranges and orange flower together, to say nothing of the honey of Mount Hymettus.
>
> He took me up with stringent logic, that any wine must be positively beastly, which pretending to be wine, tasted sweet as honey, and that it was beastly on my own showing !   I send you this report as an evidence of a curious opinion.   But drinkers of port wine cannot be expected to judge of nectar—and I hold your Cyprus to be pure nectar.

It is unusual for a connoisseur of wine to agree with

a woman's taste, but Mr. Morton Shand has lately told
us why port is little esteemed in most countries of the
vine, and that our nonconformist climate is the best
excuse for the preference for fortified wines in England.
What was the wine that Elizabeth compared to honey,
but which reminded her father of a nauseous drug?
Elizabeth speaks of its vial, its sweetness, its aroma, and
if we compare this internal evidence with the pages
devoted to the wines of Cyprus in Mr. Shand's book,[1]
probably Mr. Boyd had made her a present of the
Commanderia.   This, we learn, is stored in earthenware
amphoræ, and has an aroma often " compared to the
taste of bitter almonds."   It also has " a peculiarly
astringent after-taste "—the explanation, no doubt,
of the grimace that Mr. Barrett made when he had drunk
it.   The Commanderia, moreover, " is prepared to all
seeming with every manner of spice " and is said to be
" thick as honey and will burn like oil."

With Mr. Boyd she was now in correspondence over
the papers that, with his aid, she was contributing to the
Athenæum upon the Greek Christian Poets during the
spring and summer of 1842.   We may turn aside, for a
moment, to compare the formal prose that she was
writing professionally with her conversational and
delightful written letters.   Occasionally the two styles
impinge upon each other, as must have been noticed a
page or two back when, in the middle of a gay passage,
she suddenly exclaimed : " I must take a new paragraph
for the window."   What have paragraphs to do with
private letters?   As an unlettered American once
remarked upon some point of grammar : " We are all
equal here " !

[1] *A Book of Wine*, by P. Morton Shand. 1926.

XI

Of these two long essays, which formed a series apiece in the *Athenæum*, the first, upon some Greek Christian Poets, is the slighter in interest. Miss Barrett was a sympathetic, responsive, and well-read student, but she was not, formally speaking, a good critic. The moment when she deserts her private correspondence, the charm of her style suffers a change. She becomes self-conscious, formal, a little awkward in her critic's gown, and wears an air of strain which can also be found at times in the essays of other poetesses, for example, occasionally in Mrs. Meynell. She comes out, as we have learnt to know her in her letters, in passing asides, asides which have the grace of a poet and the ease of a conversational letter-writer. When she touches, in her comparisons, the classic writers of Greece, for example, Pindar, she has nothing original to say, and the fragments of translation, in which she introduces us to Gregory Nazianzen and nearly a score of even less familiar names, are of no special interest or merit. She loves these poets, we feel, partly because her cherished Mr. Boyd loves them, partly because she responds to the Christian note in which they abound. She is drawn to these " meek, heroic Christians, and heavenward faces washed serene by tears . . . poetical souls, that are not the souls of poets ! " If we turn our Christian pre-possessions upside down by glancing at them from the Greek point of view, the Christian attitude would have seemed romantic and feminine to such a sculptor as Lysippus, such a poet as Pindar. It is Plato, the least Greek of them all, whom Christians have adopted, because his romantic departure made him a bridge between Athens and Jerusalem. The magnanimity advocated by Aristotle lacks the colour of the charity that crowns the ethics of St. Paul. The pleasure of

E

finding a Christian pasture in the post-classic language of Homer is the secret of Miss Barrett's delight in late Greek writers. This pleasure has little to do with the value of their poetry, and is really more the proof of departure than of kinship with the Greek poets of old. Many of them endeavoured to turn portions of the Bible into hexameters. Miss Barrett was too complete a romantic to apprehend the classical spirit, a spirit which, in the words of a Greek scholar, includes " a wholesome abstention from spirituality." She seems almost to have regarded the difference between the Greek Christian and the Greek pagan poets as one of degree only. The distinction of kind is hardly marked, for she had read her Greek poets with feminine and romantic prepossessions. Her intelligence is manifested rather in her pictures of her favourites, when she confines herself to evoking the quality of a poet whom she loves. This passage upon Gregory is a good example :

> Gregory was not excellent at an artful blowing of the pipes. He spoke grandly, as the wind does, in *gusts ;* and as in a mighty wind, which combines unequal noises, the creaking of trees and rude swinging of doors, as well as the sublime sovereign rush along the valleys, we gather the idea from his eloquence less of music than of power. Not that he is cold as the wind is—the metaphor goes no further : Gregory cannot be cold . . . and gifted peradventure with a keener dagger of sarcasm than should hang in a saint's girdle.

What a characteristic, feminine, touch ! Here are a few lines from her spirited, almost hymnal, version of Gregory's poem called " Soul and Body " :

> Wilt have measureless delights
> Of gold-roofed palaces, and sights
> From pictured or from sculptured art . . .
> Broidered robes to flow about thee ?
> Jewelled fingers ?   Need we doubt thee ?
>   I most, who of all beauty know
>   It must be inward to be so !

The most vivid of these renderings, perhaps because
the subject brings the Colosseum in the time of the
martyrs near, is her version of the poem in which
Amphilochus, Bishop of Iconium, dissuades Seleucus
from the amphitheatre :

> They sit unknowing of these agonies,
> Spectators at a show.   When a man flies
> From a beast's jaw, they groan, as if at least
> They missed the ravenous pleasure, like the beast,
> And sate there vainly.   When, in the next spring,
> The victim is attained, and, uttering
> The deep roar or quick shriek between the fangs,
> Beats on the dust the passion of his pangs,
> All pity dieth in their glaring look—
> They clap to see the blood run like a brook;
> They stare with hungry eyes, which tears should fill,
> And cheer the beasts on with their soul's good will.

It is not fine verse, and the sixth line is weak, but the
spectre of the Colosseum is there, with the faint impress
of the original eye-witness.   Once or twice she mocks
lightly at learned men, and learned women, from which
class she relied upon her quick feeling to keep free.
When she writes :

> It is better and wiser in the sight of the angels of knowledge
> to think out one true thought with a thrush's song and a
> green light for all lexicon,

she makes us think of her, for she had studied and read
and written thus before she fell ill.   It had not been
precisely thinking, but feeling rather, and a feeling that
did not always pause, in Wordsworth's sense, to recollect.
Her thoughts were Christian emotions experienced in
" a green light," just as she looked at Nature, so to speak,
through a stained-glass window.   But when a fine
emotion, inspired by a Pietà, is the theme of Bishop John
of Euchaita, it seems to lose little force in her hands :

What help can we then through our tears survey,
If such as thou a cause for wailing keep ?
What help, what hope, for us, sweet Lady, say ?
' Good man, it doth befit thine heart to lay
More courage next it, having seen me so.
All other hearts find other balm to-day—
The whole world's consolation is my woe ! '

In a few of her translations she indulges her weakness
for false rhymes : ' only as ' with Apollonius; a brace
followed immediately by Choremion with ' esteem on,'
ingenuities which never saved themselves by dominating,
or by disappearing from, her verse. The poet carries
her survey from that Ezekiel, of uncertain date and not
to be confounded with the Hebrew prophet of our
Bibles, to Maximus Margunius in the sixteenth century,
a date which leads her to end upon the name of Shakespeare, whom she calls the successor of Greek poetry.
From these appreciations we discern that the writer is
better equipped to express her responses to poetry than
to discriminate between poetry and verse. She can feel
and can convey her feelings; she is less able to tell us
with convincing reasons what is good poetry and what
poor. In other words she is a sympathetic reader, but
scarcely a critic, a judge.

The second series of papers that she contributed to
the *Athenæum* during the summer of 1842 was inspired
by a forgotten anthology of English poetry. *The Book
of the Poets*, which is the text for her essay, professed to
select from the work of poets beginning with Chaucer
and ending with Beattie. Miss Barrett supplemented
it with a review of Wordsworth's *Poems, including the
Borderers*, a tragedy lately published but written long
before. As in the earlier series, we notice a wide
reading, a retentive memory, sensitive feeling but
unripe judgment. It is in effect a short history of
English poetry, remarkable in her day though neither
in quality nor range to be compared with Mr. T. Earle

Welby's masterly little volume on the same theme.[1] On the whole, however, she is more at ease with the English poets than with the Christians who wrote in late Greek. Her reputation for learning must have been firmly established in the popular mind with these two essays covering, on their special subjects, so many centuries of poetical literature. She welcomes the " book " in " the present days of the millennium of Jeremy Bentham," but finds that, except in its selection of devotional verse, it falls short of Thomas Campbell's *Specimens*, which had appeared in 1819. Langland is sacred to her for having walked on the Malvern hills : " our first holy poet-ground is there." Speaking of Chaucer who " never disciplined his highest thoughts to walk up and down in a paddock—ten paces and a turn," she has an interesting passage on English metre.

> Critics indeed have set up a system based upon the crushed atoms of first principles, maintaining that poor Chaucer wrote by accent only ! . . . It is our ineffaceable impression, in fact, that the whole theory of accent and quantity held in relation to ancient and modern poetry stands upon a fallacy, totters rather than stands. Chaucer wrote by quantity, just as Homer did before him, just as Goethe did after him, just as all poets must. Rules differ, principles are identical. All rhythm presupposes quantity. Organ-pipe or harp, the musician plays by time. Greek or English, Chaucer or Pope, the poet sings by time. What is this accent but a stroke, an emphasis, with a successive pause to make complete the time ? And what is the difference between this accent and quantity but the difference between a harp-note and an organ-note ? otherwise, quantity expressed in different ways ?

A reconciliation so simple may not find favour to-day when the wrangling over the metrical basis of English verse is keener than ever. Since no one knows how ancient Greek and Latin were pronounced, and quantity is easier to infer than accent from the verse of a dead

---

[1] *A Popular History of English Poetry*. By T. Earle Welby.

language, from which in turn our notions of the basis
of metre are derived, Miss Barrett's simple assumption
concerning the nature of rhythm in all languages may not
deserve summary dismissal. To illustrate her point,
take the word violet. The Poet Laureate, who speaks
with authority, assures us that the ' i ' in violet is short:
and pronunciation that it is accented. If this word
occurred in a poem in a dead language, would not the
inference be that the ' i ' was long, and a rule or exception
be quickly invented to cover any difficulty ? In other
words, can anything but quantity be inferred from a dead
language, and, if we are more conscious of accent in a
language still spoken, is it not well to ask whether in
poetic practice quantity is not the principle, as she
asserts ? Her instinct seems to be speaking in this
passage, one of the few in which a statement of critical
principle occurs.

Her verdicts upon individual poets are engaging but
capricious. She declares that Gower has been under-
valued, but herself, for example, undervalues John
Skelton. She has a happy term for the " long silence
from Chaucer and his disciples down to the sixteenth
century," which she calls " the trance of English poetry."
She finds Langland, Lydgate, Stephen Hawes, and the
Chaucer of " The House of Fame " to be the four
allegorical foundations for Spenser's *Faery Queen*, and, in
praise of Spenser, adds: " The highest triumph of
an allegory . . . is the abnegation of itself." Her
imagination supplies a pretty sentence for Lord Surrey :
" There are names which catch the proverbs of praise as
a hedge-thorn catches sheep's wool, by position and
approximation," and she is generous in appreciation of
Sir Thomas Wyatt, though the power that he shared
with Donne (it was a quality of the age) of combining
the metaphysical with the physical, because the only
taboos were political, escapes her. She becomes the

feminine professor in a philosophical passage in which the heavy words objectivity and subjectivity tramp through a long and muddy sentence like boots caked with clay.   It is extraordinary how she could vary from the written speech of conversational prose to these clumsy locutions, and then how her style, recovering its poetic wings, will suddenly open them in butterfly-fashion with a flash of bright imagery.   To her Sidney's poetic injunction, " Look in thine heart, and write," is " *the completest Ars Poetica.*"   It was her one guiding principle, and, if she had not read so much and so hastily, she would have written the better.   Like all who read for the sake of reading, she read too much and thought too little.

In the high tide of the Romantic reaction she is inevitably cold to Dryden and Pope, but her technical criticism of the couplet is worth quoting :

> The new practice endeavoured to identify in all possible cases the rime and what may be called the sentimental emphasis, securing the latter to the tenth rhyming *syllable*, and so dishonouring the emphasis of the sentiment into the base use of the marking of the time.   And not only by this unnatural provision did the emphasis minister to the rime, but the pause did so also.   Away with all pauses, said the reformers, except the legitimate pause at the tenth riming syllable.

This seems to overlook the caesura, essential to the antithesis that she was to criticize later on.   She makes Cowley the bridge between the Elizabethans and the Restoration poets, while she gives to Waller his due in heralding the reformers.

When she comes to Dryden himself, in spite of qualifications which do not condemn his practice so much as his example, she does not convey the sense that Dryden was a great writer, and a great writer of verse.   The romantic in her finds him " disenchanting," is disconcerted by his habit of appealing not only to the heart but to the head, and is unaware that by poetry she means romantic poetry, for the romantic is as strict a convention as any other.   There is as much artifice in the approach, epithets, favourite rhymes, and line-endings of the imitators of Keats and of Shelley as in those of Dryden. The poetry of Miss Barrett herself was a popular kind of romantic poetry.   She had not, in short, a catholic appreciation.   Her wide reading did no more than feed the romantic taste in which she was reared.   She is not aware of Pope's purely lyrical gift.   For her he stands simply as the perfecter of the couplet.   This is the weakness of her essay and her criticism, the good things in which are her occasional flashes of imagery, her sunlit passages of spontaneous writing amid much formal, and sometimes stilted, prose.   Speaking of the circumstances in which Milton wrote *Paradise Lost*, she says : " Which is hardest ? self-renunciation, and the sackcloth and the cave ? or grief-renunciation and the working on, on, under the stripe ?   He did what was hardest."   It is for these little, may we say personal, touches that her essay is most readable to-day : as when she says that Byron's poems " discovered not a heart, but the wound of a heart," and of Prior that he instinctively stretched a " hand to a sweeter order of versification than was current."   Or again that Shenstone had the gift " to utter a pretty thought so simply that the world is forced to remember it."   The Romantic revival, which she calls the " revival of poetry," is traced to Percy's Reliques, and she does not explain that romance, like Gothic, never really died but was always in the background of the eighteenth century.   This conclusion prepares the way for her added essay upon Wordsworth, which is most interesting to us now, apart from a few well-chosen and less familiar quotations, for that sentence toward the end which looks hopefully into the future :

> In the meantime the hopeful and believing will hope—
> trust on; and, better still, the Tennysons and the Brownings,
> and other high-gifted spirits, will work, wait on,

learning from Wordsworth " the cost of this life of a
master in poetry."

XII

The letters of these years enforce the hold that Tennyson and Browning among contemporary poets were
gaining upon Elizabeth's imagination. The following
passage, reminding us of the crowd of writers among
which the two (for most readers) were scarcely distin-
guishable, is worth quoting :

> Tennyson is a great poet, I think, and Browning, the
> author of *Paracelsus*, has to my mind very noble capabilities.
> Do you know Mr. Horne's *Orion*, the poem published for a
> farthing, to the wonder of booksellers and bookbuyers who
> could not understand ' the speculation in its eyes ' ? . . . I
> am very fond of Tennyson. He makes me thrill sometimes
> to the end of my fingers, as only a true great poet can.
> [In your notice of Mr. Browning's *Blot in the 'Scutcheon*]
> there is truth on both sides, but it seems to me hard truth on
> Browning. I do assure you I never saw him in my life—
> do not know him even by correspondence—and yet, whether
> through fellow-feeling for Eleusinian mysteries, or whether
> through the more generous motive of appreciation of his
> powers, I am very sensitive to the thousand and one stripes
> with which the assembly of critics doth expound its vocation
> over him, and the *Athenæum*, for instance, made me quite cross
> and misanthropical last week. The truth is—and the world
> should know the truth—it is easier to find a more faultless
> writer than a poet of equal genius.

This was one of the flashes of criticism at which she
sometimes excelled. The strictures against which she
rebelled forced her to qualify her personal enthusiasm,
and the result was a happy balance. It set her belief in
a light the stronger for the admission wrung from her

by blinder people.   While she was becoming absorbed
by the work of Robert Browning, her ardent nature was
also being carried away by Mesmerism, in which, like
the mystic from whom the word is derived, she and others
of her generation saw less a new fact of physiology than
a door opening into the unseen world.   Among Miss
Barrett's correspondents, Mrs. Martin and Harriet
Martineau were absorbed in mesmeric experiments, and
their supposed connection with occult forces nourished
the almost hysterical interest that Miss Barrett was to
display in spiritualism later on.   Her present state of
mind is condensed in a sentence from one of her
letters : " The agency seems to me like the shaking of the
flood-gates placed by the Creator between the unprepared
soul and the unseen world."   Mrs. Jameson and Miss
Mitford were equally fervent, and in this contagious air
it is perhaps wonderful that Elizabeth kept her head as
well as she did.

The chief domestic excitements of these days were the
periodical disappearances of her spaniel Flush.   He
had been a present from Miss Mitford, and rarely left
his mistress's room.   None the less he was stolen three
times by a set of rascals who were so brazen and fearless
of arrest that they returned him each time at a ransom
more extortionate than before.   He lives in our memory
now neither for his misadventures nor for the very
unequal poem that he inspired, but as the sole witness
of the meetings that she was soon to have with her future
husband.

Between her and the outer world were many doors,
and the very few who were permitted to pass them and to
climb to her lonely room justified their privilege by
discouraging any further admissions.   Even Mr. Horne
still continued to know her only through the pillar-box.
Miss Mitford had the entry, and Mrs. Jameson's per-
sistence was rewarded in the end.   No one was more

surprised than Miss Barrett herself, and she records the event as an act of fortitude : " Mrs. Jameson came again to this door with a note, and overcoming by kindness was let in on Saturday last." These exclusions seem more strange in the retrospect than they did at the time, for, though this visit was the happy beginning of an intimate friendship, Miss Barrett adds : " My heart beat itself almost to pieces for fear of seeing her, as she walked upstairs." Outside the family circle, John Kenyon was the only man whom she received, and, as we have seen, even he had never been asked to dinner. Mr. Barrett allowed no friend of his children to intimacy with the family, and if ever daughters seemed safeguarded from lovers, it was Mr. Barrett's.

His pride of possession, increased by the reputation that Elizabeth was gaining, overlooked however the dangerous curiosity that his daughter's seclusion involved. Her reputation for learning, her repute as a feminine poet, the strange mixture of her brilliance and her invisibility, were converting her into a figure of legend. Though she was only permitted to think of literary friends, the capture of a maiden confined to an enchanted castle is a poetic enterprise likely to convert any admirer into something more. Mr. Barrett had no qualms; any change in his domestic arrangements was inconceivable, yet every fresh writing that his daughter published pushed open a little further the shutters that hid her from the world. Though Mr. Barrett knew it not, it was a critical day when Moxon issued in 1844 a two-volume edition of her poetry. Its immediate success confirmed her reputation, and the circle of her admirers became wider and more enthusiastic than before.

Like almost all immediately successful books, her poetry reflected the taste of her day. It was enthusiastic but serious, romantic yet with an emphasised moral. All her reading and reflection failed to carry her beyond the popular taste, and her gift lay in her facile and ardent expression of it. Those who were moved to confide their private gratitude to her agreed on the quality of her magic. They found in her poetry a living voice, and were drawn toward the personality, tender, warm, engaging, that made the writer seem a personal friend. Her poetry, in truth, gave to her contemporaries very much the same sensation of intimacy that posterity feels in her letters. Now, as then, we glimpse the face behind the words, for the words are like glances from a lively pair of eyes. They are transparent words, words which make us feel that their writer must be a charming person.

The two volumes that had appeared in August 1844 brought to her some very pleasant letters, including, she tells us, one from Carlyle, and another from a professional critic, previously unknown to her. A new curiosity was attaching to the postman now that letters from strangers were proving the poet to be an influence beyond her own constricted circle. One day early in 1845 a letter arrived from Hatcham, Surrey, bearing the postmark January 10th. Warm as were the feelings that her verses aroused in her correspondents, Miss Barrett must have been astonished when she read the following lines from Robert Browning, the poet beyond others to whom she had been drawn :

> I love your verses with all my heart, dear Miss Barrett— and this is no off-hand compliment that I shall write,— whatever else, no prompt matter-of-course recognition of your genius, and there a graceful and natural end of the thing.
> Since the day last week when I first read your poems, I quite laugh to remember how I have been turning and turning again in my mind what I should be able to tell you of their effect upon me, for in the first flush of delight I thought I would this once get out of my habit of purely passive enjoyment, when I do really enjoy, and thoroughly justify my admiration—perhaps even, as a loyal fellow-craftsman should,

try and find fault and do you some little good to be proud of hereafter !—but nothing comes of it all—so into me has it gone, and part of me has it become, this great living poetry of yours, not a flower of which but took root and grew. Oh, how different that is from lying to be dried and pressed flat and prized highly, and put in a book with a proper account at top and bottom, and shut up and put away . . . and the book called a *Flora* besides ! After all, I need not give up all thought of doing that, too, in time; because even now, talking to whoever is worthy, I can give a reason for my faith in one and another excellence, the fresh strange music, the affluent language, the exquisite pathos and true new brave thought; but in this addressing myself to you—your own self, and for the first time, my feeling rises altogether.

I do, as I say, love these books with all my heart—and I love you too. Do you know I was once not very far from seeing— really seeing you ? Mr. Kenyon said to me one morning, " Would you like to see Miss Barrett ? " then he went to announce me,—then he returned . . . you were too unwell, and now it is years ago, and I feel as at some untoward passage in my travels, as if I had been close, so close, to some world's wonder in chapel or crypt, only a screen to push and I might have entered, but there was some slight, so it now seems, slight and just sufficient bar to admission, and the half-opened door shut, and I went home my thousands of miles, and the sight was never to be ?

Well, these Poems were to be, and this true thankful joy and pride with which I felt myself,

Yours ever faithfully,
Robert Browning.

" Such a letter from such a hand ! " were her own words in reply to him.

To appreciate the correspondence that followed, we must see Robert Browning in his own home.

CHAPTER TWO

THE YOUNG BROWNING

I

By a coincidence that associates the Browning and the Barrett families long before the birth of the two poets, the ancestors of both possessed property in the West Indies. Elizabeth is said to have been the first child of the Barretts to have been born in England for a century. The first Robert Browning of whom anything is definitely known was the poet's grandfather. In 1778, at the age of twenty-nine, he married Margaret Tittle, a lady who had been born in the West Indies and inherited some property at St. Kitts. She was therefore technically a Creole, and two attempts have been made to suggest therefore that the Browning family possessed a strain of Asiatic blood. It has been asserted often that the family was Jewish, though the evidence is not adduced, and Dr. Furnival, his ardent admirer, nursed a conviction that Miss Tittle had black blood in her veins. Mrs. Sutherland Orr, discussing the notion in her official biography, states that the chief support of this conjecture was the ivory tint of the poet's complexion in his youth. Perhaps Dr. Furnival preferred his explanation to the Jewish one current in his day. Mrs. Orr admits that the poet was sallow, but asserts that this was due to the condition of his liver. It is not until we come to his own mother that the excuse for alleging a Jewish element in his constitution becomes plausible.

The poet was the third of three Robert Brownings. His grandmother died when the poet's father was seven years old. Five years later his grandfather married again, and thereby gave a stern stepmother to the second Robert Browning. If her husband was hard and energetic, his second wife, who had been a Miss Smith, was so jealous that she made him remove the portrait of her predecessor to a garret, on the ground that he had no need of two wives. This would not have mattered very much if she had not been equally jealous of her stepson, and thereby encouraged the rift that a difference in the tastes of the boy and his father had already threatened. The grandfather was a capable and energetic man who cared for no literature beyond the Bible and *Tom Jones*. These two books seem to have provided his sole reading, for he is said to have returned to them every year of his life. The poet's father, on the other hand, was a great reader with a talent for drawing, and he became more odious in his stepmother's eyes because he had some income from his uncle, and was therefore, if no one interfered with him, free to gratify his own tastes without becoming a burden on his parents. He was anxious to go to the University at his own charge, but she induced his father to forbid him because she declared that they could not afford a similar education for their other sons. Parental despotism thus played its part both in the Browning and the Barrett families.

This was not the first check that the poet's father had received. Before asking to be allowed to go to the University, he had wished to become an artist, but when he brought his first painting to his father, his father refused it so much as a glance. The parents seemed to have triumphed over him when they sent him to St. Kitts as manager of his mother's property, but the sensitive youth found the condition of the slaves upon the estate so detestable that he threw up this well-paid position. On his return, therefore, his father presented the boy with a bill for all the expenses to which he had been put for his child's upbringing. The father had started life as a clerk in the Bank of England and in the course of fifty years had risen to the post of Principal of the Bank Stock Office. Presumably he dictated a similar career to his son, who, in the corner to which he had now been driven, sat in his turn on a high stool in Threadneedle Street. At the age of twenty-two he married Miss Wiedemann, and took a house in Southampton Street, Camberwell, where the third Robert Browning and future poet was born a year later, on May 7, 1812. The second child of this marriage was Sarianna, who was born on January 7, 1814.

Unhappy children often marry early as the most simple way of escape from home, and with the second Robert's marriage we are brought into a healthier and more happy atmosphere. The poet's mother was a lady of mixed blood, for her father was a German ship-owner of Hamburg who had settled in Dundee, and her mother a Scotch woman. The suggestion that Browning was Jewish no doubt seeks to establish itself through the Wiedemanns, and the claim is a common one against all who bear the Browning name. The poet's mother was as unlike his father's stepmother as could be. Carlyle called her " the true type of a Scottish gentlewoman," and like her father, the ship-owner, she was fond of music. Browning inherited this taste, and from her also a sensitiveness of the nerves which underlay his apparently robust physical constitution. His father was healthy, placid, and studious. The poet was robust and excitable. His father was a man of fine clay. The son, cast in the same mould, was quickened by something from his mother.

The poet's father was one of those charming men who are treasured by their friends, but unknown to the world, except when some accident of life happens to connect them with a man of genius. By every sympathy he was fitted to become the father of a poet, and the only effect of the harshness of his own parents seems to have been to encourage his sympathy for his own children. All the gifts of his famous son lurked dimly in the father, even to the rare gift of exceptional readiness at rhyming, and he taught the poet his Latin declensions, and his future grandson the names of the bones, by stringing them together in verse. He had that appetite for reading which can while a whole life away over books, and was so indifferent to discomforts that his temper seems scarcely to have been ruffled. The details of existence bored him, and he left a restaurant where he was well served because the waiter insisted that he must choose his own dishes. He was never ill though he lived to be nearly eighty-five, and he awaited death with the interest of a spectator, asking his son " Is it a fainting, or is it a pang ? " His calm, we are told, so much astonished the doctor that he turned to the old man's daughter and said in a low voice : " Does this gentleman know that he is dying ? " " He knows it," she whispered, and her father overheard. With a smile he answered : " Death is no enemy in my eyes."

Despite the behaviour of his parents, we must not think of Mr. Browning spending a penurious manhood. The Bank of England in those days was not unworthy of a man of leisure. The hours were short, the salaries good, the perquisites many. Any hour of overtime had its appropriate fee. He was placed almost in the dignified position of a Civil Servant, able to gratify his taste for collecting old books and engravings, and to give to his children the humane education that was to himself the best possession in life. He seems to

F

have had also that human quality of the scholar which makes its possessor a born teacher of the young. Not only did he like to have youngsters about him, but he liked to quicken their minds, and indeed had quickly fallen into trouble at St. Kitts for teaching a slave to read. He was possibly the happier for not being a genius, and if he had been allowed to go to Oxford or Cambridge would doubtless have become one of the best Fellows of his college. Fate reserved him for a more domestic part, and it is not easy to imagine a more delightful or appropriate father for Robert Browning.

The poet himself was a lively and mischievous little person who excused himself for putting his mother's lace into the fire by saying that it had made " a pretty blaze." He began to improvise verses almost as soon as he could speak, and was so precocious at his day school that the dame requested his removal. All the mammas declared that he was being " brought on " at the expense of their own children. He kept a childish diary, from which the statement " married two wives this morning " is the only invention that has survived. So far as he was able he turned his father's garden into a miniature Zoo, where efts and frogs were joined by owls, monkeys, hedgehogs, an eagle, " and even a couple of large snakes," nor did he torment the creatures, but wept over any fairy tales in which they came to violent ends. One of his subsequent claims to greatness, a rare claim for a nineteenth-century poet, was his mastery of the grotesque, and the instinct that expressed itself later in this artistic form may perhaps be connected with his boyish love of queer animals. Rossetti, who toyed with the grotesque, had the same affection for curious creatures and was probably drawn to the wombat not only because of its name. Browning had the run of his father's library, and he learned too easily to take much interest in the formal lessons at Mr. Ready's school at Prestham, where he made his fellows act plays that he wrote for their amusement. At home he browsed upon old Bibles, Quarles' *Emblems*, Walpole's *Letters*, and the works of Voltaire, which the catholic taste of his father did not exclude from a house where religion was far from being neglected. There is a pleasant picture of father and son in the section called " Development " from *Asolando* :

> My Father was a scholar and knew Greek.
> When I was five years old, I asked him once,
> " What do you read about ? "   " The siege of Troy."
> " What is a siege and what is Troy ? "   Whereat
> He piled up chairs and tables for a town,
> Set me atop for Priam, called our cat
> —Helen, enticed away from home (he said)
> By wicked Paris, who couched somewhere close
> Under the footstool. . . .
> This taught me who was who and what was what :
> So far I rightly understood the case
> At five years old : a huge delight it proved
> And still proves—thanks to that instructor sage,
> My Father.

The only thing that Robert Browning had to fear was the gouty foot of his grandfather, which intruded into his childhood like a forbidding finger from his father's past. It was in his father's library that he picked up much of the out-of-the-way knowledge that was later to dismay his readers, for Mr. Browning browsed on Faust, Paracelsus, and the byways of mediæval legend. According to William Sharp, Mrs. Browning used to sit alone in the twilight at her piano, and one evening,

> glancing round, she beheld a little white figure distinctly outlined against an oak bookcase, and could just discern two large wistful eyes looking earnestly at her. The next moment the child had sprung into her arms, sobbing passionately at he knew not what, but, as his paroxysm of emotion subsided, whispering over and over, " Play ! Play ! "

Possibly the memory of these evenings, in which the dark must have made his mother seem to the boy to be improvising music, produced *Abt Vogler*, and if William Sharp's anecdote be true, the recollection of that boyish emotion may well be contained in the line :

For earth had attained to heaven, there was no more far or near.

We have other glimpses of the boy sitting in the garden and watching the sun set over St. Paul's, or walking with his father across to the Dulwich Gallery, the charm of which has cast a spell on many men of letters. It was to his mother also that Browning owed the first illumination of his life, for it was she who came home one day with a copy of Shelley's poems. From the moment when he read them he discovered what his own vocation was to be.

He must have already begun to write before this volume fell into his hands, for by the age of twelve he had composed a book of verse modestly called *Incondita*. This failed to find a publisher, in spite of his father's efforts, and it was afterward destroyed. His father preserved for many years a number of these early productions, and of one of them he said, in later days, " Had I not seen it in his own handwriting I never would have believed it to have been the production of a child." A curious fact about these verses was that none had " a single alteration." Some competent friends were interested enough to make copies from the verses in *Incondita*, and one among them was Miss Flower, for whom the young Browning, nine years her junior, cherished a tender friendship. He remembered her as a remarkable and accomplished woman. She was a musician, and her sister was the author of " Nearer, my God, to Thee." Miss Flower seems the only woman to whom Browning was much attached before he made the acquaintance of Elizabeth Barrett, and we have in him a writer of love-lyrics who yet had but one passion, and that late, in his life.

Meantime he was growing at home, for he had the good fortune not to be sent to an English public school, the defect of which is to tolerate no kind of excellence except the athletic's. One can dogmatize only of one's own generation, since, for all their conservatism, nothing will change more quickly than the atmosphere of a school. Twenty-five years ago all the forces of the institution were directed to form one type of boy, a boy who should be abject before public opinion. The natural escape from this machinery of subjection was closed by compulsory games. No doubt some kind of surveillance is convenient for the recreation of boys, but there was no good reason for limiting the games to one, and no good reason why boys, provided that they occupied themselves with something, should not be free to make their choice of many. Such freedom would have broken the subjection at its most oppressive point, but it was really the subjection that was valued. The consequence was that the public school of twenty-five years ago was completely philistine. The virtues that it was supposed to produce really resided in the English toughness and decency which refuse to take cherished institutions too seriously, but the English public school deprived the boys of every poetic and imaginative influence. No art, no sculpture, no beauty, unless the buildings happened to be fine, was allowed to come near them, and any boy who showed an appetite beyond athletics was ridiculed and ostracised. Unless he could escape to the Universities where he was free to follow his own tastes, he was compelled to look back upon a philistine education.[1] In Browning's youth the con-

[1] It is still possible to pass through Marlborough without learning of the existence of William Morris, and his name does not occur in the index of the latest and revised History of the school.

dition was frankly barbarous, and there is no reason to regret that he was not sent to a public school.

At the same time, as he began to feel his own powers and had none about his own age against which to measure them, he chafed a little in this uninterrupted domesticity. The home circle was excellent, but restricted, and, not being called out of himself by a social life more varied, he became awkward and assertive in his teens. Yet his pursuits were far more varied than would have been possible at school. He studied music, singing, dancing. He rode, boxed, fenced. For two years he had a French tutor. In this humane existence, only a dash of society, a taste of travel, was missing; and when, after reading Shelley, he became a vegetarian for two years and even supposed himself to be an Atheist, his admirable parents did not actively interfere. The effect of their conduct was to make this period of his growth one on which he looked back reluctantly; with the wholesome effect of becoming his own judge, not that of his parents. None of his energies was wasted in rebellion, and the life of Browning is a valuable example of a man of genius allowed to unfold without external interference. There are no might-have-beens in his life, unless we regret that he was not born in a richer, more humane, epoch of our civilization. When we come to consider his subsequent attitude to life, what is called the philosophy of his poetry, it will be convenient to recall his youthful apostasy. This is an experience that leaves its mark, and in an imaginative nature preserves the emotions that sprang from the old faith while corroding its foundations.

The social life of a resident university would have been good for him, but his only experience of the kind was attendance at a few lectures in Gower Street. He was soon glad to leave his rooms in order to return home. This shows that he was discontented without knowing the reason, and that it was a fuller life that he needed rather than any change of atmosphere. His sister used to say that " he had outgrown his social surroundings," as any young man must who resides entirely at home. He had friends, however: Alfred Domett, the hero of " Waring," Joseph Arnould, another young barrister, and his cousins, the children of Mrs. Silverthorne, the lady who afterward offered to pay for the publication of *Pauline*. While he was interested in painting, and later in life learned to model from Mr. Story, the arts, besides poetry, for which he showed an aptitude were acting and music. Indeed, those who heard him read poetry, especially passages from *Richard III*, invariably felt his dramatic power. There were vague suggestions of the Bar, and he might have followed his father into the Bank of England, but the wise old gentleman, whose heart had never been in banking, would not hear of such a plan. It seemed a matter of course to his parents that Browning should become a man of letters, and when his own instinct was confirmed by the opinions about him, Browning, with magnificent energy, sat down, read, and mastered Dr. Johnson's great *Dictionary* from beginning to end.

II

The year of his coming of age, 1833, was remarkable for the first of his books and the first of his travels. Before we come to the poetry, let us follow the experiences of the man who wrote, in 1844, the ardent letter that we have already read to Elizabeth Barrett. With the diffidence of youth he had sent *Pauline* into the world anonymously. Not even his parents were told, and only his sister and his aunt, Mrs. Silverthorne, were aware of its authorship. He sent the poem to Mr. W. J. Fox, who praised it generously in the *Monthly*

Repository, which he edited. The poem had been published in the spring, and before the year's end Browning was unexpectedly upon his way to Russia. He had made friends with the Chevalier George de Benckhausen, the Russian Consul-General in London. When the Consul was suddenly recalled upon an urgent mission to St. Petersburg, he showed his regard for the young poet by suggesting that he should accompany him in the nominal capacity of private secretary. They sailed for Rotterdam, and were then carried by relays of six horses at express speed across Europe. Though the graphic letters that he wrote to his sister of these experiences, which were more exciting even than a first trip to the Continent must always be, have perished, there are traces of the journey here and there among the poems. " Ivan Ivanovitch," written late in his life, may have been a feat of imagination, but we know that he traversed the snow " glib as glass and hard as steel," and must have seen the wolves whose padding he rendered in trotting lines of anapæsts. The desolate distances of white over which the pines frown like bushy brows seem more endless, because less natural, than a waste of waters, and the allusion to the Neva in this poem must have recalled to him the annual ceremony of the Tsar drinking the first water on the breaking of the ice. The oldest portrait of Charlemagne, which he saw at Aix, has found, according to Professor Hall Griffin, a faithful description in the fifth book of *Sordello*. Though no record of this journey has survived, we know that Browning enjoyed it, not only for the change and the sights but also for the glimpse he had, during his absence of three months, of society in St. Petersburg. Indeed, on his return he dallied with the idea of becoming himself a diplomat. The attraction must have been strong, for, though the idea was abandoned when his application for a post in Persia was rejected, he recurred to it, and he nursed a similar plan for his own son, who, however, became an artist. Browning returned therefore to writing, and dedicated his next work, *Paracelsus*, to his friend Count de Ripert-Montclar, the private envoy of the Duchesse de Berri, whom he secretly kept in touch with her friends and supporters in France. The Count had suggested the subject of the poem, and, like other people, Browning was finding amusing and varied friends in the ranks of diplomacy.

The publication of *Paracelsus* brought to the author a new and valued friend, John Forster, who gave to the poem an ungrudging welcome in the *Examiner*, a paper then edited by Leigh Hunt. Forster was thus the latest member of a little social circle that, in those less crowded days, included the chief writers of the day.

The Brownings, who, in more senses than one, had outgrown their home in Camberwell, moved about this time to Hatcham, on the Surrey hills. The pleasant, rambling house which they had taken not only allowed ample space for old Mr. Browning's library, a collection numbering now six thousand books, but seemed designed for hospitality, and was not so far from London as to make visitors shy of making the journey. Mrs. Robert Browning had conquered the affections of the crusty but genial Carlyle, and with time even Mr. Browning's stepmother had thawed sufficiently to make her a not unwelcome neighbour in her recent widowhood. One of her own sons, a merry soul known to the poet as Uncle Reuben, through his father's influence had a place in Rothschild's bank, a connection on which the Jewish theory of the family has insisted. This uncle bought a horse, which was lodged in the stable at Hatcham, and was often ridden by the poet. Another uncle, William Shergold Browning, was settled in Paris in the Rothschild's bank there. Besides a few historical novels, and occasional articles for the " Gentleman's Magazine," this uncle was the author of a learned *History of the Huguenots*. He delighted in genealogical history, and is the author of any early claims to rank that the poet's family may have indulged.

The appearance of *Paracelsus* created little impression on the public, but it made Browning known to the Augustans of his day. It was then the custom to meet at dinner in the afternoon, and Browning was introduced to such men as Wordsworth and Landor by Mr. Fox and Serjeant Talfourd, the author of *Ion*. It was indeed Mr. Fox who asked Browning to call one evening when Macready was present, and thus introduced him to the theatrical world.

Macready kept a diary, and two entries shortly before Christmas 1835 recall the actor's impressions of the poet :

> Mr. Robert Browning, the author of *Paracelsus*, came in after dinner (at Fox's); I was very much pleased to meet him. His face is full of intelligence.
>
> Read *Paracelsus*, a work of great daring, starred with poetry of thought, feeling, and diction, but occasionally obscure : the writer can scarcely fail to be a leading spirit of his time.

Ten days later Macready invited Browning to visit him at Elm Place, Elstree, for New Year's Eve. Forster was another of the party, and Macready was even more pleased than before :

> Mr. Browning was very popular with the whole party; his simple and enthusiastic manner engaged attention, and won opinions from all present; he looks and speaks more like a youthful poet than any man I ever saw.

At this time Browning was not only extremely handsome, but also something of a man of fashion in his dress. There is a portrait of him taken in 1835. It shows a wide brow with the hair falling in a broad wave over his left forehead, a dark eye, a delicate, slightly aquiline nose, a short upper lip, a chin firm but delicately moulded, and encased in a bushy beard and whiskers apparently meeting just under the chin. The penetrating eyes are arched by narrow lines of hair, but the life of the face is as clear in the nose and the lips as in the dark eyes above them. It is a profile for a cameo, the distinction of which is appropriately set off by a great cravat and the velvet collar of a cloak hung from his shoulders. He was fond of lemon-coloured gloves, and his slim figure and quick step must have made his entry into any room memorable. He radiated intelligence and vitality, and in an ordinary drawing-room he must have looked as distinguished as a blackbird among a crowd of canaries.

Macready and he naturally discussed the stage, for Macready was painfully aware of the slough from which only a fine dramatist could save the theatre of the 'thirties. The following February (1836) he had begun to hope that he and Browning might revive the drama together:

> He (Browning) said that I had bit him by my performance of *Othello*, and I told him that I hoped I should make the blood come. It would indeed be some recompense for the miseries, the humiliations, the heart-sickening disgusts which I have endured in my profession, if, by its exercise, I had awakened a spirit of poetry whose influence would elevate, ennoble, and adorn our degraded drama.

When, therefore, Talfourd's *Ion* was produced with success by Macready on May 26, 1836, and Browning was one of the guests whom Talfourd had invited to supper on the occasion, the chance came. It was a distinguished company, for Wordsworth and Landor were among the guests. There were good wine, toasts, and speeches. Talfourd proposed the health of " the youngest poet in England," Robert Browning, and the toast was seconded by Wordsworth himself, who had not met the young poet before. When it was over, Browning and Macready left the house together, and Macready said: "Write a play, Browning, and keep me from going to America."

"Shall it be historical and English; what do you say to a drama on Strafford?"

The subject came to his lips, because he had been helping his friend Forster with a Life of Strafford that circumstances had prevented the author from completing at the time agreed. The actor had no quarrel with the theme, and, though Browning was already occupied with the composition of *Sordello*, he started on his tragedy almost at once. Macready had no doubt upon the poet's distinction, and described a note that he received from Browning while the play was being written as "the highest honour" of his life. All seemed well, and we could wish for further details than appear in the published pages of Macready's *Diaries*. It seemed to be a good combination, for Macready was making an honest endeavour to revive the drama. Besides searching the poets, he was persuading contemporary writers, such as Bulwer, Talfourd, and his friends, to provide new plays. Macready wanted novelty to balance the relatively exact texts of Shakespeare that he was resurrecting. During the autumn of 1836 Browning was a welcome visitor to Elstree, and on November 19 the play was nearly finished:

> Browning came with Dow to bring me his tragedy of *Strafford*; the fourth act was incomplete. I requested him to write in the plot of what was deficient. Dow drove me to the Garrick Club, while Browning wrote out the story of the omitted parts. . . . Browning and Dow soon summoned me, and I received the MS., started in a cab to Kilburn, where I found a chaise, *vice* fly, waiting for me. I bought a couple of cigars and smoked to Edgware.

By the following March matters had advanced, and

Macready's admiration for Browning had deepened. On the 18th he wrote:

> Received a note from Forster, appointing Monday for the visit of himself and Browning about *Strafford*. I answered him, assenting to his proposal. Walked out with the children through Aldenham Park and the wood. Read before dinner a few pages of *Paracelsus*, which raises my wonder the more I read it. Sat with the children, narrating stories to them. Looked over two plays which it was not possible to read, hardly as I tried. . . . Read some scenes from *Strafford*, which restore one to the world of sense and feeling once again.

The next day, however, some doubts had begun to insinuate themselves:

> Read *Strafford* in the evening, which I fear is too historical; it is the policy of the man, and its consequences upon him— not the heart, temper, feelings, that work on this policy, which Browning has portrayed—and how admirably.

A glimpse at the nature of the contract occurs on March 30th:

> I went to the theatre soon afterwards and read to Mr. Osbaldiston the play of *Strafford*; he caught at it with avidity, agreed to produce it without delay on his part, and to give the author £12 per night for twenty-five nights, and £10 per night for ten nights beyond. He also promised to offer Mr. Elton an engagement to strengthen the play.

Throughout Macready's diaries he complains regularly of feeble support, and his disgust with his profession seems to have been largely caused by the incompetence of the actors and staff by whom he was surrounded. We have a picture of a man supporting rather than being supported by his associates, and the ignorance of some of them was brought out during the rehearsals, at which Browning had to explain the meaning of the word "impeachment" to the cast. On April 4th, 1837,

Browning called in with alterations, &c.; sat and talked while I dined. A young gentleman came in, who spoke with a foreign accent. . . . I introduced Browning to him as a great tragic poet, and he added his name.

On April 28th, Macready became depressed about the play:

Thought over some scenes of *Strafford* before I rose, and went out very soon to the rehearsal of it. There is no chance in my opinion for the play but in the acting, which by possibility might carry it to the end without disapprobation; but that the curtain can fall without considerable opposition, I cannot venture to anticipate under the most advantageous circumstances. In all the historical plays of Shakespeare, the great poet has only introduced such events as act on the individuals concerned, and of which they are themselves a part; the persons are all in direct relation to each other, and the facts are present to the audience. But in Browning's play, we have a long scene of passion—upon what? A plan destroyed, by whom or for what we know not, and a parliament dissolved, which merely seems to inconvenience Strafford in his arrangements.

Macready seems to have kept these doubts to himself and to have been no cause of discouragement to Browning, for on May Day we read:

Rehearsed *Strafford*. Was gratified with the extreme delight Browning testified at the rehearsal of my part, which he said was to him a full recompense for having written the play, inasmuch as he had seen his utmost hopes of character perfectly embodied. Read *Strafford* in bed, and acted it as well as I could under the nervous sensations that I experienced.

Nothing is published from the diaries concerning the first and four succeeding performances of the play. It seems that Macready was nervous, as usual concerning his colleagues, though he and Miss Helen Faucit pulled it through and played to a full house on the second evening. From one of Miss Flower's letters we learn that " Browning seems a good deal annoyed at the go of things behind the scenes, and declares that he will never write a play again as long as he lives. You have no idea of the ignorance and obstinacy of the whole set, with here and there an exception; think of his having to write out the meaning of the word impeachment, as some of them thought it meant poaching." On the fifth and last performance the actor who played the part of Pym deserted, and its run, less short in those days than such a small number of performances would imply at the present day, came to an abrupt end. On the whole we may say that his first drama met with one of those accidents that have marred the success of many a play, and that the traceable causes of failure do not rest wholly upon the author.

Discontented with the theatre, Browning returned to *Sordello*. He spent the next twelve months upon it, and then, in April 1838, he started upon his first journey to Italy. He sailed for Trieste, and, though ill for the first fortnight, the two poems " How they brought the Good News from Ghent to Aix " and " Home Thoughts from the Sea " were the product of this voyage. He went to Venice, through Treviso and Bassano to " delicious Asolo," to Vicenza, Padua, Venice again. He came home by the north, touching Verona, Trent, Innsbruck, Munich, Salzburg, Frankfort, Mayence, down the Rhine to Cologne, then to Aix, Liège, Antwerp, and across to London. It is interesting to learn what were his own dramatic ambitions. In an undated letter written about the date of this journey's end, Browning declared to Miss Haworth : " I want a subject of the most wild and passionate love, to contrast with the one I mean to have ready in a short time. I have many half-conceptions, floating fancies : give me your notion of a thorough self-devotement, self-forgetting; should it be a woman who loves thus, or a man ? " Thus, no doubt, *A Blot in the 'Scutcheon* and the tragedies

of *King Victor and King Charles* and *The Return of the
Druses* were foreshadowed.

In *Pauline* he had declared himself to have been self-
centred, indeed sufficient to himself, and only to have
felt the need of God, in whom his faith had weakened.
Here, by way of a change from historical subjects merely,
he thinks of human love, and it is permissible to imagine
that he is still thinking of love impersonally, save,
perhaps, for a flutter of the heart that was beginning,
however faintly, to be aware of itself. It is remarkable
that a great poet should have known so little of love as
Browning at the age of twenty-seven. The emotion
of worship was an instinct in him, and until he could
relate this emotion to his feeling for a beloved woman
human love remained for him unfound and scarcely
desired.

Among those to whom the works of Browning had
personally introduced the poet John Kenyon was not
yet one, but a man so welcome for himself and so well
known in the society that Browning was frequenting
was sure to make his appearance sooner or later. One
night in 1839 at Serjeant Talfourd's house, 56 Russell
Square, Kenyon and Browning were among the guests,
and before the evening was over Kenyon took Browning
aside and inquired if he were not the son of his old
schoolfellow, Robert Browning. Learning that he had
guessed rightly, Kenyon said that he and the elder
Browning had been friends in their schooldays, but had
lost sight of each other. Naturally interested, on his
return home Browning asked his father what he recol-
lected of Kenyon. The old gentleman took pen and
paper and made a drawing of a boy's head which Browning at once recognized. Thus Kenyon entered afresh
into the life of the Brownings and became one of the
most intimate of the poet's friends. Whenever Wordsworth visited London he used to stay in Kenyon's house,

and when Browning made his residence in Italy it was often with Kenyon that he lodged on his arrival in London.

In the following year, 1840, *Sordello* appeared. It is still one of the most familiar of Browning's titles, and has had the curious fate of becoming famous for every quality that can make a poem obnoxious to a reader. Its appearance plunged Browning into twenty years of neglect at the very time when he was beginning to attract admirers. Against the forbidding barrier that he had thus unwittingly raised, nothing that even he could write availed. It still hangs like a dark cloud between him and his due, and has never found any but qualified defenders. It is the classic example of the harm that a writer can do to himself by length, by expecting an equal knowledge on the part of his readers, by a condensed style that makes hard reading. Few realize even to-day that *Sordello* was the work of Browning's immaturity, and that it was published twenty-eight years before *The Ring and the Book*. It has not been enough to dislike and condemn this poem. The qualities for which it has been attacked have been predicated of almost everything written subsequently by its author. Yet any student of the poet's growth will perceive that *Sordello* marked a term, and that he became himself for the first time with the work that immediately followed. *Pippa Passes*, published in 1841, as the first of a series of booklets collectively called *Bells and Pomegranates*, from the splendid burst of poetry with which it begins has every quality of beauty, vividness, and colour that can charm the reader. It is, in truth, an amazing transformation, as sudden and mysterious as the budding of spring. The flooding of sunrise, with which *Pippa* begins, marks the daylight's arrival of Browning's genius. Hitherto he had been writing, or rather groping, in a twilight fitfully lit with flashes of

G

great beauty. Now he was the master of his own gifts, and the first fact of which we are conscious as we start reading *Pippa Passes* is that, whatever qualities it may have, it is great writing. There is a splendid vigour in its use of idiom, and we recognize a poet who is master, not of a limited language of beauty, but of the wide resources of the English tongue.

The series of pamphlets known as *Bells and Pomegranates* ran to eight numbers between 1841 and 1846, and included the two tragedies already mentioned, the *Dramatic Romances and Lyrics*, *Luria*, and *A Soul's Tragedy*, and the two latest of his plays, namely, *A Blot in the 'Scutcheon* and *Colombe's Birthday*. From this it will be seen that Browning had not permanently wearied of the theatre. Indeed, both Macready and himself had reason to hope for a greater success with another play. *A Blot in the 'Scutcheon* was the product of their aspirations. Macready not only wanted it, but he wanted it in a hurry, and it is said to have been written in five days. Unfortunately, Macready's published *Diaries* contain none of the entries that he must have made, for the production of the play was the occasion of a quarrel. When Sir Frederick Pollock, who edited the *Diaries*, published them in 1875, Browning was still living, and the details, contained in one of Browning's letters to be found in his Life by Mrs. Sutherland Orr, are not worth much attention. The vital thing is that Browning had reason to believe that the play was inadequately produced, and resented, since it met with applause, the legend that only Macready had saved it from failure. " If," wrote Browning in the letter mentioned, " applause means success, the play thus maimed and maltreated was successful enough: it ' made way ' for Macready's own Benefit, and the Theatre closed a fortnight after."

One of the admirers of the play was Charles Dickens,

though the letter in which he expressed his opinion to Forster was never seen by Browning until it appeared nearly thirty years later in Forster's biography of the novelist. Browning was deterred from writing for the stage less by the failure of his plays than by the mischances and circumstances of theatrical production, in which the moods and needs of the moment are always liable to interfere. When he and Macready met again, shortly after both men had become widowers, Browning caught the actor by the hand and the past was buried. On the other hand, Browning remembered gratefully the behaviour and the acting of Helen Faucit (Lady Martin), and declared in a letter that this was to him " the one gratifying circumstance connected with " the play. It was she who took the chief part in *Colombe's Birthday* when this was produced at the Haymarket Theatre in 1853. It was performed in America in 1854 and by the Browning Society in 1885, and Mr. Arthur Symons has quoted the opinions of an eye-witness on each occasion : the American to show how the audience was held during the close of the fourth act, and the English to testify that " it is more direct in action, more full of delicate surprises than one imagines it in print." Though rarely seen, both *King Victor and King Charles* and *The Return of the Druses* have been played to the admiration of some good judges. Browning declared that he wrote them for performance, and that he must not be supposed to have been a playwright in any other sense.

On the other hand, it cannot be said that any of the plays have held the stage by intrinsic interest; they have been revived to challenge the exaggerated legend of their failure, before audiences of admirers of the poet, and it is hard to believe that the defection of a single actor in a secondary part would have caused the withdrawal of a piece that had promised to be commercially

successful. One of the great advantages of a subsidized
theatre in England would be the opportunity to test
from time to time, and as a matter of course, plays in
the same category as Browning's tragedies. In such a
theatre the plays would have a fair chance. They would
thus escape neglect and an artificial determination to
applaud them simply for the sake of their authorship.
As things are, criticism has small means of deciding.
Against a few chequered performances and privately
arranged revivals, we have the praise of a few, sometimes, like Dickens, readers merely. It is the reader,
then, who will be most impressed with the effect that
A Blot in the 'Scutcheon made upon Dickens, who wrote :
" Browning's play has thrown me into a perfect passion
of sorrow. Nothing in any book I have ever read so
affecting as Mildred's recurrence to that ' I was so
young—I had no mother.' I know no love like it,
no passion like it, no moulding of a splendid thing after
its conception like it." How far Browning could hold
an audience equally well from the stage of a theatre
remains a question which has not really received the
decisive test, unless the absence of revival be decisive.

A Blot in the 'Scutcheon had been published, as No. 5
of the pamphlets known as *Bells and Pomegranates*,
in 1843, and was followed by *Colombe's Birthday* a year
later. The year 1844 was notable for two other events
in Browning's life. He went a second time to Italy,
paid his first visit to Rome, and on his return found the
two entrancing volumes of Elizabeth Barrett's poetry
awaiting him. On this second Italian journey Browning
made for the south, and in Naples once again asserted
the personal charm that had led the ship's captain on
his former voyage to offer him a free passage to Con-
stantinople. The new friend was a Signor Scotti, who
insisted on arranging all the details of their common
journey, which, after visits to Sorrento and Amalfi,

brought the pair to Rome, where they used to spend their evenings under the hospitable roof of the Countess Carducci, an old acquaintance of the poet. She must have been proud of her visitors, for there are many records of Browning's good looks, and she herself called the young Italian the most handsome man that she had ever seen. He disappears tragically from our view, for soon after he and Browning had separated he committed suicide for some reason never published or forgotten. On his way home Browning presented a letter of introduction to E. J. Trelawney, then living at Leghorn, but this natural wish to see the last person who had been with Shelley did not bear fruit. The two men met and parted without much liking on either side. The poet carried away a pleasant memory of Naples, where he once thought of making a home for himself in old age. His poem "The Englishman in Italy," published in *Bells and Pomegranates* during the year after his return, was the immediate outcome of this journey.

If a man so self-confident, so active, and so healthy ever paused to consider what he had made of his life, what would Browning have glanced back upon at the end of his travels in the autumn of 1844? He had met with nothing but sympathy in his determination to become a poet. At the age of thirty-two he was the author of three long poems including an epic, of five published plays, two of which had been acted, but the private expectations that he had aroused had scarcely been fulfilled. He was far from making a living by his pen, and the appearance of *Pippa Passes* in 1841, which means so much to his reputation with posterity, had failed to dissipate the cloud that *Sordello* had raised. He had thought, he had read, he had travelled, but he had not fallen in love, had never received that intimate sympathy from a woman or a stranger which, at the moment of its arrival, means more to a young poet than

anything else.   He was still unacknowledged and alone,
with an uphill course before him.   Much had been done,
but little accomplished, for his life's work.   Friends and
acquaintances he had in plenty; some critical appreciation too; but the kind of recognition that he would
most have prized, the voluntary tribute from an imagination that had stirred his own, had not been forthcoming.
Critical appreciation, though gratifying to a young
writer, remains external unless it leads to some intimate
friendship, and with none of the poets whom Browning
had yet met was he naturally in sympathy.   Most were
his seniors.   One of Wordsworth's actions had suggested the theme of " The Lost Leader " to him.   Landor
he liked better, but their imaginations were poles apart,
and there was none who had that personal appeal for
his imagination that Byron's writing had aroused in his
boyhood or that Shelley had exerted twenty years before.

It is true that he felt a latent attraction toward Elizabeth Barrett, for Kenyon was an intimate friend of hers
and had previously offered to introduce him.   The
attempt had miscarried, but Browning, who was already
sympathetic toward her work and had heard much of
the dim room to which she was confined, felt almost as
if he knew her.   Probably he did not realize how ready
he was to be stirred if any chance should bring them
together.   Had he anticipated such a chance, it would
have seemed remote.   Miss Barrett was a confirmed
invalid who received no one but Kenyon, and Kenyon
had failed to gain admittance for his friend.   That she
would make a move in Browning's direction could
hardly have entered his head.   It was, then, with
sympathetic interest and no more, that Browning opened
the two volumes of her verses which he found on his
return from Italy.   Some quality in her work appealed
to his imagination more than anything which he had
met in contemporary poetry, and when, thus quickened

to eager attention, he turned the pages of " Lady Gerald-ine's Courtship " and found his own name mentioned by her in an admiring line, he discovered that she was not impossibly remote, since the spell was reciprocated. His books had penetrated into her room, and had found there a reader after his own heart, a reader the quality of whose imagination had just come home to him triumphantly. The shock of surprise and pleasure carried him away. He was accustomed to keep his sense of enjoyment to himself. Unlike Shelley, he had never been tempted to approach his literary idols. In personal relations he was somewhat reserved, a man who, though he liked society, had no desire to invade other people's lives, or to introduce himself to strangers. But Miss Barrett could hardly be so considered. Browning knew as much of her as anyone could know outside her immediate circle. Kenyon had mentioned him to her, and now she herself had proved to have taken a vivid interest in his own work. Thus he felt justified in abandoning his habitual reserve and in giving full rein to his feelings in the letter that we have already quoted.

It is now convenient to recall the early poetry which had led Miss Barrett to bracket Browning with the more popular Tennyson in the verse that led him to write to her.

CHAPTER THREE

HIS EARLY WORKS

I

THE earliest of Browning's writings are full of interest for those who realize how inadequate is the name of optimist which has hung itself upon him. *Pauline, Paracelsus, Sordello* unfold a chequered spiritual development, and this record is fascinating because it is the record of a great man, a man of warm heart but restless intellect, which pull him to opposite conclusions. His imagination and his feelings are in love with the teachings of tradition, but his intellect was curious of the thoughts and criticisms of his day, and thus fed his imagination with food that, left unprompted, it would have rejected. In this way he became a spokesman of his age, and, being the poet who expressed the age most variously, it was natural that his works should be examined for the support that they might give to the beliefs most debated in his time. The traditional party found in him feelings sympathetic, and from these feelings endeavoured to decipher a philosophy that should justify their own feelings to themselves. The temptation was great, because the eye of the poet was open to all the matters raised by their opponents, and his imagination was great enough to present every point of view poetically. Literally, all sorts and conditions of men were delineated in his works. He rarely spoke in his own person; and then usually in the heat of a challenge in which his own feelings could be overheard.

A poet so vivid and so various necessarily repelled or dazzled his contemporaries. Toward the end of his life he became a cult, and when the cult languished it was forgotten that his poems had been, not only arguments, but stories, the range, telling and style of which are unapproached in their kind. A great poet and a great story-teller died with Browning, and yet he has scarcely been considered simply as a man of letters. Before tracing his early development, it is well to set his major qualities as a man of letters in the foreground.

Browning is the only modern poet whose range, humanity, humour, mastery of language, and variety of gifts invited comparison with Shakespeare. If he had shown a faculty for dramatic action equal to his faculty for dramatic speech, the plays of the two would have been compared inevitably. There are the songs and the soliloquies, in and out of Browning's plays, ready to our hand, and his wealth of characters, his variety of motive, his power of painting unforgettable scenes and situations in verse show how nearly he came to being the chief dramatic poet of the nineteenth century. Browning, being a dramatist at one remove, offers comparison with dramatists and with novelists. If we confine ourselves to the soliloquy, it is not praise, but truth, to speak of Browning's mastery. This was not shown, however, in the wider field. Now the enduring success of a play does more for the fame of its author than continued reprints of a book. The theatre touches a wider audience, and lasting success in it confers not only immediately greater rewards but a wider renown. The recent revival of *The Beggar's Opera*, for example, has given a prestige to the name of Gay that would not have been his by the printing-press only. When, therefore, a poet like Browning touches closely upon the borders of the drama, it is well to remember that, had he been a playwright, his great qualities would have been seen in a much stronger

light.   As it is, he peopled his poetry and not the stage
with a great procession of characters.   It is this richness
of personality, the many-sidedness of his nature, which
makes us curious of the growth of his mind.

As beautiful poems in themselves, however, *Pauline*,
Paracelsus, and *Sordello* detain few readers.   They may
be read for incidental beauties, but they are chiefly
interesting as examples of a method that was later to be
brought to perfection, and for that which they reveal of
the great poet who wrote them in his immaturity.
Already we see, in this early work, a passionate curiosity
about life in all ages and in every type of individual.
The poet is preparing to sweep into his pages as many
portraits, as many motives, as varied situations, as he
can.   His great contemporaries could be more faultless
in this kind or in that, but none of them was free of so
many kinds as Browning.   The quality that binds him
to his age was not an artistic limitation, but the emotional
disappointment that infected it.   It is in *Pauline*, composed at the age of twenty-one, that we find the clue to
his trouble.   His boyish verses, written under the
influence of Byron, have perished.   *Pauline* recalls the
crisis of awakening produced after Shelley had fallen
into his hands.

II

The effect was twofold and contradictory.   From the
first Browning was endowed with a passionate instinct
for religion, which allied itself naturally with the imagination of the poet.   In Shelley he found what must have
seemed to his boyish inexperience an extraordinary
paradox.   On the one hand was an imagination as
aspiring as Browning's own, with a poetic ardour for
divine truth and beauty.   On the other, an indignant
repudiation of revealed religion.   The boy Browning

was thus compelled to recognize that the one could exist without the other, a conclusion that probably had not occurred to him before. Over many unorthodox poets the question would not have arisen. The atmosphere of Byron, for example, is so clearly secular that any blasphemies awaken no surprise. Shelley, however, constantly touches religious feeling. His poem to Intellectual Beauty is a hymn that a religious mystic almost might have written. Throughout his verse he not only stimulates the shyest of spiritual desires, he brings back glimpses from that world of which our universe is but a shadow. One of Shelley's sonnets contains a definition of fame which shows how quickly he will pass from human concerns to a divine fulfilment. The lines that call fame " that shadow of the unborn hour cast by the envious future on the time " imply a standard to which the Invisible Church or the Communion of Saints is an obvious parallel. Had Browning not been a poet himself, he might have denied Shelley's poetry in recoil from his explicit doctrine: the implied doctrine in Shelley is religious enough. Being a poet, Browning held fast by the poetry and only temporarily surrendered the Christian faith in which he had been reared. But the faith that he recovered had suffered a change. No longer was it the ' glad, confident ' faith of a fellowship with others. It had diminished to a personal feeling, maintained in spite of the world. Faith dwindled to hope; certainty became courage; belief, as he afterwards called it, ' a dream ' :

> All my days I'll go the softlier, sadlier,
> For that dream's sake !

The courage indeed is constant, but *Fears and Scruples* is the title of the late poem that contains this statement of a watered creed.

No doubt Shelley only hastened a process that was

inevitable. A poet so sensitive to impressions as Browning could not have escaped the century in which he lived. What ultimate beliefs in the English-speaking world are generally accepted as a matter of course? This is an unavoidable but unhealthy condition of affairs, and overshadows the poetic imagination as much as the consciousness of critical listeners would interfere with the thrushes and the robins. A poet should sing from the overflow of his feelings, not with the knowledge that every one of his assumptions may be thought a matter in dispute. Dante could be serene because both ecclesiastical and secular society accepted his premises. Browning, like Shakespeare, is interested primarily in isolated Men and Women because so little else of interest remains common to us all.

It is the driving of Browning to this limitation that *Pauline* reveals :

> O God ! where does this tend—these struggling aims !
> What would I have ? What is this " sleep," which seems
> To bound all ? Can there be a " waking " point
> Of crowning life ?

The question tortures him because :

> Is it not in my nature to adore,
> And e'en for all my reason do I not
> Feel him, and thank him, and pray to him ?—*Now*.
> Can I forego the trust that he loves me ?
> Do I not feel a love which only ONE . . .
> O thou pale form, so dimly seen, deep-eyed,
> I have denied thee calmly—do I not
> Pant when I read of thy consummate deeds,
> And burn to see thy calm, pure truths outflash
> The brightest gleams of earth's philosophy ?
> Do I not shake to hear aught question thee ?

He adds that he will " give all earth's reward " but to believe, and to believe that he is " not unloved," for divine no less than human love becomes a torture with the presumption that it is not returned. The poem ends

with a statement of faith " in God, and truth, and love."
If Shelley had endorsed the Christian definition of Love
as well as endowing with unearthly music the religious
feelings that this definition implies, he would have been
the poet of poets to Browning. Among the beautiful
passages on which we have not time to linger is the first
reference that Browning makes to music, an art which
inspired many of his later poems. Music, he says,

> is earnest of a heaven,
> Seeing we know emotions strange by it,
> Not else to be revealed.

The entire poem has this great interest. It is a description of the poet's gifts by himself, a statement of that
faculty of sympathy for all forms of life which was later
to project itself into a thousand separate creations of
different beings. Just as Shelley, invoked throughout
the poem, tantalizes us by having the essence without the
form of religion, so Browning kept the emotions without
the assurance of the Christian creed.

III

Paracelsus, published two years later, in 1835, is the
first of Browning's character-studies. The waning
certainty confessed in the earlier poem modifies the treatment of the subject. Again the soul of a seeker is set
before us, but this time with the proviso that, in our
twilight and with our limitations, the test of integrity
will be the motive of a man, not the failure or success of
his efforts. The aim of Paracelsus, as befits the first
of Browning's heroes, is more ambitious than that of
his successors. It has the inordinacy of youth : to
possess the philosopher's stone, to master all human and
divine knowledge. We may fancy that the poet Aprile,
who produces the crisis in the development of Paracelsus

in the second scene of the poem, is an idealized sketch of Shelley. His effect on Paracelsus is reminiscent of the influence of Shelley upon Browning himself. Aprile might be the author of the song:

> I love all that thou lovest,
> Spirit of delight!

To Paracelsus the visible world is the garment of God, and it is toward the Wearer that he presses. In the well-known lines the poet himself may be overheard:

> I go to prove my soul.
> I see my way as birds their trackless way.
> I shall arrive! what time, what circuit first,
> I ask not: but unless God send his hail
> Or blinding fire-balls, sleet or stifling snow,
> In some time, his good time, I shall arrive.

And there is the noble, if tragic, conviction:

> It all amounts to this—the sovereign proof
> That we devote ourselves to God, is seen
> In living just as though there were no God.

Though there are several descriptive passages of great beauty, the narrative power of the poet is still undeveloped, and the circumstances and historical setting are not much more strongly etched than before. While the subject of *Paracelsus* was suggested by the friend to whom the poem is dedicated, Browning through his father had become familiar with many shadowy figures of the Middle Ages. Here he fixed upon one who may well have seemed the typical baffled seeker that Browning now felt himself to be.

Though the poem is divided into four sections, in which Paracelsus twice " aspires " and twice " attains," its intellectual weakness is that each attainment is elusive. Paracelsus pursues knowledge till he is convicted by the poet Aprile of having overlooked love in his search. He loses faith in himself and in God, to discover on his death-bed the shadow of that confidence in both which had once upheld him. Aprile, who

> would supply all chasms with music, breathing
> Mysterious notions of the soul, no way
> To be defined save in strange melodies,

in the manner of Shelley, goes on to make an unconscious prophecy of Browning's future :

> Common life, its wants
> And ways, would I set forth in beauteous hues :
> The lowest hind should not possess a hope,
> A fear, but I'd be by him, saying better
> Than he his own heart's language. I would live
> Forever in the thoughts I thus explored.

Paracelsus declares that he differs from Aprile in that :

> I cannot feed on beauty, for the sake
> Of beauty only; nor can drink in balm
> From lovely objects for their loveliness;
> My nature cannot lose her first intent,
> I still must hoard, and heap, and class all truths
> With one ulterior purpose : I must know !

Here the imagination and the intellect of Browning are given separate voices, and the two sides of his nature, which combine in many of his poems, are analysed. In a generation more disillusioned than his own, this subordination of interest to an " ulterior purpose " is often resented. The undercurrent has enabled interested people to uphold Browning as a tedious poet, and the relation of his stories and studies of character to a purpose beyond them has prevented many from enjoying the stories and the portraits themselves. His work and his name, however, unavoidably raise the question what was his own opinion, and the best answer, for he did not change, is to follow his development through his early work, after which we can content ourselves with the enjoyment of his creations as pure poetry.

Paracelsus had once despised the aids of men and of tradition. Then he became content rather to help man by his knowledge than to know. There are splendid passages in his final speech, where he reviews all forms of life, finds these proceeding from God, and declares that, even in the loves of savage creatures, " God renews his ancient rapture." The poem ends, in fact, with the germ of the evolutionary theory, looking backward toward the appearance of man, and in man himself for the signs of desires that shall surpass him as he is :

> Man's self is not yet man. . . .
> But in completed man begins anew
> A tendency to God.   Prognostics told
> Man's near approach : so in man's self arise
> August anticipations, symbols, types.

He says that a few men,

> Serene amid the half-formed creatures round
> Who should be saved by them and joined with them,

are conscious of these signs :

> Such was my task, and I was born to it.

As it happened, however, Browning, despite this intention, did not absorb the new faith which, right or wrong, adequate or inadequate, came to men through the acceptance of the hypothesis of evolution. In his day the theory was studied, very naturally, less for its own content than for the statements that it opposed; but had Browning been born half a century later it might have inspired him to a poem that the world unfortunately still waits for. This is a pity, for at present we are in a sad case. Every generation born here since 1860 has the theory in its blood, but the theory is never affirmed, never professed, because it has not yet passed from the minds of men into their feelings, and, with very few exceptions, it has not yet moved imaginative writers.

People hear of it in the books in which one man of science criticizes another, and the theory is open to as many objections as any other revelation. If we suppose the Churches deprived of their liturgies, and religious writings confined to discussions of the authorship of the Fourth Gospel or of the Epistle to the Hebrews, we discover a parallel. Yet the assumption of most educated persons is in this plight at present, and will remain so until a poet of Browning's powers shall use his art to show how far human cravings can find a satisfaction in this hypothesis. It transforms rather than discards many traditional and cherished hopes. The incidence of pain and of evil, the notion of the Fall, the instinct for immortality, the indifference (that an inner voice gainsays) of the universe to man's sufferings, the infinite unimportance of the individual matched with his sense of an infinite of which he is a part, all have an explanation in the notion of neo-Lamarckian evolution. It does not matter whether this notion is right or wrong. The facts that matter are that here is an assumption which many men believe, and that its corollaries remain sterile because poetry has not touched them into life. All religions thrive upon the arts, which give to them their liturgies, their images, their songs, their stories, and their temples. A belief without its liturgy is as unsatisfying as a beautiful liturgy without belief.

Browning was a man of forty-seven when the *Origin of Species* made an inadequate statement of the theory popular. His heart was too much with the beliefs of childhood then challenged, his imagination too stored with the art that they had created, to see the corollaries of the theory then distorted in the dusty pages of Darwin's book. Until poets have brooded upon its implications, and made fables of its story and songs of its aspiration, many will remain ashamed of an assumption which they tacitly accept, unless, indeed, they accept nothing. In

H

Browning's poetry we have the shock of the situation in which his generation was involved. Thus Shelley's intuitions, soaring as they did beyond the confines of any controversy, are less tied down to a period than many of Browning's. In all ideas there is something prosaic, but the "desire to know" which Browning had confessed in *Paracelsus* might have occasioned a fascinating poem if Browning had been born late enough to feel the attraction, not the shock, of this new—and unproved—conception of man's possibilities and origin.

IV

Sordello is the first of his reincarnations, for it is more personal and detached than *Paracelsus*. The troubadour is less abstract than the nameless hero of *Pauline*. The interest is still rather with intellectual motives and points of view than with human character, for when the old literature becomes questioned and an alternative is unsure, a restless intellect will turn to motives and points of view for crumbs to feed on. This psychological epic in six books is not easy even to criticize. It is one of the few hard poems which deserve their immediate reputation, and have not become much easier with the passage of time. This suggests that the defects belong as much to the poet as to his readers, and are therefore not to be explained away as a few staunch admirers have averred.

Belonging to the group of immature works, *Sordello* differs from the two preceding poems in that it is not written in blank verse but in heroic couplets. This proves an added difficulty. Though Browning was a great master of rhyme, the rhymes in *Sordello* interrupt, and do not lighten, our reading. The verse throughout is jammed, and often so crabbed that the lines are more distinguished for their jars than for their movement.

Few couplets provide rest by being complete in themselves. A pause after the opening word is common enough to become almost a mannerism. It is as if the poet, having been compelled by some convention to write in rhymes, had determined to obliterate their presence so far as possible. The style is condensed and elliptic; parenthesis within parenthesis abounds; the person to whom a pronoun refers is often doubtful. According to Mrs. Orr, we owe this staccato style to a privately repeated criticism.

Caroline Fox wrote a letter to one of Browning's friends which the friend passed on to him. Miss Fox reported that John Sterling had recoiled from the "verbosity" of *Paracelsus*. Browning therefore apparently determined to avoid verbosity by omitting conjunctions and the like, by packing explanations into exclamation marks, and by leaving out connections of all kinds. The effect of the criticism was unfortunate, but it was also foolish, or carelessly expressed. Browning, always concise in expression, was often prolix in treatment, and prolixity, not verbosity, was his besetting sin. Moreover, a very concise style in poetry is best suited to short poems, and it is in fact his shorter poems that contain most of his masterpieces. It is also in the single vivid sentence that he excels, but his teeming brain and incandescent imagination would often star his sentences with clauses each of which contained a separate image or idea, one inside another, like a Chinese puzzle. Here, again, prolixity of ideas, and not of words, was his true characteristic. This is nowhere more conspicuous than in *Sordello*. Another fault in the poem is that the historical setting hampers the narrative, which suddenly stops to introduce us to the tangled relations of a political group of people who distract our attention from the "growth of the soul" that is the main theme. The economy which he afterward perfected is absent, and he yielded to the youthful failing of using many more ideas and facts than his treatment or the poem required.

A strange light upon Browning's method of composition at this time is thrown by a passage in W. M. Rossetti's *PreRaphaelite Brotherhood Journal*. Under the date February 26, 1850, Westland Marston is quoted as follows :

> Marston says that Browning, before publishing *Sordello*, sent it to him to read, saying that this time the public should not accuse him at any rate of being unintelligible. Before our involuntary smile has vanished we are told : " Browning's system of composition is to write down on a slate, in prose, what he wants to say, and then turn it into verse, striving after the greatest amount of condensation possible; thus if an exclamation will suggest his meaning, he substitutes this for a whole sentence."

No other evidence in support of this contention, so far as I know, exists, but it is conceivable that a long poem might be so written, and *Sordello* reads as if such a method might have been employed upon it. Another fact worth notice is the quality of Browning's prose, which is never fluid, easy, or very natural. Whether we look at his single essay, prefixed to some spurious letters of Shelley, or to his own letters to friends, we find a dry style, a twisted and exclamatory manner. The following awkward sentence, taken from a letter to Domett, dated May 15, 1843, is an instance : " I am dull, in every sense, this dull evening. . . . Some call me over from time to time (*there* lies note the last, which I stopped this to say ' no ' to); but these are away—so are not you." Keep the awkward construction unchanged, aim at greater concision, put the sentence into verse, and you would have a few ribbons of line in Browning's rough manner. If the supposed prose version upon his slate were, as seems likely, a kind of shorthand already, the ultimate form of many sentences in *Sordello* would be explained. It is also interesting to recall a sentence from another letter to Domett, dated November 8, 1843, in which Browning alludes to the growth of his style :

> The fact is, in my youth (*i.e.* childhood) I wrote *only* musically —and after stopped all that so effectually that I even now catch myself grudging my men and women their half-lines, like a parish overseer the bread-dole of his charge.

No doubt cultivation had something to do with his crabbed manner, but it is hardly an exaggeration to say that his prose is never musical or harmonious. An occasional phrase, which belongs to the poetry of his mind, will slip into the prose, but only to emphasize the grit of its unnatural surroundings. He seems to have little natural sense of prose-harmony, whereas, however grotesque his verse may be, a sense of verse is never wanting. That is why patience with the verse is generally rewarded; and there is ground for accepting the assertion that whoever will read *Sordello* three times through may be at ease with it. This is a stiff test. Epics are considered long by those who do not read them, but it is unnecessary to deny that *Sordello* could have been pruned to its advantage.

Briefly, the " study in the development of a soul " is obscured by minute details of the politics in a city-state. The outward story is a hindrance to our interest rather than a help, and the prolixity of the poem is better testimony to the ardour of the poet's temperament than to the extent of his harvest. His religious instinct suffered from the scepticism of the age, and he became drawn toward apparent failures, seeking exercise for his restless intellect in the casuistry of motives that an atmosphere of scepticism invites. Had he lived during the War, we should have had a few splendid songs of patriotism and some analytical studies of spies or those who refused military service. We can imagine a vivid picture of a call for volunteers, in which some man who had the moral courage to hold back would be contrasted with the brave and the adventurous. In the twilight of ultimate beliefs Browning was driven back upon his defences, and courage came to take the place of religious faith in the inspiration of his poems. An early example of disinterested courage is the Sordello of his poem.

V

The theme is not unlike that of *Paracelsus*, though the action takes place less in the study than in the world. Both men are egoists. Sordello, a troubadour of the fifteenth century, is conscious of great ambitions, and early imagines some high rôle for himself in the world. Like that of Paracelsus, the ambition of Sordello is much vaster than his powers, but he is more quickly conscious of the disparity. It partly paralyses him, so that he is tempted to dream the act rather than to risk the performance. He imagines himself, not the fulfiller of his own dreams, but Apollo or some contemporary hero. His weakness is a weakness of the will. His strength the strength of his imagination. Because he cannot achieve his dream in the splendid act of dreaming, he shrinks from the slow steps by which alone great dreams are realized. There is enough of the man of action in Sordello to torment the poet in him, enough of the poet to make the man of action seem a vulgar schemer. His sudden success in the poetical contest with Eglamour intoxicates Sordello, and leads him from the quiet corner of Goito into the busy political life of Mantua. Before long he becomes disillusioned with diplomacy and sickened by intrigue. In self-disgust at having thrust his own shoulders into such a crowd, he turns his back on Mantua, and, in the meditation proper to his nature, recovers his poetic self. Yet a lurking ambition continues to gnaw his heart, and this cannot be fulfilled in solitude or without the aid of the human creatures he has learned to scorn.

He is now anxious to serve the populace whose miseries he has been investigating. They seem to be crying for such a man as he when the unexpected chance comes to him of a political career. In the service of these unhappy ones shall he not find his own fruition? A Ghibelline himself by family connection, he comes to believe that the popular cause is better represented by the Pope's party, the Guelphs. But before he takes a decisive step to change sides he discovers that he is not, as he had always thought, an archer's son, but the child and heir of the Ghibelline lord Salinguerra. Moreover, his future is otherwise splendid, for the beautiful and exalted Palma, a charming sketch of a woman, loves him, and she is no less ambitious for him than he is for himself.

The crisis comes when he is appointed Ghibelline and Imperial representative in North Italy. In passing we may recall how Browning himself endeavoured to enter diplomacy, the only career that ever competed with poetry in his regard. Thus Sordello's dream of worldly power is suddenly fulfilled as he had once willed it; and to accept in silence, not to act, is all that destiny requires of him. The temptation is shrewdly contrived. All that Sordello has to do is to shelve his unuttered and recent convictions. In the excitement of the news he is almost carried away, and, after all, what could a humble layman on the Pope's side accomplish? If he goes over to the Pope's side, terrible actions will be required of him, for he will be renouncing, not only his father, but the party with which he has been identified from his birth. The struggle overwhelms Sordello, but none the less he makes his choice. The insignia of office are found cast aside, and the soul of the dead man is thus shown to have been true to its convictions. Something has

delivered him from egoism and merely personal aims,
and his need for that something is the old religious need
that lay at the core of Browning's own nature.   We are
also reminded that poetry is the finest service of a poet,
and that he is not called upon to compete with men of
action.   The little that Sordello accomplished in the
eyes of the world is not the measure of Sordello.   His
honour, not his failures, is the test of him, and the little
poetry that he left, we are told, served a greater purpose.
Sordello was the precursor of Dante.

VI

Having admitted the defects of the poem, which are
more familiar than its beauties, let us glance at some of its
splendours, landscape-pictures most of all.   Here is a
picture of Goito in autumn :

> A pressure shuddered through the welkin; harsh
> The earth's remonstrance followed.   'Twas the marsh
> Gone of a sudden.   Mincio, in its place,
> Laughed, a broad water, in next morning's face,
> And, where the mists broke up immense and white
> I' the steady wind, burned with a spilth of light,
> Out of the crashing of a myriad stars.
>
> > (Bk. III)

Here a portrait and a landscape in one :

> In this castle may be seen,
> On the hill tops, or underneath the vines,
> Or southward by the mound of firs and pines
> That shuts out Mantua, still in loneliness,
> A slender boy in a loose page's dress,
> Sordello : do but look on him awhile
> Watching ('tis autumn) with an earnest smile
> The noisy flock of thievish birds at work
> Among the yellowing vineyards; see him lurk
> ('Tis winter with its sullenness of storms)
> Beside that arras-length of broidered forms,

On tiptoe, lifting in both hands a light
Which makes yon warrior's visage flutter bright. . . .
Look, now he turns away ! Yourselves shall trace
(The delicate nostril swerving wide and fine,
A sharp and restless lip, so well combine
With that calm brow) a soul fit to receive
Delight at every sense; you can believe
Sordello foremost in the regal class
Nature has broadly severed from her mass
Of men and framed for pleasure as she frames
Some happy lands that have luxurious names
For loose fertility; a footfall there
Suffices to upturn to the warm air
Half-germinating spices, mere decay
Produces richer life, and day by day
New pollen on the lily-petal grows,
And still more labyrinthine buds the rose.

(Bk. I)

Or take this quiet corner, like one of Rossetti's pictures :

That eve-long each by each
Sordello sate and Palma : little speech
At first in that dim closet, face with face
Despite the tumult in the market-place
Exchanging quick low laughters : now would gush
Word upon word to meet a sudden flush,
A look left off, a shifting lips' surmise—
But for the most part their two histories
Ran best thro' the locked fingers and linked arms,
And so the night flew on with its alarms
Till in burst one of Palma's retinue.

(Bk. III)

The pages in which the elusive details of the story interject are scarcely worth deciphering, and the real objection to the style is that it is a poor style for narrative of such length. Innumerable little pools of light and beauty do not make a stream of narration, and, except when telling the simplest of stories, such as *Hervé Riel*, *The Boy and the Angel*, or *An Incident in the French Camp*, the natural method of Browning was not a rhythmical sequence. He preferred to seize a crisis, to throw all his cards upon the table, and to develop a situation from within, usually with reflections on the retrospect from the principal character. The method can be admirable for short stories, and probably no poet in English or any other literature has written such a long and magnificent series of short stories as Browning.

VII

While he was writing *Sordello*, it will be remembered, Browning was introduced to Macready and, on his suggestion, turned to the writing of plays. The half-dozen dramas that followed, though neither the blank failures nor the artistic successes that they have been variously described, show no genius for the stage, but a talent occasionally quickened by genius for a particular speech, piece of dialogue, or a good curtain. Neither in plot nor conception is there dramatic originality. To bring poetry nearer to drama than any other poet is not necessarily the same thing as to possess an instinct for the theatre. Browning did not bring anything new to dramatic themes or dramatic technique. The subject, treatment, and climax of his plays are conventional. For the theatre Browning wrote as an amateur, and his nearest approach to direct drama, *A Blot in the 'Scutcheon*, is clearly the work of an apprentice who is not the master of his medium, though this was Browning's fourth play.

This is interesting; for the two half-plays, *Pippa Passes* and *In a Balcony*, are both original conceptions. For the rest, in between the finer passages there is a void, and the action moves by fits and starts to relieve the dramatic monotony of the speeches. The poet supplies what is necessary without feeling his form or fusing its elements. The end of *The Return of the Druses*, the final love-scene of *Colombe's Birthday*, do not redeem the subject of the first or the unsatisfactory drama of the second. When we turn to the *Dramatic Lyrics* we are in a different world. In the plays Browning uses the conventions as best he can without natural aptitude. In the poems, with scarcely an exception, he is the master of his method. This is most obvious, as it happens, in the two half-plays already named. The conception of the loveless Queen suddenly supposing herself to be desired in middle age, and of the unseen Pippa vitally affecting the lives of those she passes unknown to herself, are both inventions. Browning's plays may be compared to poems ' adapted for the stage ' with the incomplete success of the more common ' adapted novel.' The story of each could be told in a monologue at the moment of crisis by the chief actor, because the chief actors stand apart, and it is for their dramatic poetry that the plays are most worth reading. If there is a defect in Mr. Arthur Symons' extraordinarily understanding and patient *Introduction to the Study of Browning*, it is that he treats the plays and the poems as if they were upon the same level. He discusses the poetry in the dramas, but, except in relation to two scenes, he does not bring the plays to the dramatic test.

In a good tragedy, and it would be hard to find a stricter example of technique than *The Father* by Strindberg, the story should seem to tell itself. We should become so much absorbed in the process of unfolding that, however deeply moved we may be by this or that character or by the fate that overtakes them, the story should dominate both us and the protagonists themselves. Moreover, in a stage-play, and Browning resented the notion that his were intended for the study, every psychological crisis should in some way become visible to the eyes. The drama should pass before us in a series of inevitable pictures, each step emerging from the one before like the unfolding of a terrible flower. There are few such stage pictures in Browning. It is in isolated speeches that he excels. The argument is there, the speech is there, but they do not combine to produce a picture in the rhythm of which the characters are borne along. Browning had an analytic and expository imagination. He could indeed tell a story. He could not let it tell itself, and, with half a dozen plays from his hand, it is too much to pretend that he was given no chance of proving his quality. Had the instinct been there, can anyone doubt that he would have been as superior to the inadequate presentment of his dramas as he was to the delayed recognition of his poems? He was tempted by Talfourd and Macready into play-writing; he was fond of going to the play; he had written some kind of drama for his schoolfellows. None of these facts is enough to rebut the evidence of his plays that he was not born to be a dramatist.

The play to prove this is *A Blot in the 'Scutcheon*, which is also the most actable and direct. A girl on the eve of her marriage is discovered to have been receiving an unknown man at night. Her brother, a stickler for the family honour, therefore kills the young man, and the girl dies in time to explain that her nocturnal visitor was her future husband. Will anyone pretend that this is not a conventional and threadbare story? It would require a very rich imagination to make a tragedy of an incident like this. Browning does not lead up to the situation, show us how the two were thrown together, how, with the unwitting aid of the family, their intimacy grew, or how these fatal secret meetings seemed to be natural. The lover's share is not directly brought out. He comes, in secret fear, to make his formal proposal. He re-enters on the evening when he is killed, but he remains a fragment of machinery, and the impatient killing of the lover is a device too familiar to move us. Except that the piece is written by a poet, and that the heroine and her sister have charm and character, the play is a melodrama, not a tragedy, and it is the nearest to an effective tragedy that Browning wrote. There is no before and after. There is but an incident, hurriedly led up to and catastrophically resolved. Poetry so rich in situations as Browning's tempts us to forget that dramatic aptitude is not common. Were it otherwise, the most lucrative form of literature would not have so few recruits, nor the theatre be abandoned to wretched plays because no better are forthcoming. What is wrong with our theatre to-day is an economic mess : extravagant rents with consequent speculation. What is wrong with the drama is the want of good dramatists. Poetic drama is very rare. It is a sad pity that Shelley was lost to it; for however obvious the central defect in *The Cenci* may be, the dramatic gift of the author is unmistakable. Browning was trying his hand at a form for which his virtuosity in the dramatic lyric was really a disqualification.

VIII

It was in 1842, in the third number of *Bells and Pomegranates*, that the peculiar genius of Browning was first displayed. The Dramatic Lyrics then published were the first batch of poems to be followed by the kindred groups of Dramatic Romances and Men and Women. The " Cavalier Tunes," " Porphyria's Lover," " Johannes Agricola in Meditation," " Rudel " and " In a Gondola " were all contained in this. Moreover, to the printer's request for a poem to fill up a blank at the end of its sixteen pages, Browning made the royal reply of " The Pied Piper of Hamelin." These poems are now so familiar that criticism would be otiose did they not display a common quality that is apt to be overlooked. The language of poetry is of many kinds. The elaborate rhetoric of the Elizabethans, the cunning workmanship of Donne and his later kin, the incomparable daintiness of Herrick, the scholarly splendour of Milton, the polished idiom of Dryden and Pope, the unearthly beauty of Blake and Shelley, the fine rattle of Byron, are types. Browning, while he could vie with almost all of these, is distinguished for drawing upon the great commonalty of English speech. He uses the whole tongue. His realm really is that of the King's English. In reading him we have the exhilarating sense of hearing a whole language on his page, not the sense that he has refined, however exquisitely, upon a province or corner of it. The daily speech of men and women, the living idiom of the language, is the basis of the whole, to which the poet, the scholar, the man of the world, the student of technical terms contribute their splendid tributaries.

A comparison with Byron is instructive. An orator rather than a poet, Byron was a master of parlance. The vigour of his verses does not display a subtle sense of language. He can rattle and rhyme, and sometimes attain eloquence and sonority, but he delights in fitting the rags of expression into the pattern of his stanzas so that the incongruity shall be part of the effect. We are surprised to meet these things in poetry. We never feel that they are part of it, and the imagination that employs this mixture is often on a par with the phrases used. We are always acutely conscious of the author, who seeks to amuse us by his sudden changes of tone, to follow a fine line with a splenetic anticlimax, to retrieve a vulgarism by a flash of genuine fire. The antics of the style are deliberate and self-conscious. The poet, like the man, was lamed. With Browning, who possessed an incomparably finer ear and a very much richer vocabulary, the poet is almost always in control. His style seems to be less the invention of a single man than the natural outburst of a language equally fit for poetry and for common use. The ease with which the written and the spoken idioms run into one another has the effect of losing the author in his style, and the poems come before us as if they were anonymous creations in which we are hardly concerned with the writer himself.   Once we have over-come our surprise that the written and the spoken idioms combine, at their best, so easily, we read the poems as children read " The Pied Piper ": they belong to the language rather than to any author's works.   This verdict would have seemed paradoxical to his con-temporaries because, in spite of the innovations of Wordsworth and Byron, they were looking in their poets, not for the whole gamut of English, but for some exquisite modulation sacred to verse.

Browning is the master of an enormous vocabulary used with ease.   Who, since Shakespeare, has approached him in wealth, or fusion, or variety ?   It is not merely a matter of words.   No turn of speech, no trick of idiom, seems to have escaped him, and these idiomatic turns were controlled by a fine ear, so that, instead of descend-ing from poetry to parlance with a jerk, there is, for the most part, no question of the poetry of the whole.   One effect of this naturalness has been to obscure the artistry of his style.   He went further.   He played with English. " The Pied Piper " is a riot of rhymes; rhymes not arduously contrived but pouring out, as if in spate, into the generous stanza that he fashioned for their reception. The consequence is that the lines and phrases which we remember are often moving because, while familiar, we had not noticed the fineness of their cadence before. When Wordsworth begins a notable sonnet with the phrase " It is not to be thought of," we are delighted because he shows us the beauty of a cadence that we have heard every day but not, till now, admired.   This, I think, is the mark of a great style, as distinguished from the majestic, the polished, or the ethereal.   Browning is very rich in common treasure.   How beautifully the phrase " him even " closes a reference to Keats, and the following are bare reminders of examples familiar to us all :

> The town's true master if the town but knew !
> I must learn Spanish one of these days.
> For I intend to get to God.
> You and I will never see that picture.
> In fifty different sharps and flats.
> What, and is it really you again, quoth I ?
> I never saw a brute I hated so.
> How well I know what I mean to do.
> Not verse now, only prose !

Detached thus roughly from their context, they fall back into the rank and file of speech, but Browning translated them by poetic right into a poetry of which they should be an integral part without sacrificing either its dignity or their own virtue.   There was no poetic or unpoetic language to this poet, who was an artist so thorough that he could handle all materials with a like skill, and the wider his choice the more happy his conscience.   In this idiomatic style there can be no patching, no slurring over weak places which a more selected and artificial vocabulary allows.   To use it is a test that would trip many distinguished writers.   Moreover from the same note struck with the finger of a single common word, Browning can soar or play as the mood takes him easily. " Day " introduces the splendid spurt of poetry with which *Pippa* opens, as " rats " heralds the most rollicking of his rhymes to the " Pied Piper."   He did not despise the enchantments of the magicians, but, like another Shakespeare, he proved that the rarest height is less rare than the whole range, peaks and all.   In other poets we have exquisite kinds of music : in Browning the living language of a people, which is splendid, sonorous, idiomatic, grotesque in turn, and sometimes at once.

If we may judge by Shakespeare and Browning, such a range of language is naturally accompanied by the widest human sympathy so that there is no character so commonplace or perverse, no point of view so shamefaced or casuistical, that escapes them. Both are draughtsmen of the human soul. Neither contributed much to the stock of human ideas. If many attempts have been made to formulate the philosophy of both, this is because their works contain immortal presentments of common experience. But whereas Shakespeare was content with human character, and in Hamlet showed the turmoil of a soul which had outgrown the prevailing conception of duty and found no alternative with which to replace his disbeliefs, Browning was chiefly positive in lamenting the recoil from Christianity and in praising the courage that no ultimate destiny can shake. All the passages quoted in support of his Christian leanings ache with the admission that the old assent has gone. What remained for the thinker in him but innumerable points of view to investigate and chronicle ? Indeed we learn from " How it Strikes a Contemporary " that the faithful record of men's thoughts and doings became Browning's definition of the modern poet's function before God.

Thus extreme individuals had a peculiar attraction for him. With that love of the grotesque which was his glory, he began with two portraits of fanatics, Porphyria's lover and the determinist Agricola, originally grouped together under the title of " Madhouse Cells." The first murders his mistress in order to eternalize the moment of her surrender ; the second poem is a faultless lyrical expression of the mood of one who believes himself to have been the predestined and elected of God. The soliloquy, which fixes each speaker in a mood of isolated egoism from the rest of the world, here justifies itself triumphantly, and neither poem extends beyond the reader's willing absorption. A barely

I

perceptible modulation of this monologue makes " My Last Duchess " the story of two lives.   These poems are admirable examples of apparently spontaneous English which the poet's ear and the scholar's cunning have touched to a finer tone.   They have a completeness that is independent of their period, so that it would not be easy to date them were their authorship not known.

The Dramatic Romances and Lyrics, which appeared in the seventh number of *Bells and Pomegranates* in 1845, are of similar kind and quality.   " How They Brought the Good News from Ghent to Aix," one of Browning's fine poems upon horsemanship; " The Lost Leader," one of the great poems of indignation which covered the deserter with dishonour and not hate, and showed how Browning, had he cared, could have become the spokesman of a people; the " Home Thoughts " that immortalize the English thrush in a famous passage; several examples of his vivid landscapes, are all here.   The monologues show a mastery that he was to rival but hardly to surpass, and again at a length that was not to defeat its intensity.   " The Bishop Orders his Tomb in St. Praxed's Church " deserves its undying popularity. From the time when Ruskin praised it, the poem remains a fadeless picture of the Renaissance mind in Italy.   By a series of cunning strokes, a picture is evoked, not of one character, but of an epoch.   The contradictory elements in the Latin character are shown in turn with a cunning variety of language in which nothing is too homely, nothing too lyrical, to be excluded from so complex an effect.   The literary pleasure in reading this poem is intense.   As we lay down the page we say, What a great man of letters is here !

Other poets use, as it were, an English purified : Browning pure English in its many kinds.   In the distant future Browning's works may be treasured for their style, a storehouse of English idiom in the nineteenth century. Indeed, our common style may seem richer than we know it when the record to be studied will be the noble English of Browning's verse. How fresh and vigorous and pure it seems in his own handling! This breadth and freedom, and a finish that is not to be detached, was indeed a service, for it came late in the day, near a century after the knell tolled by the appearance of the first great dictionary. Under the shadow of this sophistication, Browning took the language and renewed its sap, and, in this sense, he was the greatest writer of his time. It would have seemed odd to his contemporaries that he should be upheld as a master of style because their own sense of style was too literary and narrow. He seemed rather to have no style at all, because the English that he wrote was peculiar not to one man but to a people.

CHAPTER FOUR

I

THE poems at which we have glanced were those that Miss Barrett had been reading, but they did not chiefly impress her with the sense of a master of English. Her warm heart and emotional nature, inclined to religion like his own, responded to the living pulse of his aspirations. Ever since she had read *Paracelsus* Browning had been the " king of the mystics " in her eyes. It is not a phrase that posterity would use, but it is worth notice by any curious of the precise causes of the attraction that each found in the writings of the other. The first quality that they had in common was a warmth of personality which made the immediate life of their writings even more striking than the beauties into which it would flower. She might be weak, and he rough, in many places, but both the weakness and the roughness belonged to ardent and generous spirits who made themselves felt by readers in an intimate and almost personal fashion. While it is possible to read the productions of Landor or Wordsworth or Tennyson or Coleridge for the sake of the poems themselves, as complete and independent creations, without special interest in the personal characters of these writers, the poems of Miss Barrett and of Robert Browning have a way of making us ponder on the charm and the vitality of the people who have written such things. The subjects and the thoughts of both, moreover, are never

116

far from men and women, round whom their imaginations prefer to play rather than to create independent worlds of abstract thought or ideal beauty. All the learning that she had mastered in her own studies she found contributing additional life to his poems, as if the books that he had read had stepped down from their shelves and introduced themselves in the persons of their once suffering and active creators. Not so much the alert thought as the vivid thinker attracted her to him, in whom she seemed to meet living ideas, and not the cold theories of learning. The life that she had aspired to keep in her own studies she found inspiring his poems, which were full of thoughts, of characters, of experiments in metre. In this work, so learned and alive, there appeared to her the realization of an aim dear to herself.

Being a shrewd reader of contemporary poetry with no undue satisfaction in her own, she recognized his genius, and was indeed one of the first competent readers to appreciate fully his range, his quality, and his power. From his point of view, there was no contemporary poetess to compare with her. Each found a completely sympathetic reader in the other. The human voice that could be heard by all in her writings had a peculiar warmth for him because, not only was she without a living feminine rival in her art, but he, heart-whole and expecting to remain so at the age of thirty-three, suffered in his otherwise delightful home from a lack of intellectual companionship. There were also minor ties in their experiences of authorship. She had been criticized for obscurity, which was the charge levelled against him. She was reputed to be a learned woman, and he was supposed to put needless difficulties in the way of his readers by his fondness for recondite subjects. Her style was rebuked for roughness and false rhymes, for almost such faults as his was attacked.

Indeed there need be little doubt that, to their contemporaries, the similarity between the poets was thought to be closer than any later criticism would allow. An ardent temper and great natural fluency they had possessed, as they were to discover, from infancy.

In his approach to her, and apart from the chivalry of his nature, a chivalry nourished for a particular reason in his own home, there was a reason for his humility that must not be overlooked. Of the two, she was the popular author. Consciousness of the reputation that she had won, and for which he must still wait, was present to him. However secure he might be in the reality of his gift, his generous nature did not doubt that she deserved this popularity. There must also have been for him something peculiarly winning in the perfection of her escape from the " fears and scruples " about the old religion that troubled him in the atmosphere of his time. On that integrity of trust his own reverence could repose, for, whether she composed religious dramas such as *The Seraphim* or lyrics such as *Cowper's Grave*, she remained, despite her acquaintance with sceptical philosophers, at peace and untroubled. No poet of the century, till we come to the incomparable Christina Rossetti, was more at one with Christian beliefs. Elizabeth Barrett's poetry too was thoroughly feminine, a quality that would endear it to a man already attracted by the writer.

Attentive readers of the first of Browning's letters will have noticed two things. He had been moved by the poetry as if it had been by a charming woman, and he had expressed his feelings with the tender audacity that was one of her own engaging gifts. His first letter to her, in temper if not in tone, is extraordinarily like one of her letters. Probably he had deepened the likeness from having given himself up to her two volumes for the whole of the previous week. If he was to write to her at all, he had adopted the style most likely to please her. Evidently it came from his heart when he said : " Your work is a living flower—how different from lying to be dried and pressed flat, and prized highly, and put in a book." No wonder, with her admiration for him, that she was " thrown into ecstasies." She replied immediately, and from that morning onward an exchange that was to last for eighteen months, by which it had become daily, began. Two closely-printed volumes, running to nearly twelve hundred pages, were to enshrine this correspondence. Each preserved the letters of the other, and Browning handed the complete collection to his son, to do what he liked with, not long before he died. Coming late, as they did, to the knowledge of the world, these letters were not available to the official biographers, and their successors have dismissed in a chapter the record of a love-story which must either be read in detail, as it stands, or else carefully followed if we are to watch the progress of a beautiful attraction inch by inch along a path that seemed to be beset with impassable difficulties.

To understand the attitude from which the correspondents started, we must recall two facts about her and two about him. Born with an intense capacity for affection, her heart had been crushed by the death of her brother, the only person with whom she had been able, in her limited circle and under the eye of her strange father, to form any intimate tie. The blow had fallen when she was already an invalid. It seemed to confirm her isolation, and she recovered no more than to acquiesce in the hopeless confinement that weighed upon her. The flicker of life that remained found an outlet in her poetry, which was the utmost life that she fancied to be within her reach. The poetry had brought her some success and some response, but in the main from people whom her shyness did not desire to see. Browning's letter was one of the few that came from a stranger whom she valued, and with whom her sympathies were at ease. The temptation to respond more than formally surprised herself, and she resented what seemed a weakness, but she felt something of the spell that had similarly attracted him. He, for his part, imagined that she was an incurable invalid, suffering from a disease of the spine that would keep her on her back always, and indulged no more than the hope of doing some service to a nature that he felt to be in unison with his own. He had no doubt that he would meet in the poet what he had recognized in the poetry, for he was too complete a poet and whole-hearted a man to expect a separation between the two. He was still anxious to return to Italy, and had supposed that he would never marry, since no woman of kindred nature or capable of sharing the quiet life, devoted to poetry, for which he had put aside all thoughts of other ambitions, had come or now seemed likely to come his way. With a common friend in Mr. Kenyon, with Miss Barrett's allusions to his own work, fate seemed to be drawing the two toward friendship. He was on the side of this tendency, and happy in it, but his ardent letter meant no more. From January to May the postman carried increasingly long letters between them, but it was not till May 20, 1845, that Browning was at length admitted to the house. It is the degree of intimacy that is possible to mere letter-writers which we follow during this first period of four months.

II

"I love your verses with all my heart, dear Miss Barrett," he had begun, and her rejoinder, "Such a letter from such a hand," was too sincere to be a compliment. It expressed exactly her feeling after reading his letter. She added words that must have touched him : " Sympathy is dear, very dear, to me : but the sympathy of a poet, and of such a poet, is the quintessence of sympathy for me." It is scarcely fanciful to assert that Browning's letter had touched a chord which had lain unquickened since her brother's death, so close had been the sympathy between them. She hopes that Browning will really criticize her poems, though she does " not pretend to any extraordinary meekness under criticism." This dash of self-confidence in the midst of her acknowledgments is a graceful example of the skill with which she could make her letters smile or sigh, so that her pen seems to follow the changes of expression on her face. She is even bold enough to hope that the lost chance of their meeting may recur some day, sufficiently vague to be reassuring. " In the Spring, we shall see . . . and in the meantime I have learnt to know your voice, not merely from the poetry but from the kindness in it." They had recognized each other from afar, and on his initiative she had suddenly stirred in her corner like a dormouse after a long sleep. He replied at once and, fixing on her talk of faults, admitted that he was tempted to expand upon her poetry, " for an instructed eye loves to see where the brush has dipped twice in a lustrous colour, has lain insistingly along a favourite outline, dwelt lovingly in a grand shadow." He makes us feel what he means by declaring that her poetry accomplishes what he has always wanted to do : " You speak out—I only make men and women speak." There is no doubt that the directness with which she expressed herself in her poetry greatly appealed to him, for in a much later letter he declared that he wrote dramatically because something seemed to stand between him and the direct utterance of his feelings. It was this difference between them that led him constantly to exaggerate her gifts. This second letter, twice as long as his first, ended with the admission that, whereas he can usually achieve only laconic notes, he finds his pen running away with him when she is his correspondent.

This led Elizabeth into a pretty picture of her own nature, as vivid as a pencil sketch upon the wall. Her Italian master used to say that the one word to describe her was headlong, an adjective on which she improvises with pleasure : " Headlong I was at first, and headlong I continue—precipitately rushing forward through all manner of nettles and briars instead of keeping to the path; guessing at the meaning of unknown words instead of looking into the dictionary—tearing open letters, and never untying a string—and expecting everything to be done in a hurry, and the thunder to be as quick as the lightning." Though he could afford to smile at this, the erudite Browning, who had drained Dr. Johnson's *Lexicon* at a draught, had made a famous slip in *Pippa Passes*, which is duly recorded for the curious who will look up the word twat in the *Oxford English Dictionary*. Miss Barrett, who invented, alas, the word oftly for the sake of an easy rhyme, was certainly headlong there, but she had a juster sense than he of the respective quality of their poetry. In his poetry, she tells him, she has discerned two worlds; the subjective and the objective are both in it. " Then you are ' masculine ' to the height—and I, as a woman, have studied some of your gestures of language and intonation wistfully, as a thing beyond me far ! and the more admirable for being beyond."

With such criticism, curiously enough, he was unable to compete. He never did discuss her poetry in any detail, and this not only because it was too near and like herself to criticize, but because in prose the analysis of art was as difficult to him as the analysis of motive in verse was easy. There never was a writer, even in these letters to her, who was more manifestly uncomfortable in prose. His sentences are often twenty lines long; the construction will change in the middle; the asides and explanations suggested by the original thought sometimes go so far as to make him break off with the admission that the thread has snapped and that he is unable to finish, when an expressive dash is the means by which he will scramble out of the muddle. What then, apart from the spell of personal attraction, did she find to praise so often in his letters? Vitality was the word that she used. He was vexed that the writing of his letters should be considered by her at all. Except in their sincerity, his are the exact opposite of hers. Grace, vividness, charm are not the qualities of his side of their correspondence. His letters are rugged, and rough, and tender, and patient, and considerate, and strong. They are choked with the feeling that he fears to offend her by expressing, and it is the royal nature from which they come, the reliant strength, made tender by his affection, that enthralled her. The miracle, to her, was that such a nature should go out of its way to place her first in its regard, to think the world well lost for the pleasure of seeing her in her loneliness, to prefer her in her weakness and dependence to all the other opportunities within its reach. He soon taught her to believe that he would be content merely to write to her and to receive her replies, and that she could never give too little to content him. As we read his side of the correspondence, we come to share her own belief and wonder, which is not less because we know that his professions were to be fulfilled even in detail. She had been so secluded, and had possessed so much more affection than she could spend since her brother died, that it becomes clear on reflection why she was amazed that such a man as Browning would make any sacrifice to maintain intimacy with her.

From the moment when their first letters passed, he is convinced that this intimacy is vital to him. In a fortnight he tells her that when his " head strikes work " he turns to her two green volumes, and that he would feel repaid if he could boast a reader equally responsive. It is a relief to write, but then, since she knows next to nothing of himself, he must stop, with the Spring to look forward to, however! This was a natural wish, for he " hates writing to nearly everybody," and if she feels the same let her answer no more. With her fondness for delightful scribbling, and few can have written more letters than herself, she replies that everybody likes writing to somebody, and that " this talking upon paper " is as good as any social pleasure, and, by implication, the only social pleasure at her hand. She boasts of those which her friends have written, and says that Miss Mitford's letters, in a drawer near by, would make a folio worthy to stand beside the Fathers, should they ever appear in print. Heart-warm and soul-warm they were. Her admission that she never thinks letters too long or too frequent was an invitation that the poet was not slow to accept. " I can read (she says) any MS. except the writing on the Pyramids," and " if you agree to send me a blotted thought whenever you are in the mind for it, I will be your regular correspondent." She wants to know how he takes criticism, whether he is pained by cold words and neglect, or whether the writing of poetry is joy enough for him. Who are his favourite poets? who his special sponsors : questions to fill out the knowledge of him which, whatever he may think, she has gained from his works. Her letter, twice as long as any that either had written hitherto, provoked a generous reply. To such a point had the new friends come by the end of February.

He chewed her delightful curiosity for a week, and then this lamed correspondent spends a page to explain

that he would rather hear from her than from anybody.
He intends to ' speak out ' in his own person, for his
published poems contain ' nothing ' of him but evidence
of ability and ' a dramatic sympathy with certain modifications of passion.' He says that he is pent in; he can
only flash out through a chink in the tower that holds
his inner self like a lamp in a lighthouse. As to criticism,
the sense of his vocation is too sure to be affected by
the opinions of other people, but it is tiresome that his
admirers will often praise the wrong things. He cannot
understand why Keats and Tennyson should complain
of a gruff word or two. "Tennyson reads the
' Quarterly ' and does all they bid him with the most
solemn face in the world—out goes this, in goes that,
all is changed and ranged. Oh, me ! " Browning complained that Tennyson's revisions always spoilt something. Turning to himself to ask if his writing is
illegible, he provokes the reply that small writing
attracts her. Miss Barrett adds slyly : " Mr. Landor,
for instance, writes as if he had the sky for a copybook,
and dots his i's in proportion." This leads her to an
ingenious apology for facility. Just as a man may
count six without using his fingers, so he may spend no
more labour on writing a hundred lines in one day than
on writing three. Her own verses were headlong, like
their author, and nothing could alter that. Everything
that he has told her she seemed to know before, in the
same way that she has often amused her sisters by
describing the faces of their friends from their bare
names, though she has never set eyes upon them. " But
you," she confesses, " are different. You have to be
made out by the comparative anatomy system. . . . You
have taken a great range—from the high faint notes of
the mystics, which are beyond personality, to dramatic
impersonations, gruff with nature, ' gr-r-r you swine ';
and when these are thrown into harmony, as in a manner

they are in *Pippa Passes* (which I could find it in my
heart to covet the authorship of more than any of your
works), the combination must always be striking and
noble." She has a horror of the idea of writing for the
stage, and of having her works 'ground to pieces'
between the teeth of insensitive actors. This was well
enough in Shakespeare's day, but now the printing press
has the advantage that the theatre then possessed.
Browning, by the way, would never write for the
papers except to oblige a friend in need, like poor
Hood, and he had a feeling for seeing plays to correspond
with her preference for reading them. She speaks of
criticism in a charming image. "The denial of contemporary genius is the rule rather than the exception.
No one counts the eagles in the nest, till there is a rush
of wings; and lo! they are flown. And here we speak
of understanding men, such as the Sydneys and the
Drydens." With a flick of her pen she gives a graceful
thrust at Carlyle: a delicate thrust of the deadly sort
that the heavy-going sage too rarely encountered.
"Does Mr. Carlyle tell you that he has forbidden all
singing to this perverse and froward generation, which
should work and not sing? And have you told Mr.
Carlyle that song is work, and also the condition of
work?" It is curious that her keen intuitions, which
ran away with her pen when she wrote the verse that
came so readily, produce a graceful prose free of redund-
ancy. How different from Browning, who, with an
equal facility, was muddy and involved in his prose.
His prose, as a rule, is the must and the scum of his
vintage, and would lead one to fancy that he could
never write verse with the effortless mastery that is
really his characteristic. He had little wit or fancy in
prose to set beside such a sentence as the following
from the same letter: "The curious thing in this world
is not its stupidity, but the upperhandism of the stupidity.

The geese are in the Capitol, and the Romans in the farmyard—and it seems all quite natural that it should be so, both to geese and Romans!" She is a delightful prose-writer. Her letters are as excellent in their own kind as his lyrics could be.

At the end of February, 1846, Browning reminds her that it is Spring, and that "the birds know it. 'I shall see you,' I say!" He was occupied with *Luria*, and found himself, like a true dramatist, sympathising equally with all his characters, whether rascals or the reverse. He is wanting to write, as she has advised, a poem in his own person, but the old doubt recurs: "what is to be done now, believed now, so far as it has been revealed" to him? It was the thorn in his soul that he could not pluck out. He amuses her with a sketch of Carlyle reading, with gossip of the spider who lives in a skull in his room, and with John Mill's remark on his boyish verses: "the writer possesses a deeper self-consciousness than I ever knew in a sane human being." The letter ends, as it began, with the words: "tell me if Spring be not come."

To conceal the inner fear that something unforeseen would come of such a meeting, she answers: "to me the snowdrop is much the same as the snow: it feels as cold underfoot," and the voice of the turtle is drowned by the east wind. The end of May is Spring, she says, in England, and, to the very end, she pleads for little delays before every step in advance that he puts in front of her. On the subject of his dramatic poems she shows insight. "Your great dramatic power would work more clearly and audibly in the less definite mould, that is to say, outside the theatre." She too is contemplating a monologue, Aeschylus sitting, a blind exile, on the flats of Italy, returning to the past "just before the eagle cracked his great massy skull with a stone." The germ of the poem that proved to be *Aurora Leigh* is

also stirring in her mind, which revolves " a poem as
completely modern as ' Geraldine's Courtship,' running
into the midst of our conventions and rushing into
drawing-rooms and the like." Meantime the idea waits
upon a story, a story that she wishes to invent and not
to find, so that she may be free to take any liberties with
it. She has known about his spiders without being
told, as anyone may in these ' days of mesmerism and
clairvoyance.' We hear his voice in the rejoinder,
" you shall laugh at the East wind yet ! " He could
not escape the contrast that the past of each of them
presented. He has been ' spoiled ' so thoroughly that
he feels free to imperil his whole future, for his past is
gained, secure, recorded. She replied that she had been
spared the cruelty of the world, " the unworthiness of
the dearest," and thus, as we have seen, had grown to
regard Mr. Barrett with the same inevitableness as a
rough wind. But " it is delightful to be broad awake
and think of you as my friend." They had advanced to
that assurance by the beginning of March.

Confidence that she would yet grow stronger, an
intuition perhaps that she was not encouraged to get
well, makes him move an inch nearer. Will she always
put in one line about herself ? From the first he realized
that her health was the main obstacle, though to what
event he had scarcely yet defined. He applauded her
literary projects, and sketched for her another version
of the *Prometheus Bound*, to pass insensibly to his own
belief : " if there were no life beyond this, the hope in
one would be a blessing." Was it in innocence or as
an argument that he should end by saying that he will
be off on his travels again, and so once more raise the
question of their meeting ? He makes the odd remark
that he has always ' hated society,' a fact that his habit
of frequenting it belies. Perhaps he was obscurely
discontented with his bachelorhood and, now that he

had found a woman poet for his particular friend, was beginning to find other society empty. He goes on to declare that the act of writing gives him no pleasure, though he finds this in the fulfilment of a vocation. She, he fancied, enjoyed 'making music,' but, for himself, "my heart sinks whenever I open this desk and rises when I shut it." In other words, the new influence streaming in was making every other interest seem unprofitable.

In her turn, Miss Barrett waited a week before writing her reply, through ill health resulting from the bad weather. Who could be well in such a wind? However April will come, and perhaps allow a meeting, but does he have any notion "how, when the chance comes to see a living human face to which I am not accustomed, I shrink and grow pale in spirit"? She will also be afraid. "You are Paracelsus, and I am a recluse with nerves." Then follows the description of her girlhood which was given on an earlier page. Of course she likes to write: "I seem to live while I write—it is life for me"; and, whatever he may say, it must be the same for him. This was her first piece of lengthy self-revelation, which invited him to similar confidences. They seemed to her to be at the opposite ends of experience. He is sated with all that she wishes to see. Is it possible that he is really tired of reading? The latest novel is still as attractive to her as a piece of plum cake to a child. She "could have forgotten the plague listening to Boccaccio's stories." She was not drawn to the new version of *Prometheus* that he suggested: "the old gods are dethroned." We want new forms as well as new thoughts. Why should we go back to the classics? Was he not going direct to life while recommending antique models? Then, as if taking his own ground, she adds: "Christianity is a worthy myth, and poetically acceptable." Lastly, does he really mean that he is about to go away?

K

Ten days later, on the eve of April, Browning bursts his shackles and tumbles out his thanks to her for her letters in a sentence over thirty lines in length. Here surely, and in his prose, not under the influence of any reported criticism, is the explanation of the involved style of *Sordello*? When he was thinking in verse, when his imagination had not fired and fused his feeling, in the cumbered ground of his mind he would flounder as in clay. Hardly one of these letters reads as if it had been written with ease. Yet the pleasure that he took in them, the feeling that she aroused, in kind if not yet in degree, was to flow into the rocking rhythm of *One Word More*, a few years later. The prose of many, indeed of most of the poets, is often so attractive that the contrast between the verse and prose of Browning is extraordinary. We expect the strength and scintillations of granite, but grit and awkwardness are what we find. The clock is striking ten on this sunny morning, and the sun makes his thoughts flow toward her. Will she tell him, when next she shall write, if she felt better at that hour?

A gap of a fortnight intervened, and it was Browning who wrote again to ask if the wind had been responsible. She had not been well, and in her reply twitted him with having gone out of his way to avoid her house because he had not received her permission to pass it. She *had* felt better on that morning, and clearly he cannot have been thinking of her since, for she has not been well on the following days. At the end of April he had a sheaf of her questions to answer, but excused himself in a sentence as long and devious as a Devonshire lane. Conscious of the tangle, he says that this page "is pretty sure to meet the usual fortune of my writings—you will ask what it means." By way of apology he added: "Remember, I write letters to nobody but you, and that I want method." He was soon to confess that he was certainly not gravelled for matter, but that he dared not write all that was in his mind. Nevertheless he never found it easy to express himself in correspondence, and he had a strain of reserve, almost an inhibition, when the subject was very personal to himself.

The month of May begins with her confession that she finds his style Sphinx-like at times. She plagues him with questions about books to find out the extent of their sympathies, and to see him, as it were, by refracted lights. He jumped at the chance to explain his meaning afresh. With her for friend, it seemed foolish to write long letters about a parcel of books. A man, who has wanted all or nothing, like himself, is apt, if he cannot have the all (of her, implied), to be disinclined to chat about anything else. He had startled her by saying that there was next to no pure poetry in Dante, and that Italy was " stuff for the use of the North," but he meant only that one has to go to foreign visitors like Shelley if one would discover what kind of trees and flowers Italian poets see. Then, in a flash, his own enjoyment in visible things : " This world has not escaped me, thank God." He has been troubled by constant headache, he who thought he could never be unwell. These headaches lasted throughout the eighteen months of their correspondence, and it seems probable that they were the physical counterpart of the emotional desire that was flooding him thus late in his life. He finds that the headaches are relieved by violent exercise, so he has been " polking all night and walking home by broad daylight to the surprise of the thrushes in the bush here." An allusion of hers to " The Flight of the Duchess " drew the explanation that the poem was " only the beginning of a story written some time ago, and given to poor Hood in his emergency at a day's notice." Browning, by the way, in a letter to one of

his men friends, called " The Bridge of Sighs " a poem
" alone in its generation, I think." He would like to
send her *Saul*, but " nobody ever sees what I do till it
is printed." The wind that sets the blossoms on his
chestnut tree " rocking like fairy castles in an earth-
quake " is surely the South wind, a mild wind, a wind
of Spring.

The mother in her is up in arms at his avowal that
he has been up at nine after three hours' sleep. " Do
tell me how *Lurias* can ever be made out of such ungodly
imprudences . . . when we all know that thinking,
dreaming, creating people like yourself have two lives
to bear instead of one, and therefore ought to sleep
more than others." This may have moved him, but
there was a tantalizing surprise to follow : " You are
going to Mr. Kenyon's on 12th (May) and yes—my
brother and sisters are going to meet you and your
sister there one day to dinner. Shall I have the courage
to meet you soon, I wonder ! If you ask me, I must
ask myself. . . . You are not going away soon—are
you ? In the meantime you do not understand what it
is to be a little afraid of Paracelsus."

Browning, whose head " took to ringing a literal
alarum," suddenly felt so unwell when dressing for
dinner one night that he cancelled his engagement and
warned Mr. Kenyon not to expect him a few days later.
Mr. Kenyon, of whose shrewd eyes we shall hear more,
hurried round with the news to Miss Barrett. She
snatched her pen, and at midnight dashed off the following note : " May I ask how the head is ? Mr. Kenyon
was here to-day and told me such bad news that I cannot
sleep to-night (although I did once think of doing it)
without asking such a question as this, dear Mr. Browning. . . . I had been thinking so of seeing you on
Tuesday with my sister's eyes—for the first sight." By
return of post she received a very warm letter, telling

her that he has cancelled all his engagements, that his London season is done with, that instead of dining out he will walk in the garden and go to bed at ten. The exclamation, " Oh, the day when I shall see you with my own eyes," may have increased her trepidation. How could her weakness and her admiration withstand a man who, on correspondence alone, could found expectations so urgent as this ? Indeed he wrote the next day another letter in which an apology for these superlatives may be read between the lines. He is at one with her in her praise of Horne, the author of *Orion* and *The Spirit of the Age*, and speaks of the ingratitude of many whom Horne had helped. " I feel grateful to him I know. . . . I am not the one he would have picked out to praise had he not been loyal." Browning leaves the date of their meeting to her, only begging her to take the permanence of his request for granted.

At length her surrender came. On May 16 she wrote : " To prove I am not ' mistrustful,' if you care to come to see me you can come, and that it is my gain (as I feel it to be) and not yours whenever you do come. You will not talk of having come afterwards I know, because . . . I *cannot* admit visitors in a general way." She would not wish to make a spectacle of herself, or to seem to hold out a beggar's hat for sympathy from her sofa. Then she warned him not to expect an illusion. " There is nothing to see in me, nor to hear in me—I never learnt to talk as you do in London, although I can admire that brightness of carved speech in Mr. Kenyon and others. If my poetry is worth anything to any eye, it is the flower of me "—a remark which is an unconscious injustice to her letters, letters so lively and spontaneous as to keep a sympathetic recipient on the tip-toe of expectation concerning her. " Come then. There will be truth and simplicity for you in any case ; and a friend. . . . You must choose whether you would like best to come with Mr. Kenyon or to come alone—and if you would come alone, you must just tell me on what day . . . any day after two and before six."

It was always at six o'clock in the afternoon that Mr. Barrett returned home from his mysterious activities in the City.

Browning received this letter on May 17th. By return of post he wrote: " I will call at two on Tuesday. . . You see it is high time you saw me, for I have clearly written myself out." He may have opened the one that arrived for him on the following day with a trembling hand, but it was to say that Tuesday was all right. But, once more, let him not misapprehend her. " You have lashed yourself up into an exorbitant wishing to see me . . . because I was unfortunate enough to be shut up in a room and silly enough to make a fuss about opening the door." With her sense of the disparity between herself and him, in capacity and in circumstance, she had yet to be convinced that pity was not the motive that made him turn toward her.

On May 20, 1845, Browning at last knocked at the door of 50 Wimpole Street, and was conducted to the shaded room upstairs.

III

There was no witness except her dog Flush to this and most of their subsequent meetings, and a new phase in their relation began. It lasted from May to the following August, when the second climax occurred. In the most recent of her letters she had disclaimed all doubt and any curiosity concerning him. What figure of a man was she to see? Except in their indication of a warm and generous heart, his letters do him less justice than his poems, and have scarcely revealed more than

the ardour of the mood which possessed him. They
leave to our imagination the likable man that we know
him to have been in society, and the " author of Paracelsus," as Miss Barrett thought of him, is better presented by his friend Arnould, " afterwards the well-
known Indian judge, one of whose judgments, on a
question of liberty of conscience, was circulated by
grateful natives in letters of gold." [1]   Writing to Domett
about a year before Browning had found his way to
Wimpole Street, Arnould says :

> Browning's conversation is as remarkably good as his
> books, though so different : in conversation anecdotal,
> vigorous, showing great thought and reading, but in his
> language most simple, energetic and accurate. From the
> habit of good and extensive society he has improved in this
> respect wonderfully. We remember him as hardly doing
> justice to himself in society; now it is quite the reverse—no
> one could converse with him without being struck by his
> great conversational power; he relates admirably.

Miss Barrett knew the poet, and the reluctant letter-
writer. It was a vigorous, well-groomed man of the
world, with a hearty voice and impulsive gestures whom
she was to see; a man who left her room fearing lest he
had talked too loudly.

A new chapter in their correspondence opened. They
had become firm friends. He had now penetrated to
her inner circle. They continued to meet, and to write
between meetings that soon averaged themselves into
three a fortnight. Her following letter does not betray
how agitating to her this interview had been. When
she heard his knock on the door and his foot on the
stairs, her heart failed her. She felt really ill. The
genial strength of the man luckily dissipated these
tremors, and she even wrote asking him to come again,
if he cared to do so, regularly. This invitation pro-

[1] *Robert Browning and Alfred Domett.*   Edited by F. G. Kenyon.

duced an incontinent reply. His actual words can be guessed only, for, in a panic, as much for his sake as for the shock this declaration caused by suddenly transforming the friend into the lover, she administered a gentle but firm rebuke. On receiving this he begged for the return of his outburst, and immediately thrust it into the fire. All we have, then, is the delicate rebuke that reduced him to apology. The window that she had opened was swung back by a sudden breeze, and, unprepared, she spent the twenty-four hours after his letter came in great agitation. Then, on May 2nd, she plucked up her courage and replied to him. As this was the single episode in which he did not treat her fairly, the one error that he retrieved with such care, it is worth a glance. Her words were:

> I intended to write to you last night and this morning, and could not,—you do not know what pain you have given me by writing so wildly. . . . You have said some intemperate things, fancies, which you will not say ever again, nor unsay, but forget at once, and for ever, having said at all; and which (so) will die out between you and me alone, like a misprint between you and the printer. . . . Now if there should be one word of answer attempted to this; or of reference; I must not . . . I will not see you again—and you will justify me later in your heart.

So far he had acted excusably, but he now had to extricate himself, and, in his eagerness to do this completely and at once, he did not withdraw his words, but said that she had misunderstood them, thereby not pausing to consider that he was putting her interpretation of his fervour into an invidious light. It was a desperate attempt not to forfeit the confidence that he had gained. It was made in a panic; otherwise he would have reflected that the effect of his excuses was to put the innocent correspondent in the wrong. Two such successive examples of impulsive feeling might well

have shaken her belief in his stability, but what we have
to notice is the delicacy with which she evaded the
presumption that his recantation implied. " I could
almost smile," he dared to say, " at your misapprehension of what I meant to write "; but he will be on his
good behaviour in the future. This apology, apart from
the injustice to her, was not too penitent, as who should
say : Need we exaggerate a stumble that had no malice
in it ?

She was distressed and uncomfortable, for to be forward was the major offence with which a Victorian
woman could be charged. If she had been angry, he
would have richly deserved it, but she was too gentle,
and too fond of him, for a stern rebuke. The pathos of
her rejoinder, " I assure you I never made such a mistake
in my life before," is irresistible. With humorous
generosity she takes refuge in declaring him obscure,
and recalls the popular verdict upon his poetry to
support her. Not only was she the last person in the
world to deserve such an imputation, but as she was a
recluse and he a man of the world, the vulgar likelihood
was that she might have been guilty of feminine vanity.
Let them both begin afresh, she pleaded, and forget all
about this ' exquisite nonsense.' He received therefore
an invitation to come again.

After their second meeting the skies cleared, but she
begged not to be left to fix his days for him. One dis-
agreeable experience had made her careful : " I cannot
help being uncomfortable in having to do this—it is
impossible." She then allows a gleam of light to fall
upon her household : " But if you knew me—I will
tell you ! if one of my brothers omits coming to this
room for two days, I never ask why it happened ! if my
father omits coming upstairs to say ' good night ' I
never say a word; and not from indifference." It is
not for her to choose the days, but for Browning. She

must feel that, just as she feels that when Mr. Barrett did not choose to come upstairs she was held to have offended autocracy. Browning must not look to her for instruction in anything; there is nothing that she can teach him "except grief." Assured of her friendship now, he askes to be entrusted with any little commissions for which her brothers may be too busy, or Mr. Kenyon not available. Meantime, the secret that he has become her privileged visitor is jealously preserved from the world.

In a discussion of poetry Browning has some interesting confessions of faith : " I know, I have always been jealous of my own musical faculty (I can write music).— Now that I see the uselessness of such jealousy, and am for losing it and letting it go, it may be cramped possibly." He meant that in his boyhood he had written smooth verse with too much ease, and since then had determined to sacrifice sound to sense whenever they threatened to conflict. " Your music (he continued) is more various and exquisite than any modern writer's to my ear. One should study the mechanical part of the art, as nearly all that there is to be studied—for the more one sits and thinks over the creative process, the more it confirms itself as ' inspiration,' nothing more or less. Or, at worst, you write down old inspirations, what you remember of them—but with that it begins." We come now to an interesting passage which helps to show part of the attraction that she had for him. In his own home, as we shall be reminded presently, despite Mr. Browning's scholarly pursuits, there was little community of taste between father and son, and in none hitherto had Browning found a complete and competent response to his own poetry. In her eyes he still seemed to be so far above her that the following confession must have brought her nearer to him than he knew : " You do not understand (he wrote) what a new feeling it is for me to have someone who is to like my verses or I shall not ever like them after!"

The 'first yellow rose' was enclosed in this envelope because one of her poems tells of some 'flowers in a letter' that she had received. She thought it worth while to mention that the flowers had come from her sister Arabel. It was now the middle of June, and we hear more than once that she is better. Indeed it is clear that something was beginning to nourish her vitality at last. The opening door was in her mind, to which Browning had found the key, for the state of her room with its generally shut windows may be guessed from the quickness with which her friends' flowers would pine and wither in their vases. Though lively, he is still troubled by headaches, and when she suggests that a trip abroad might cure them, he replied: "That is just the thing I most want to avoid (for a reason not so hard to guess perhaps). . . . So, till to-morrow —my light through the dark week." She had become this for him, in words even, by the end of June.

The arrival of visitors at Wimpole Street interfered with his coming, and she was fagged by conflicting arrangements. Outside, it was full summer, and, she told him, "now that the windows may be open the flowers take heart to live a little in this room." For the first time we hear also of her growing interest in mesmerism, a discovery supposed by herself and many others in her day to be of spiritual significance. "Miss Martineau is practising mesmerism and miracles on all sides, and counts Archbishop Whately as a new adherent." From the first Browning reserved his judgment, though mesmerism seemed to imply religious unbelief to him: "An old French friend of mine, a dear, foolish, very French heart and soul, is coming presently—his poor brains are whirling with mesmerism in which he believes, as in all other unbelief." Though not published till

Men and Women appeared in 1855, Browning's most breathless lyric, called "Mesmerism," was perhaps the outcome of the letter from Miss Barrett and this discussion with his friend. Very characteristically, he makes the hero of this poem concentrate upon the thought of his mistress until she actually appears. The tensity of his expectation is conveyed in fifteen stanzas in which there is not a single full stop, and the whole poem races to its end with scarcely a breathing-place. As the mesmerist uses his power to draw the absent woman to his side, so, we may be sure, would Browning have pursued the study of it could such a power have come within his reach at this time. During their marriage he and his wife did not correspond for they were never separated, but ten years previously we can overhear him saying: if mesmerism will bring you to me at will, I will become a mesmerist to some purpose.

The position that she was beginning to hold in the world at large is indicated by the arrival of a letter from America addressed to 'Elizabeth Barrett, poetess, London.' The Post Office wrote on the package, "Enquire at Paternoster Row," whereupon someone added, "Go on to Mr. Moxon," and in the end the missive reached Wimpole Street. The innocent belief of the Americans that English poets existed for our Post Office led her, to the subsequent scandal of her feminist admirers, to confess her belief in the intellectual inferiority of women: "Only one woman, and only that one down all the ages of the world, seems to me to justify for a moment the opposite opinion—that wonderful woman George Sand . . . so full of a living sense of beauty, and of noble blind instincts toward an ideal purity—and so proving a right even in her wrong." He must not tell this to Mrs. Jameson, for Miss Barrett had "had a sensation of cold blue steel from her eyes."

On this topic Browning refused to be drawn. The

July day was hot and he was doing all he could to overcome her reluctance to be moving. He hoped that she
had ventured to leave her room, to go out even, and
that she will not allow herself to be discouraged by any
subsequent fatigue. In these promptings we may detect
Browning's growing dissatisfaction with her enforced
helplessness. His common-sense and his personal observation of the invalid suggest to him that the sofa and the
absence of fresh air may have been tried long enough.
Having gained admittance to her cloister, he now begins
to encourage the mildest rebellion against its accepted
rules. We can picture his excitement when she tells
him : " I have really been out ! and am really alive after
it, which is more surprising still." Why must it be
assumed that the slightest movement will kill her ?
" One of my sisters (he learns) was as usual in authority,
and ordered the turning back just according to her own
prudence and not my self-will." His private ' privilege '
of seeing her makes him grateful, a word which they
both use but never succeed in explaining to each other.
Yet he would rather miss her than that she should not
go out, a confession to prove that her health had become
for him the first obstacle to be removed. She admitted
that she was inclined to cling to excuses for remaining
indoors, and he was clearly the only member of her
circle who did not approve of them. Her excuse at the
moment was " any sign of thunder," because her nerves
could not support the noise. She attributed this to one
of the great storms that she had witnessed in the Malvern
Hills, and her description of it and of her old home is
too good to be passed over :

> We lived four miles from the roots (of the hills), through
> all my childhood and early youth, in a Turkish house my
> father built himself, crowded with minarets and domes, and
> crowned with metal spires and crescents, to the provocation
> (as people used to observe) of every lightning of heaven.
> Once a storm of storms happened, and we all thought the

house was struck—and a tree was so really, within two hundred yards of the windows while I looked out—the bark rent from top to bottom—torn into ribbons by the dreadful fiery hands, and dashed out into the air, over the heads of other trees, or left twisted in their branches—torn into shreds in a moment as a flower might be by a child. Did you ever see a tree after it has been struck by lightning? The whole trunk of that tree was bare and peeled—and up that new whiteness of it ran the finger-mark of the lightning in a bright beautiful rose-colour (none of your roses brighter or more beautiful!), the fever-sign of the certain death—that the branches themselves were for the most part untouched, and spread from the peeled trunk in their full summer foliage; and the birds singing in them three hours afterwards! . . . So I get 'possessed' sometimes with the effects of these impressions. . . . When my father came into the room to-day and found me hiding my eyes from the lightning, he was quite angry and called it ' disgraceful to anybody who had ever learnt the alphabet '—to which I answered humbly that I knew it was—but if I had been impertinent, I might have added that wisdom does not come from the alphabet but in spite of it. Don't you think so?

When Mr. Barrett peered round her door, his daughter must have wondered what mood was ' possessing ' him at the moment. The sympathy that her story drew from Browning was of a more positive kind. She is told to set herself against any irksomeness caused by the carriage drives, to think of the delight her returning strength will give to her friends, to remember that this month of July is the time of times for going out. In return for her description of the storm-struck tree, he sends her an account of a storm that he saw at Passagno. The styles of the pair are well contrasted in the parallel.

It was at Passagno, among the Euganean Hills, and I was at a poor house in the town—an old woman was before a little picture of the Virgin, and at every fresh clap she lighted, with the oddest sputtering, muttering and mouthful of prayer imaginable, an inch of guttering candle which, the instant the last echo had rolled away, she as constantly blew out again for saving's sake.

From her description " he sees " the tree. From his we see to the life the old Italian peasant under the stress of the storm. He added an equally amusing account of another storm, which 'Leigh Hunt had from Byron,' and again it is its revelation of human character that fetches him. On his promising to bring the completed draft of " The Flight of the Duchess " to her, she relates her poetic talent to his own : " To judge at all of a work of yours, I must look up to it, and far up—because whatever faculty I have is included in your faculty and with a great rim all round it besides." Her judgment was not deceived, perhaps it was privately confirmed, by the difference in their popularity. That he *will* exaggerate the quality of her poetry brings a pretty rebuke to him : " I do wish that you would consider all this reasonably, and understand it as a third person would in a moment, and consent not to spoil the real pleasure I have had and am about to have in your poetry by nailing me up into a false position with your gold-headed nails of chivalry, which won't hold to the wall through this summer." She has forbidden Mr. Kenyon to show Browning her *Essay on Mind*, which she agrees with the daughter of Coleridge in now calling a 'girl's exercise.' " Bad books (she asserts) are never like their writers you know—and those under-age books are generally bad." There can be no doubt that she was still attributing his attentions to the 'chivalry' and pity of his nature, and that she lived in the expectancy of his waking from his dream concerning her. If his judgment was astray over her poetry, as she knew it to be, how likely it was that he was equally mistaken in the quality of his feelings for herself. To foresee that possible awakening, and to retain his friendship when it came, was one reason why she continued to discourage him in the use of any expressions he might come to repent. Moreover she herself was only half-aroused in her quiet corner. She will have surprised some readers by adding in the same letter: "Sometimes—it is the real truth—I have haste to be done with it all," and again, some of his friends "are weary even unto death of the uses of this life." Existence was indistinguishable from the prison in which she was confined. Even now she did not indulge the hope of escaping, though "Papa and my aunt are discussing the question of sending me off either to Alexandria or Malta for the winter. . . . In every case, I suppose, I should not be much consulted." Poor Miss Barrett! She was wrong in thinking that all her better poems had been written last year, that is to say in 1844. "The best was yet to be," though she did not know it. That she received a present of carnations from Browning's sister shows that his family were in the secret of his new friend.

For a remarkable example of his ragged prose, we may turn to his undated letter written about July 18. It contains his doctrine of the soul expressed, or rather involved, in a sentence twenty-three lines long. The main assertion is that, were this present life everything, we should not possess qualities beyond its immediate uses. The body is self-sufficient for natural ends, but the soul is inarticulate and possesses depths which we discern but dimly, and these argue qualities to be developed hereafter. To Browning this life was a test and no more. The capacity revealed by our defeats and endeavours would survive us. He found an immediate application for this belief in Miss Barrett's attempts to walk, and was overjoyed that a journey should be proposed for her. He implies that he will follow wherever she shall go, and soon came to think that her salvation depended upon her removal from home and its influences to warmth and freedom in the South. He can call as easily "to-morrow at the Muezzin as next Wednesday at three!" This letter, he remarks,

was a second draft, and we can imagine some of the
things that he omitted. The heart that he had failed
to storm he was now nursing like a candle-flame in the
hollow of the hand that wrote to her.

Her letters now trespass into literary criticism, and she
was a good critic of *his* poems from the start. Indeed
she was generally more discerning with modern literature than with the classics, which somehow, and in
spite of her ardour, came to her as dead books, or at
least partly paralysed her mind. She has been turning
to his poems : " first to the St. Praxed's which is of
course the finest and most powerful, and indeed full
of the very power of life and of death. It has impressed
me very much . . . and the Garden Fancies . . . with
that beautiful and musical use of the word ' meander-
ing,' which I never remember to have seen used in
relation to sound before. It does to mate with your
' simmering quiet ' in *Sordello*, which brings the summer
air into the room as sure as you read it." Her criticism
fixes on a " tendency, which is almost a habit and is
very observable in (The Laboratory) I think—of making
lines difficult for the reader to read—see the opening
lines of this poem. Not that music is required everywhere, nor in them certainly, but that the uncertainty
of rhythm throws the reader's mind off the rail . . .
and interrupts his progress with you and your influence
with him. Where we have not direct pleasure from
rhythm, and where no peculiar impression is to be produced by the changes in it, we should be encouraged by
the poet to forget it altogether, should we not? . . .
And how could it be that no one within my hearing
ever spoke of these poems. . . . I was quite unaware
of your having printed so much with Hood. . . . The
world is very deaf and dumb, I think—but in the end,
we need not be afraid of its not learning its lesson."
She breaks off to go out for a drive, and signs herself

L

for the first time with a warmth new to her side of the correspondence. The result is a tiny note from him, the shortest of the collection: " I cannot write this morning—I should say too much, and have to be sorry and afraid." The effect was somewhat spoilt for her by another statement, that he had found her *Essay on Mind* " wonderful." What better proof could she have that he did not know his own? The man who appealed to her so convincingly was expressed more truly in the words: " I would rather go without your letters, without seeing you at all, if that advantaged you—my dear, first and last friend." If he was disinterested to that degree, she could be sure that he was not deceiving himself. The possibility that this might be so was now becoming real to her. During the remainder of the summer the conviction slowly grew.

In answer to his fear that he stayed too long on these Wednesdays she becomes transparently clear: " As long as I live and to the last moment of life, I shall remember with an emotion which cannot change its character, all the generous feeling that you have spent on me, wasted on me." In the poet she was rediscovering some of that intellectual sympathy which had perished for her when her favourite brother had died. But this was accompanied by the fear lest her friendship in some way should come between Browning and his proper life and work. Mr. Kenyon was growing interested in this friendship, and, in answer to his inquiry, she had told him that she " was not disappointed in Mr. Browning." This leads her to ask him " to say just as little about your visits here and of me as you find possible even to Mr. Kenyon as to every other person whatever. As you know, and yet more than you know, I am in a peculiar position—and it does not follow that you should be ashamed of my friendship, or that I should not be proud of yours, if we avoid making it a subject of conversation in high places, or low places." Ought he not also to go away and cure his headaches: "you could write to me, you know, from the end of the world." But Browning did not travel this summer, and Miss Browning sent cakes to Flush, like a tactful and devoted sister.

A new bond between them was revealed by her account of her former visits to dissenting chapels with her father, for Browning too had been nurtured in Nonconformity. The simplicity had appealed to her, but she found "a narrowness among the dissenters which is wonderful; an arid, grey Puritanism in the clefts of their souls."

The reticence that she has asked upon the subject of their friendship he tells her is strictly kept: "The talk of my visits, it is impossible that any hint of them can ooze out of the only three persons in the world to whom I ever speak of them—my father, mother, and sister." It was, on the other hand, fear lest any rumour should reach the ears of Mr. Barrett that led Elizabeth to be so fearful of report. The contrast between the Browning and the Barrett families must have been painful to her, and made her remember, whenever she was tempted to day-dream, how her own father would dash such hopes as Browning's to the ground. It was more cheerful to listen to Browning's vivid praise of her "Vision of the Poets," in which the graphic portraits were a little in the manner of his own. He found a lively image to convey his pleasure: "a line, a few words, and the man is there—one twang of the bow and the arrowhead in the white—Shelley's 'white ideal all statue-blind' is perfect—how can I coin the words?" He was delighted to find that they had both been brought up among the Independents: "Can it be you, my own you past putting away, you are a schismatic and frequenter of Independent Dissenting Chapels? And you confess this to me—whose father and mother went this very morning to the very Independent Chapel where they took me, all those years back, to be baptised—and where they heard, this morning, a sermon preached by the very minister who officiated on that other occasion ! " He believes that all their supposed differences will turn out, when carefully examined, to be ties and coincidences of this kind.

She had been scratching out lines and words in her letters, and he called this a giving and taking away, as if he were not as much interested in her first thoughts as in her second ones. Is she spending on letters to him time that could be spent upon writing fresh poems ?

It is not letters that tire her, " but the bodily exercise is different, and I do confess that the novelty of living more in the outer life for the last few months than I have done for years before, makes me idle and inclined to be idle—and everybody is idle sometimes—even you perhaps—are you not ? For me, you know, I do carpet-work—ask Mrs. Jameson—and I never pretend to be in a perpetual motion of mental industry." Her doubts of the feelings that he was beginning once more to indulge are expressed in the words : " Do not talk again of what you would ' sacrifice ' for me. If you affect me by it, which is true, you cast me from you farther than ever in the next thought." Thus far had he lured her by the middle of August, far enough to be convinced of his devotion, but not far enough to doubt that she could be anything but a hindrance to himself. Yet after seven months she could no longer disguise from herself the direction in which she was being swept.

With unswerving faith in the possibility of her recovery, he tells her that her ' health ' will assure ' all ' eventually, and that she must never lose a sunny day for anyone, not even for him. He sends her some more flowers, and learns that she imperilled their leaves by hunting for a note among them, " not a word, even under the little blue flowers." Then, to make him more fully aware of the conditions of her home-life, she draws the curtain a little aside : " Do you conjecture sometimes that I live all alone here, like Mariana in the moated Grange ? It is not quite so; but where there are many, as with us, and my father is out all day and my brothers and sisters are in and out, and with too large a public of noisy friends for me to bear . . . and I see them only at certain hours . . . except of course my sisters. And then, as you have a ' reputation,' and are opined to talk generally in blank verse, it is not likely that there should be much irreverent rushing into this room when you are known to be in it." He is her ' dearest friend ' now, so much a friend that he dares to say, for reasons given at length, " I am not George Sand's—she teaches me nothing—I look to her for nothing." Though he is very bold, he escapes lightly, perhaps in order that he may be tempted into further confidences. Her eyes seem to rest upon him when she says that she is con-stantly amazed at his curious knowledge of books and men, both general and peculiar, " and you looking none the older for it all." Her pen runs on in imitation of the rain outside which keeps her to her room this after-noon. She was astonished to learn on one of these visits that he was weary in his soul, for a sigh seemed to come unnaturally from a man of his vitality. It must be that he is in need of change, and is missing his regular trip abroad.

He had evidently been inquiring into her life of tute-lage, which she was at some pains to excuse, since she was always ready to excuse her father. She has been free, she says, to read and to think. For the rest, " my own sense of right and happiness on any important point of overt action has never run contrariwise to the way of obedience required of me—while in things not

exactly overt, I and all of us are apt to act sometimes
up to the limit of our means of acting, with shut doors
and windows, and no waiting for cognisance or submission. Ah—and that last is the worst of it all perhaps! to be forced into concealments from the heart
naturally nearest to us; and forced away from the
natural source of counsel and strength!—and then, the
disingenuousness, the cowardice, the 'vices of slaves,'
—and everyone you see—all my brothers—constrained
bodily into submission, apparent submission at least, by
that worst and most dishonouring of necessities, the
necessity of *living*, everyone of them all, except myself,
being dependent in money-matters on the inflexible will
—do you see? But what you do *not* see, what you
cannot see, is the deep tender affection behind and below
all those patriarchal ideas of governing grown-up
children. . . . The evil is in the system—and he simply
takes it to be his duty to rule, and to make happy according to his own views of the propriety of happiness—he
takes it to be his duty to rule like the kings of Christen-
dom, by divine right. But he loves us through and
through it—and I, for one, love him! and when, five
years ago, I lost what I loved best in the world beyond
comparison and rivalship—far better than himself as he
knew . . . I felt that he stood nearest to me on the
closed grave. . . . And I will tell you that not only has
he been kind and patient and forbearing to me through
the tedious trial of this illness (far more trying to standers-
by than you have an idea of perhaps) but that he was
generous and forbearing in that hour of bitter trial, and
never reproached me as he might have done and as my
own soul has not spared—never once said to me then
or since, that if it had not been for *me*, the crown of his
house would not have fallen. [It was at her entreaty
that her brother had joined her at Torquay.] He *never
did*—and he might have said it and more—and I could

have answered nothing. Nothing, except that I had
paid my own price—and that the price I paid was
greater than his loss—his! For see how it was; and
how, ' not with my hand but heart,' I was the cause or
occasion of that misery—and though not with the intention of my heart but with its weakness yet the occasion,
any way!

" They sent me down you know to Torquay—Dr.
Chambers saying that I could not live a winter in London.
The worst—what people call the worst—was apprehended for me at that time. So I was sent down with
my sister to my aunt there—and he, my brother whom
I loved so, was sent too, to take us there and return.
And when the time came for him to leave me, *I*, to
whom he was the dearest of friends and brothers in one
—the only one of my family who—well, but I cannot
write of these things. . . . *I*, weakened by illness, could
not master my spirits or drive back my tears—and my
aunt kissed them away instead of reproving me as she
should have done; and said that *she* would take care
that I should not be grieved—she—and so she sate down
and wrote a letter to Papa to tell him that he would
' break my heart ' if he persisted in calling away my
brother. . . . And Papa's answer was—burnt into me,
as with fire, it is—that ' under such circumstances he
did not refuse to suspend his purpose, but that he considered it to be *very wrong in me to exact such a thing.*' So
there was no separation then : and month after month
passed—and sometimes I was better and sometimes
worse—and the medical men continued to say that they
would not answer for my life—they! if I were agitated
—and so there was no more talk of a separation. And
once *he* held my hand—how I remember! and said that
he ' loved me better than them all and that he *would not*
leave me—till I was well,' he said! how I remember
that! And ten days from that day the boat had left

the shore which never returned; never—and he *had*
left me! gone! For three days we waited—and I
hoped while I could—oh—that awful agony of three
days! And the sun shone as it shines to-day, and there
was no more wind than now; and the sea under the
windows was like this paper for smoothness—and my
sisters drew the curtains back that I might see for myself
how smooth the sea was, and how it could hurt nobody
—and other boats came back one by one.

"Remember how you wrote in your *Gismond*

> What says the body when they spring
> Some monstrous torture-engine's whole
> Strength on it? No more says the soul,

and you never wrote anything which lived with me
more than that. It is such a dreadful truth."

This letter, dated August 25, 1845, as these extracts
will have shown, is crucial in the series. It reveals
why she held herself to blame for the accident to her
brother; it throws a searchlight also upon Mr. Barrett,
and helps to explain why she was ready to make so
many excuses for him. She admits, a few lines lower,
that it would have been cruel of her father to reproach
her, yet his kindness in not being cruel was a positive
thing. The effect upon third parties, however, is not
equally grateful, and this letter marks a further stage in
Browning's intimacy with her. To no one else had she
ever confided the story; to no one else could she bear
to speak of it. Browning had been admitted to the
sanctuary of her heart, and had begun to form a definite
image of Mr. Barrett in relation to his daughter.

This image she endeavours to modify, for she tells
him: "Wilson (her trusted maid) tells me that you
were followed upstairs yesterday . . . by somebody
whom you probably took for my father. . . . No, it
was neither father nor other relative of mine, but an

old friend in rather an ill temper." Browning had now been 'good' for several months, and the temptation to respond ardently to her confidences, recurring strongly with her recent letters, had been resisted. At the end of August, however, he can hardly hold out: " I believe that when you bade me, that time, be silent—that such was your bidding and I was silent—dare I say I think you did not know at that time the power I have over myself, that I could sit and speak and listen as I have done since? Let me say now—this only once—that I loved you from my soul, and gave you my life, so much as you would take,—and all that is done, not to be altered now: it was, in the nature of the proceeding, wholly independent of any return on your part. . . . If I thought you were like other women I have known, I should say so much !—but (my first and last word, I believe in you)—what you could and would give me of your affection, you would give nobly and simply and as a giver—you would not need that I tell you (tell you !) what would be supreme happiness to me in the event—however distant. . . . I will never recur to this, nor shall you see the least difference in my manner next Monday: it is indeed always before me—how I know nothing of you and yours. But I think I ought to have spoken when I did "; and in a postscript, " I trust you see your, dare I say your *duty* in the Pisa affair, as all else must see it." Under his encouragement she had begun to rise from her sofa, to leave her room, even to go out. It was now his conviction that she must abandon Wimpole Street, must go abroad. Then, once let her escape to Italy, and he would see !

It was a difficult situation in which she found herself. She was receiving a lover's letters, the letters of a man who had a great future, a great present, she was sure. She was immensely drawn to him, but if she showed a fraction of the feeling that he aroused, he would be building hopes that were impossible, because she was an invalid, because she would not be a burden, because she was a prisoner in her father's house. " Your life ! (she answered) if you gave it to me and I put my whole heart into it, what should I put but anxiety, and more sadness than you were born to ? What could I give you, which it would not be ungenerous to give ? Therefore we must leave this subject "; and, if she shall go to Pisa, he must not be there " before or as soon." To him the condition of her health was the vital question. Once she was well enough to move, he could be at her side. As he told her exultantly, " Surely the report of Dr. Chambers is most satisfactory—all seems to rest with yourself." He insisted on this text, and it was agreeable to hear that she is just off to Regent's Park, " twice round the Inner Circle is what I can compass now—which is equal to once round the world, is it not ? " She sent to him the American edition of her poems, full of blunders, and the news that the American publisher had sent her a cheque for £14, a tenth of his profits, so that her writings have now a commercial value as well. The chance of Pisa looms nearer with the doctor's favourable report, and Browning was convinced that if once she could be transported anything good might be expected for them both. It was true that Mr. Barrett would have to be consulted, but presumably he wished his daughter well. September opened, full of hope, and with this renewed declaration of Browning's love for her, the second phase of their correspondence ended.

IV

With the autumn and winter of 1845 a new stir and activity came into the life of Miss Barrett, or rather the quickening influence brought to her health and her hopes by Robert Browning was beginning to bear fruit. As Michaelmas approaches she is full of steamers and the like, " but, now that the day seems so near, and in this dead silence of Papa's, it all seems impossible, and I seem to see the stars constellating against me, and give it as my serious opinion to you that I shall not go." She has had, she added, the kindest of letters from Mr. Kenyon urging it. After thanking Miss Browning for presents of flowers that have now become a weekly thought, Elizabeth asked her lover's mercy: "You do not know the courage it requires to hold the intention of it fast through what I feel sometimes. If it (the courage) had been prophesied of me only a year ago, the prophet would have been laughed to scorn." As we know, the prophet would have been reckoning without the gentle but inflexible pressure of Robert Browning.

The figures in the somewhat dim interior at Wimpole Street are lit for us by a description of her sisters which Elizabeth sends in answer to Browning's admission that he was unable to distinguish between them : " Henrietta is the elder, and the one who brought you into this room first; and Arabel, who means to go with me to Pisa, has been the most with me through my illness and is least wanted in the house here, and perhaps—perhaps —is my favourite, though my heart smites me when I write that unlawful word. They are both affectionate and kind to me in all things, and good and lovable in their own beings—very unlike, for the rest; one most caring for the polka—and the other for the sermon preached at Paddington chapel—that is Arabel. . . . Henrietta always managed everything in the house even before I was ill, because she liked it and I didn't, and I waived my right to the sceptre of dinner-ordering."

The pair now observe that they have met seventeen times, and that her last letter was the fiftieth from her. Browning pressed her to go to Italy, and added that his

wishes were always fulfilled. He puts his love for her
into frank words, and records the change that she has
brought into his scheme of existence. Glancing at his
past, he wrote: " My whole scheme of life (with its
wants, material wants at least, closely cut down) was
long ago calculated—and it supposed *you*, the finding
of such an one as you, utterly impossible, because in
calculating one goes upon chances, not on providence
—how could I expect you?" There seems no other
record of the following experience in his life: " Anyone who can live a couple of years on bread and potatoes
as I did once on a time, and who prefers a blouse and a
blue shirt (such as I now write in) to all manner of dress
and gentlemanly appointments, and who can, if necessary, groom a horse not so badly, or at all events would
rather do it all day long than succeed Mr. Fitzroy Kelly
in the Solicitor-Generalship—such an one need not very
much concern himself beyond considering the lilies how
they grow. But now I see you near this life, all changes,
and at a word I will do all that ought to be done." He
recalled that Charles Kean had once offered to give him
£500 for any play that he might find suitable, and he
had no doubt that by the drama, or diplomacy, or whatever course was best approved by such influential friends
as he could boast, he would be able to earn the income
necessary for a husband. With a fervour the sincerity
of which we cannot doubt, he added that he would do
anything to serve her, or her husband if she had one.
" Neither now nor formerly (she told him) has any man
been to my feelings what you are." She would accept
the great trust of his happiness, ' would' not ' does,' but
was not the best future that could be hoped for her
precarious? Thus he must be persuaded to look elsewhere; besides " my own father if he knew that you
had written to me *so*, and that I had answered you so
even, would not forgive me at the end of ten years . . .

because he never does tolerate in his family (sons or daughters) the development of one class of feelings." Then she mentioned a humble but significant fact. Though she does not desire riches, she could not be very poor even if she wished " with three or four hundred a year of which no living will can dispossess me." Nevertheless " the subject will not bear consideration—it breaks in our hands."

This merely circumstantial objection was another step gained for the poet, and her possession of a private income swept away her argument that he must never be allowed to sacrifice the freedom of his leisure for herself. The obstacles at which she still hints he cannot imagine, but he takes her word for it that they exist. The otherwise implied gift of herself finds him not unworthy in that she has been the only love in his life. " Having for many years made up my mind to the impossibility of loving any woman, having wondered at this in the beginning, and fought not a little against it, having acquiesced in it at last, and accounted for it all to myself, and become if anything rather proud than sorry, I say when real love, making itself at once recognized as such, did reveal itself to me at last, I did open my heart to it with a cry, nor care for its overturning all my theory . . . nor apprehend that the new element would harm what was already organized without its help." He will therefore " work blindly at removing these obstacles," like a mole, shall we say, at the foundations of Mr. Barrett's household rule.

A final sacrifice he offers : " one I could cheerfully make, but a sacrifice, and the only one : this careless ' sweet habitude of living '—this absolute independence of mine, which, if I had it not, my heart would starve and die for, I feel, and which I have fought so many good battles to preserve—for that has happened too—this light rational life I lead, and know so well that I lead; this I could give up for nothing less than—what you know—but I would give it up." One must not be too old to make such a change, and he felt sure that "along with what you have thought genius in me, is certainly talent; and I have tried it in various ways, just to be sure I *was* a little magnanimous in never intending to use it." In a charming confession to illustrate this contention, he mentioned what must be the most obscure and unsuspected of his works: "In more than one of the reviews and newspapers that laughed my *Paracelsus* to scorn ten years ago—in the same column often, of these reviews, would follow a most laudatory notice of an Elementary French book, on a new plan, which I *did* for my old French master, and he published —' *that* was really a useful work '! So that when the only obstacle is that there is so much per annum to be procurable, you will tell me."

He had won her heart; the financial difficulty had vanished on her own showing; he had still to win her consent, and to spirit her away. To do this last, her loyalty to her father had to falter, and none but her father himself could bring that about.

V

At this moment a crisis was approaching in Mr. Barrett's relation with her, which together with the state of her health was the only real obstacle in the way. On September 17, 1845, she wrote: "It is all over with Pisa; which was a probable evil when I wrote last, and which I foresaw from the beginning—being a prophetess, you know. I cannot tell you now how it all happened—only do not blame *me*, for I have kept my ground to the last, and only yielded when Mr. Kenyon and all the world see that there is no standing. I am ashamed almost of having put so much earnestness

into a personal matter—and I spoke face to face and quite firmly—so as to pass with my sisters for the 'bravest person in the house' without contestation."
It was no less marvellous that she should have had the strength than the spirit to protest against parental inclinations. If she must have put heart into the poet by saying : " I had done living, I thought, when you came and sought me out! and why? and to what end? That, I cannot help thinking now "—these symptoms of physical and mental vigour may have presented themselves to Mr. Barrett in another light.

Her desire to go to Pisa, a state very different from acquiescence in being sent there or elsewhere by himself, could not but suggest the thing that he most hated in his children, independence and a will of their own. From the moment when the plan began to be put forward on his daughter's part, Mr. Barrett became opposed to the idea of it. That there could be a conflict even of wills was hateful to him. With an infatuation blind to the revolution he was provoking, he appeared to his daughter in his most estranging guise : " Papa has been walking to and fro in this room, looking thoughtfully and talking leisurely—and every moment I have expected I confess some word (that did not come) about Pisa. Mr. Kenyon thinks it cannot end so—and I do sometimes—and in the meantime I do confess to a little 'savageness' also—at heart! All I asked him to say the other day was that he was not displeased with me— and he *wouldn't ;* and for me to walk across his displeasure spread on the threshold of the door, and moreover take a sister and brother with me, and do such a thing for the sake of going to Italy and securing a personal advantage, were altogether impossible, obviously impossible! So poor Papa is quite in disgrace with me just now—if he would care for *that !* "

It was Mr. Barrett's mistake at this time not to care

how she might regard his attitude. He had had the licence of this disregard too long to value the affection which was the final support of his authority, and he refused to contemplate a loyalty to another that any of his children might indulge. Believing himself absolute and secure, he had come to value obedience for its own sake, and to ignore the fact that, away from the planta- tions, and no longer even there, the moral strength of authority rests on the willingness with which it is accepted. He did not know that his daughter was turning her starved affections to the poet, and that the poet was a convinced, though cautious, critic of this authority. At this news Browning's self-control, astonishing throughout in respect of his future father- in-law, nearly gave way. Meantime the family backed up Elizabeth as far as they dared, and this new spirit encouraged Mr. Barrett to despotic obstinacy. Her brother George had promised to speak; the doctor had spoken, and " Arabel had the kindness to say yester- day that if I liked to go she would go with me at what- ever hazard—which is very kind—but you know I could not—it would not be right of me. . . . As to being the cause of any anger against my sister, you would not advise me into such a position I am sure—it would be untenable for a moment." He will not hear of her suggestion that he should go to Italy alone: " Italy *just now*—oh, no ! " Meantime she confessed to having " more strength to lose " which is " so sure to be still better." Browning's courageous facing of the facts, and determination to overcome them, sustained him still.

Her next news is the little spurt of self-assertion before her unbending father : " I have spoken again, and the result is we are in precisely the same position; only with bitter feelings on one side. If I go or stay they *must* be bitter; words have been said that I cannot

easily forget, nor remember without pain; and yet I
do almost smile in the midst of it all, to think how
I was treated this morning as an undutiful daughter. I
tried to put on my gloves—for there was no worse
provocation. At least he complained of the undutiful-
ness and rebellion (!) of everyone in the house—and
when I asked if he meant the reproach for *me*, the answer
was that he meant it for all of us, one with another.
And I could not get an answer. He would not even
grant me the consolation of thinking that I sacrificed
what I supposed to be good, to *him*. I told him that
my prospects of health seemed to me to depend upon
taking this step, but that through my affection for him
I was ready to sacrifice these to his pleasure if he exacted
it—only it was necessary to my self-satisfaction in future
years to understand definitely that the sacrifice was
exacted by him and was made to him—and not thrown
away blindly by a misapprehension. And he would not
answer *that*. I might go my own way, he said—*he*
would not speak—*he* would not say that he was not
displeased with me, nor the contrary : I had better do
what I liked : for his part, he washed his hands of me
altogether. . . . George himself admits I can do no
more in the way of speaking—I have no spell for charming dragons. . . . I feel aggrieved of course and wounded
—and whether I go or stay that feeling must last—I
cannot help it. But my spirits sink altogether at the
thought of leaving England *so*—and then I doubt about
Arabel and Stormie—and it seems to me that I ought
not to mix them up in a business of this kind where the
advantage is merely personal to myself. On the other
side, George holds that if I give up and stay even, there
will be displeasure just the same. . . . But shall I give
it up ? Do think for me."

What could a lover say to this, a lover who had
observed that the first signs of improved health in her

M

dated from the breath of independent love and interest
that he had brought? "I truly wish," he wrote in
impotent anxiety, "that you may never feel what I
have to bear in looking on, quite powerless and silent
while you are subjected to this treatment, which I
refuse to characterise—so blind is it *for* blindness."
Then, on almost the sole occasion when he ventured
to criticize her father, and in language so guarded as
to emphasize every word by the contrast of his own
charity, he spoke. By instinct, or the very tact of love,
he found an argument even higher than her view of
dutiful forbearance to undermine her supposed obligation
to obey.

> I think I ought to understand what a father may exact,
> and a child should comply with; and I respect the most
> ambiguous of love's caprices if they give never so slight a
> clue to their all-justifying source . . . but now here, the
> jewel is not being over-guarded, but ruined, cast away. And
> whoever is privileged to interfere should do so in the posses-
> sor's own interest—all commonsense interferes—all rationality
> against absolute no-reason at all. And you ask whether you
> ought to obey this no-reason? I will tell you: all passive
> obedience and implicit submission of will and intellect is by
> far too easy, if well-considered, to be the course prescribed
> by God to Man in this life of probation—for they *evade* pro-
> bation altogether, though foolish people think otherwise.
> . . . In your case I do think that you are called upon to do
> your duty to yourself; that is, to God in the end. . . . Every
> interest that appears to be affected by your conduct should
> have its utmost claims considered—your father's in the first
> place . . . and this examination made, with whatever earnest-
> ness you will, I do think and am sure that on its conclusion
> you should act in confidence that a duty has been performed
> —difficult, or how were it a duty? Will it not be infinitely
> harder to act so than blindly to adopt his pleasure, and die
> under it? Who cannot do *that*?

It was skilful, and sound, advocacy. Thus the new
love that was displacing the old was taking higher
ground also. It was proving, not only claiming to be,

the superior. It forced the daughter to recognize that Mr. Barrett *would* rather see her dead than free from him. The poet has also gathered courage from another corner.

"How 'all changes'—when I first knew you, you know what followed. I supposed you to labour under an incurable complaint—and of course to be completely dependent on your father for its commonest alleviations. . . . When you lately told me that 'you could never be poor'—all my solicitude was at an end —I had only myself to care about. . . . Now again the circumstances shift—and you are in what I should wonder at as the veriest slavery—and I who *could* free you from it, I am here scarcely daring to write. . . . Now while I dream, let me once dream! I would marry you now and thus—I would come when you let me, and go when you bade me. . . . I deliberately choose the realisation of that dream (of simply sitting beside you for an hour every day) rather than any other, excluding you, I am able to form for this world—of any world I know."

She was convinced at last, but still inexorable. She confessed that by this letter, the first of his in which the word marriage occurs, " the tear-marks went away in the moisture of new, happy tears. . . . You have touched me more profoundly than I thought even you could have touched me—my heart was full when you came here to-day. Henceforth I am yours for everything except to do you harm. . . . It is all I am able to say, and perhaps all I shall be able to say. However this may be, a promise goes to you in it that none, except God and your will, shall interpose between you and me,—I mean that, if He should free me within a moderate time from the trailing chain of this weakness, I will then be to you whatever at that hour you shall choose——."

He had won her; the obstacle of her health was
melting in his sunlight, of her will in his consideration.
Even her willing surrender to Mr. Barrett had vanished
away. Mr. Barrett was indeed a formidable barrier,
but his attitude over the Pisa affair had undermined his
authority, and had thus played unconsciously into the
lovers' hands.

VI

Browning continued to press his advantage in the
inch-by-inch progress with which he was moving open
her imprisoning doors. " Now (he tells her) you must
think the boldlier about whatever difficulties remain,
just because they are so much the fewer . . . and do
make ' journeys across the room ' and out of it, mean-
while, and *stand* when possible—get all the strength
ready now that so much is to be spent. Oh, if I were
by you ! " He is, and knows he is, her best physician,
and there was still some faint idea of Italy, to which
friends were offering to take her, if Papa would allow.
She was afraid that she had made him look an ogre,
and begged Browning not to feel too severe. There
was, she explained, another side to her father's character
which Browning had not been privileged to view. She
did not dare to accept her lover's offer of a cloak : " Papa
knowing it would not like it," and the present might
awaken suspicions that it was most necessary not to
arouse. Besides, she was still dallying with the question
of steamboats despite the expressed pleasure of Papa.
She says that she walks upright every day, and is not
losing courage. " Be sure I shall be ' bold ' when the
time for going comes—and both bold and capable of
the effort . . . If I stay it will not be from a failure in
my resolution—that will not be—shall not be . . . and
now I feel as if I should *not* stay in England, which is

the difference between one five minutes and another."
When she thought of herself, she felt equal to the effort.
When she thought of her father, she knew that he could
bear her down; "scenes," of which we are to hear
something, are really more than sensitive people can
endure. Either these people must escape or collapse
beneath them.

Her letter of October 11, 1845, admits us into this
household, an Ibsen household, which only the robust
vitality of Robert Browning, poet and lover, was strong
enough to sweep clean of its gloom, its cobwebs, its
presiding genius of bane. "Well, George will probably speak before he leaves town, which will be on
Monday! and now that the hour approaches, I do feel
as if the house stood upon gunpowder and as if I held
Guy Fawkes' lantern in my right hand. . . . To show
the significance of those evening or rather night visits
of Papa's—for they come sometimes at eleven and
sometimes at twelve—I will tell you that he used to
sit and talk in them, and then *always* kneel and pray
with me and for me, which I used of course to feel as
a proof of very kind and affectionate sympathy on his
part, and which has proportionally pained me in the
withdrawing. They were no ordinary visits you observe
—and he could not well throw me further from him
than by ceasing to pay them—the thing is quite expres-
sively significant. Not that I pretend to complain, nor
to have reason to complain. One should not be grateful for kindness only while it lasts : that would be a
short-breathed gratitude. I just tell you the fact proving
that it cannot be accidental."

Mr. Barrett was coming perilously, invisibly near to
forfeiting his daughter's loyalty, but even now Browning
gives him the benefit of one last doubt. "If after all
you do not go to Pisa, why we must be cheerful and
take courage and hope. I cannot pretend but to see

with your eyes and from your place you know—and
will let this be all one surprising and deplorable mistake
of mere love and care—but no such other mistake ought
to be suffered, if you escape the effects of this. . . .
Oh, these vain wishes—the will here, and no means."
To be by her: he can 'stop at that, but not before.'
To cheer her he reported that her publisher says that
her poems are selling well and will show a clear profit;
that Moxon spoke encouragingly of his own prospects,
that Tennyson has received his pension of £200 a year.
There was a scare that one of her brothers had a fever,
but the elder Brownings did not fear contagion, and
the poet continued to call. Then the critical interview
occurred between George and Mr. Barrett.

"Do not be angry with me (she pleaded), do not
think it my fault, but I do not go to Italy. It has ended
as I feared. What passed between George and Papa
there is no need of telling: only that the latter said
that 'I might go if I pleased but that going it would be
under his heaviest displeasure.' George, in great indignation, pressed the question fully, but all was in vain,
and I am left in this position—to go, if I please, with
his displeasure over me (which, after what you have
said, and after what Mr. Kenyon has said, and after my
own conscience and deepest moral convictions say aloud,
I would unhesitatingly do at this hour!) and necessarily
run the risk of exposing my sister and brother to that
same displeasure—from which risk I shrink and fall
back and feel that to incur it, is impossible. . . . And
so tell me that I am not wrong in taking up my chain
again and acquiescing in this hard necessity. The
bitterest 'fact' of all is that I had believed Papa to have
loved me more than he obviously does—but I never
regret knowledge."

It was Browning and not Mr. Barrett who had finally
taught her what love means, and the difference in the

fruits of selfishness and of affection. But the habit of
obedience is not easily shaken off, and the wisp of it, so
to speak, clung to the plea of what her family would
have to endure if she rebelled. It was not really valid
so long as she did not carry them with her from London,
but the fascination of her story is the slow and human
stripping, one by one, of the swathes that tied her, in
body, mind, and habit, to her father's heels. She
promised, if possible, to keep well during the winter,
and that she ' will not be beaten down if the will can
do anything.' We feel that Mr. Barrett must have
wondered what was happening to the obedient and
dutiful invalid upstairs. She herself was astonished at
the contrast.

" I admire how, if all had happened so but a year
ago (yet it could not have happened quite *so*) I should
certainly have been beaten down—and how it is different
now—and how it is only gratitude to you to say that it
is different now. My cage is not worse but better since
you brought the green groundsel to it—and to dash
oneself against the wires of it will not open the door.
We shall see—and God will oversee. And in the meantime you will not talk of extravagances; and then
nobody need hold up the hand : as I said and say, I
am yours, your own, only not to hurt *you*." She continued to be afraid of plucking the feathers from his
wings, of being a drag upon his feet, a hindrance to his
work. Since he was now more to her than all the
world beside, to hurt him would be to wound her hopes
at their tenderest. We watch the slow barometer of her
trust and courage rise degree by degree, in these letters
of the winter 1845–6, and by October she had come to
the point of declaring, " I will never fail to you from
any human influence whatever." Mr. Barrett was
dethroned. Only her precarious health hindered her
from making an explicit promise to marry Browning.

Meantime she counselled caution less for her father's sake than for her own. "We must be wise in the general practice and abstain from too frequent meetings for fear of difficulties." At his next visit Browning asked certain questions, and she lets us overhear her reply : " I believed I had sufficiently made clear to you long ago how certain questions were ordered in this house, and how no exception was to be expected for my sake or even for yours. . . . The weekly one visit is a thing established and may go on as long as you please —and there is no objection to your coming twice a week now and then, if now and then merely—if there is no habit, do you understand ? . . . Let Pisa prove the excellent hardness of some marbles ! . . . the other obvious evils the late decision about Pisa has aggravated beyond calculation—for as the smoke rolls off we see the harm done by the fire." Of his new poems she liked ' supremely ' the ' Lost Leader ' and the ' Thoughts from the Sea,' " those grand sea sights in the long lines."

She had been accustomed to tease him with questions concerning the reason for his affection for herself, which always stood, to her, in need of explanation. He found the convincing reason at last : " I love you because I love you," because there was no reason but his love itself. She was human enough, woman enough, to surrender completely to this argument, which indeed is the only satisfactory reason, and perhaps we may date the fourteenth of her Sonnets, which expounds it, from this time. She was afraid of his impulsiveness, his chivalry, his pity, none of which could be expected to endure by themselves the strain that a permanently invalid wife must fear to be. As we shall see, his was the reason that she had instinctively given in her girl-hood when the subject was under discussion by some of her friends. She passes on to explain that no caution need apply to her brothers and sisters : " the caution referred to one person alone. In relation to whom there will be no getting over . . . but though I have been a submissive daughter, and this from no effort, but from love's sake, and because I loved him tenderly (and love him) and hoped that he loved me back again even if the proofs came untenderly sometimes—yet I have reserved to myself always that right over my own affections which is the most strictly personal of all things."

Browning's headaches are better, and he urges her by every means to grow well : " Think what telling me that you grow stronger would mean . . . so try, try, dearest, every method, take every method of hasten-ing such a consummation. Why, we shall see Italy together ! " He has become her 'angel at the gate of the prison '; and all she is now afraid of, except Papa, is Mr. Kenyon ' when he puts on his spectacles.'

Her mind is equally busy with the past, and she let Browning now see the state in which she first received him. " When I wrote that letter to let you come the first time, do you know, the tears ran down my cheeks —I could not tell you exactly why : partly it might be mere nervousness. And then I was vexed with you for wishing to come as other people did, and vexed with myself for not being able to refuse you as I did them." Here is further evidence, if we needed it, of the ideal that Browning had represented to her imagination before the two had met. In his works she had recognized the voice of a great poet, and he in hers the rare voice of a poet who was also an exceptionally charming Christian woman. His reply admitted that " from the beginning the personal interest absorbed every other, greater or smaller," and these last words clearly included her poems. They had been drawn to each other, not only as man to woman, but as poet to poet, the strongest double magnet two hearts can feel. Their correspondence was like a recognition, their acquaintance a taking-up of already familiar intercourse, their love the completion of the vision they had seen. From the first he had been carried away, and if she had hesitated it was because the reality seemed a good beyond her power to return.

VII

It is roughly with November that the love-letters proper begin, for she started that month by asking him if she might have back the missing letter, the one that had brought him into trouble and which he had begged to have returned in order to destroy. He had burnt it, but her request showed that she accepted it now. Another little sign was Mr. Kenyon, who had been scanning her with his spectacles, and had talked of its being a mystery how Browning had made his way ' here.' Another surprise was that she had walked, instead of being carried, downstairs. In six months she had recovered the use of her limbs, though this feat seemed to her to be due as much to audacity as to vigour. Their differences now are but the light and shade of their affection. She rebukes him genially for speaking of her ' glorious genius,' and says that it was not until he had found an ' irrational reason ' that she was convinced that he really loved her for herself. Indeed, years ago, when some young women were discussing how best an attachment should begin, she had declared that the motive should lie in the feeling itself and not in its object, and that " the affection which could (if it could) throw itself out on an idiot with a goitre would be more admirable than Abelard's."

She tells him that the rhythm of " The Flight of the Duchess " more and more strikes her to be " a new thing," and her chance admission, that opium is pre-

scribed for her occasionally, awakened his fears. He
assured her that his love had always been independent
of his admiration for her poetry, and the best proof,
clearer to us than to him, was that he had originally
responded to the character that her poems revealed.
" Always remember," his letter proceeded, " I never
wrote to you, all the years, on the strength of your
poetry, though I constantly heard of you through Mr.
Kenyon, and was near seeing you once." He distinguished himself carefully from " the foolish crowd
of rushers-in upon genius—who come and eat their
bread and cheese on the high altar and talk of reverence
without one of its surest instincts—never quiet till they
cut their initials on the cheek of the Medicean Venus to
prove they worship her." His admiration had gone its
natural way in silence, but when her two volumes
appeared, and Browning found his name there, and
began to speak to Mr. Kenyon about them, and Kenyon
had said that she would be pleased to hear, then " I did
write, on account of my purely personal obligation,"
but still without prescience of all that followed; for he
was " scheming how to get done with England and go
to my heart in Italy." Her sonnet, " Past and Future,"
affects him ' more than any poem I ever read.'

Meditating the stages of their intimacy, she repeats
that her only doubt of him had been whether he was
not self-deceived. The resolution of this doubt had
been ' something between a dream and a miracle,' for
he, who had the world about him, yet made her the
centre of his life. Indeed she continued to protect him
against herself until the last distinction had died. On
his part, he does succeed in convincing us that there was
only one woman in the world for him, and that had he
missed Elizabeth he might never have married. He,
who has never kept a journal in his life, has counted and
recorded every meeting and minute spent with her, and

these last, when added together, have amounted to
'nearly two days now.' By the end of November he
has begged for a lock of her hair. Every new advance
terrified her a little, as one by one the past foundations
of her prison-life were sapped. She insisted on an
exchange, and in the letters on the subject, which explain how she had repeatedly refused such gifts to girls,
she insists how she has believed in him despite that
piece of disingenuousness in the past. "Did I not
believe you even in your contradiction of myself—in
your Yes and No on the same subject—and take the
world to be turning round backwards and myself to
have been shut up here till I grew mad—rather than
disbelieve you either way." This reminder was the
price that he had to pay for a lock of her hair.

By December 1845, Browning has begun to confess
that these meetings and letters are insufficient, and to
force her to see that matters cannot rest where they are.
In return he received another sketch of the situation in
her family. "It is not my fault if I have to choose
between two affections, only my pain. . . . I shall be
thundered at; I shall not be reasoned with—it is impossible. I could tell you some dreary chronicles made
for laughing and crying over, and you know that if
once I thought I might be loved enough to be spared
above others, I cannot think so now. In the meantime
we need not be for the present afraid. Let there be
ever so many suspectors there will be no informers.
. . . So it has been in other cases than ours—and so it
is, at this moment in the house, with others than ourselves. . . . Unless you said it was all a mistake (will
you, again?) . . . anything less would be something
worse than nothing: and would not save me—which
you were thinking of, I know—would not save me the
least of the stripes. . . . It is an obliquity of the will,
and one laughs at it till the turn comes for crying.

Poor Henrietta has suffered silently, with that softest of possible natures, which hers is indeed, beginning with implicit obedience, and ending with something as unlike it as possible; but, as you see, where money is wanted, and where the dependence is total, see! And when once, in the case of the one dearest to me; when just at the last he was involved in the same grief, and I attempted to make over my advantages to him (it could be no sacrifice you know—I did not want the money and could buy with it nothing so good as his happiness) why then, my hands were seized and tied, and then and there, in the midst of the trouble, came the end of all! I tell you all this just to make you understand a little." She went on to speak of her favourite uncle: "It is through him in part that I am richer than my sisters, through him and his mother—and a great grief it was and trial when he died a few years ago in Jamaica. . . . Once he said to me, 'Do you beware of ever loving! If you do, you will not do it by half: it will be for life and death.'"

Thus by the end of the year the house in Wimpole Street was seething with quiet conspirators, and active rebellion was being plotted both upstairs and down. Elizabeth, whom Mr. Barrett, in the belief that she would never desire to marry, had once called the ' purest ' of his children, was using the word marriage in her letters to the weekly visitor known to Mr. Barrett as the ' pomegranate man.' She shared her uncle's estimate of her nature: "The capacity of loving is the largest of my powers I think—I thought so before I knew you—and one form of feeling. . . . From out of the deep dark pits men see the stars more gloriously—and de profundis amavi." Referring to her family name of Moulton, which her brothers thought ought to appear upon her title-pages as well, she wrote: "I would give ten towns in Norfolk (if I had them) to own some purer lineage than the blood of the slave. Cursed we are from generation to generation ! "

The year 1846 opened with her scruples conquered but not removed. She foresaw, for instance, that Mr. Kenyon would say : " It is ungenerous of her to let such a risk be run." He made her nervous with " his all-scrutinising spectacles, put on for great occasions, and his questions that seem to belong to the spectacles, they go together so—and then I have no presence of mind, as you may see without the spectacles. Two or three times I fancied that Mr. Kenyon suspected some-thing—but if he ever did, his only reproof was a redupli-cated praise of you—he praises you always and in relation to every sort of subject." She often brooded on the stages by which the abstract poet, the personality that was Mr. Kenyon's friend, the man who wished to write to her, had become what cannot now be expressed. Then she gave the account of the country life that she had hated, as we read it in an earlier chapter, and these reminiscences brought Browning to confess his own taste for wild country things, especially vermin. Speak-ing of his liking for toads and snails, he wrote : " I always loved those wild creatures God ' sets up for themselves ' so independently of us, so successfully, with their strange, happy minute inch of a candle, as it were, to light them, while we run about and against each other with our great cressets and fire-pots." The extent to which she herself had lived in books and imagination can be judged from a curious remark. She told Browning that, for a long while, his letters brought him nearer to her than his presence. No doubt the visible vitality of the man took, as it were, her breath away. She had always been a little afraid of too much concentrated life. There used to be a great ancient toad in her garden, which, though she was sure that he wore a jewel in his head, she had not dared approach too nearly. She had the common horror of bats, " which come sailing, without a sound, and go, you cannot guess where," the most supernatural-seeming of natural creatures. She thinks of Browning, she tells him, as prisoners think of liberty. " Is it wonderful that I should stand as in a dream, and disbelieve, not you, but my own fate ? Was ever anyone taken suddenly from a lampless dungeon and placed upon the pinnacle of a mountain, without the head turning round and the heart turning faint, as mine do ? "

VIII

Before January 1846 was over, he had advanced to the point of pressing her to fix a time for their marriage. In a panic she said that it was " advisable to hurry nothing," because at the slightest suspicion Browning would be refused admission to her house, and any letters that he wrote to her would " infallibly be stopped and destroyed—if not opened." This was not timid imagining but dire experience. " I look back with shuddering (she wrote) to the dreadfulness in which poor Henrietta was involved who never offended as I have offended— years ago which seem as present as to-day. She had forbidden the subject to be referred to until that consent was obtained—and at a word she gave up all, at a word. In fact she had no true attachment, as I observed to Arabel at the time—a child never submitted more meekly to a revoked holiday. Yet how she was made to suffer. Oh, the dreadful scenes ! and why, because she had seemed to feel a little. I told you, I think, that there was an obliquity, an eccentricity, or something beyond, on one class of subjects. I hear how her knees were made to ring upon the floor, now ! She was carried out of the room in strong hysterics, and I who rose up to follow her, though I was quite well at that time and

suffered only by sympathy, fell flat down upon my face
in a fainting fit. Arabel thought I was dead. I have
tried to forget it all—but now I must remember—and
throughout our intercourse I *have* remembered. . . . Do
you remember, besides, that there can be no faltering
on my part, and that, if I should remain well, which is
not proved yet, I will do for you what you please and
as you please to have it done. . . . My sisters know.
Arabel is in most of my confidences, and being often
in the room with me taxed me with the truth long ago
—she saw I was affected from some cause—and I told
her. We are as safe with both of them as possible.
. . . My brothers . . . are full of suspicions and con-
jectures which are never unkindly expressed. I told
you once that we held hands the faster in this house
for the weight over our heads. But the absolute knowledge would be dangerous for my brothers. . . . My
life was ended when I knew you, and if I survive myself
it is for your sake."

Nothing could be more generous than the self-control
which Browning, even when thus fully informed, preserved. He replied that such a state of affairs resembled
his peculiar nightmare, in which he is standing by
powerless before the infliction of cruelty on some unresist-
ing beast. " Let no one try this kind of experiment on
me or mine," was his only comment. Had Mr. Barrett
ever tried it on Elizabeth in Browning's presence, it is
hard to say what might not have occurred : possibly the
martinet would have crumpled up at the first sign of
genuine anger from an independent man. " I do hold
it (the poet continued) the most stringent duty of all
who can to stop a condition, a relation of one human
being to another which God never allowed to exist
between Him and ourselves." Then we have the contrast provided by the interior of his own home : " If I
went with this letter downstairs and said simply ' I want

this taken to the direction to-night, and am unwell and unable to go, will you take it now?' my father would not say a word, or rather would say a dozen cheerful absurdities about his ' wanting a walk,' ' just having been wishing to go out,' etc. At night he sits studying my works—illustrating them (I will bring you drawings to make you laugh)—and yesterday I picked up a crumpled bit of paper—' his notion of what a criticism on this last number ought to be, none that have appeared satisfying him.' So judge what he will say! And my mother loves me just as much more as must of necessity be." He said that the one trial that he would never be able to bear would be " the repetition of these scenes— intolerable, not to be written of."

It is interesting to have Mr. Kenyon's view of Mr. Barrett, which his daughter reported to the poet : " Mr. Kenyon says broadly that it is monomania, neither more nor less. Then the principle of passive filial obedience is held, drawn (and quartered) from Scripture. He *sees* the law and the Gospel on his side. Only the other day there was a setting forth of the whole doctrine, I hear, downstairs—' passive obedience, and particularly in respect to marriage.' One after the other, my brothers all walked out of the room, and there was left for sole auditor Captain Surtees Cook, who had especial reasons for sitting it out against his will—so he sate and asked ' if children were to be considered as slaves,' as meekly as if he were asking for information. I could not help smiling when I heard of it. He is just succeeding in obtaining what is called an adjutancy, which with half pay will put an end to many anxieties."

The question whether she shall begin to receive Browning standing and no longer from her sofa agitates them. If she does show that new sign of vigour, he says, " I should not remain master of myself I do believe." Despite the inchmeal progress of the past

N

year, and the grim obstacle of Mr. Barrett, by the end
of January 1846 Browning was confident. "All steps
secured but the last, and that last the easiest! Yes, far
easiest! For first you had to be created, only that;
and then, in my time; and then, not in Timbuctoo but
in Wimpole Street, and then the strange hedge round the
sleeping Palace keeping the world off—and then . . .
all was to begin, all the difficulty only begin : and now
—see where is reached!" This brings her reminder
that "for *him*—he would rather see me dead at his foot
than yield the point : and he will say so, and mean it,
and persist in the meaning."

The letter from her, dated January 27, 1846, gives a
vivid and painful chronicle of the repulses which her
heart had undergone at her father's hands. It is too
long to quote, but it amplifies the picture with which
we are already familiar. Her "heart has struggled in
towards him through the stones of the rock—thrust off
—dropping off—turning in again and clinging," till the
final rebuff over the Pisa affair proved to her beyond
doubting that Mr. Barrett was fonder of his authority
over her than of herself. She concluded by saying :
"After all he is the victim. He isolates himself—and
now and then he feels it—the cold dead silence all round,
which is the effect of an incredible system. If he were
not stronger than most men, he could not bear it as he
does. With such high qualities too !—so upright and
honourable—you would esteem him, you would like
him, I think." She explained that she could never give
Browning the chance of making his own way in the
household. "I have not influence enough for *that*.
George can never invite a friend of his even." Captain
Surtees Cook, who eventually married her sister Henrietta, comes "by particular license and association";
but once when, in return for Mr. Kenyon's particular
kindness, she had asked that he should be invited to

dinner, he "an old college friend, and living close by
. . . it was in vain."

Subject to her health growing no worse, Browning
now claimed the fulfilment of her promise, " say, at the
summer's end : it cannot be for your good that this
state of things should continue. We can go to Italy for
a year or two and be as happy as day and night are long."
Her last excuse is that this decision shall not be regarded
as binding until the hour to act upon it shall have come.
It is her final plea for delay, the lingering fear that somehow her hopes would be disappointed of their fulfilment.
When she does indulge them, she declares, whether in
Italy or England, " we shall have sufficient or more than
sufficient means of living, without modifying by a line
that ' good free life ' of yours."

In February she still insisted that it must be called a
conditional engagement, but throughout the spring he
strengthened her conviction in the certainty of their
future. He assumed their early marriage time after
time, and said that together each of them will accomplish
all that each was intended to do. Like other lovers they
refined upon each other's thoughts, explained, and
created, minute misunderstandings, and occasionally
indulged in superstitious freaks. Browning, on a
sudden impulse, consulted the ' sortes ' in the pages of
an Italian grammar, and hit upon a saying that more
than satisfied their hearts. He was often laid up with
headaches, and these may well have been due to the
emotions, so ardent but so controlled, under which he
was living. For her part, his visits produced a reaction :
the light and life that he brought with him began to ebb
the moment he had shut the door behind him, and she
was her lonely captive self once more.

One of their interesting discussions turned upon the
question whether letters should be published or burnt,
and his reserve elsewhere was so strict that, without this

passage, we might wonder if even his admiration for
her letters was sufficient to explain the consent to their
publication implied by leaving the discretion to his son.
He affirmed that " real letters " limiting the experience
to two persons might be burnt, but that clever and amusing letters like Miss Martineau's or Miss Mitford's to
Elizabeth could be read by all the world.   Miss Barrett's
view was different, and probably influenced Browning's
decision in regard to the eventual publication of her
own.   " I for my part (she wrote) value letters (to talk
literature) as the most vital part of biography, and for
any rational being to put his foot on the traditions of his
kind in this particular class does seem to me as wonderful
as possible.   [Miss Martineau allowed her letters to be
shown, but forbade them ever to be published.]   Who
would put away one of those multitudinous volumes
even which stereotype Voltaire's wrinkles of wit—even
Voltaire ?   I can read book after book of such reading,
or could.   And if her (Miss Martineau's) principle were
carried out, there would be an end !   Death would be
deader from henceforth.   Also it is a wrong selfish
principle and unworthy of her whole life and profession,
because we should all be ready to say that if the secrets
of our daily lives and inner souls may instruct other
surviving souls, let them be open to men hereafter, even
as they are to God now.   Dust to dust, and soul-secrets
to humanity—there are natural heirs to all these things.
Not that I do not intimately understand the shrinking
back from the idea of publicity on any terms—nor that
I should not myself destroy papers of mine which were
sacred for *me* for personal reasons—but then I would
never call this natural weakness virtue, nor would I, as
a teacher of the public, announce it and attempt to justify
it as an example to other minds and acts, I hope. . . .
All the letters in the world are not like yours and I would
trust them for that verdict with any jury in Europe, if

they were not so far too dear . . . but nobody in the world writes like you—not so vitally." It was, no doubt, the memory of the opinion in this letter of hers, dated February 17, 1846, that justified Browning in preserving this intimate correspondence for posterity. His own letters were probably included as the foils and excuses for hers.

That Browning himself could have indulged other ambitions is clear from a remark that is apt to be overlooked. In the same month he told her that he had received a strictly private letter "proposing that I should start in a few days for St. Petersburg, as secretary to somebody going there on a ' mission of humanity.' " She begged him not to go, and he was genuinely vexed that she should consider the quality of his letters. He never felt less of a writer than when corresponding with her, and she had some difficulty in extricating herself. Who could indulge irrelevant feelings over notes that were to him no less than the beatings of his heart ? It is a good instance of the difference between the poet and the man in him. His imagination was oblique and dramatic. He had confessed that he could not write poems in the first person to express his thoughts. Thus when he was personal, as in his love-letters, the letters, as letters, are not remarkable except for the generous heart and excellent courage that they reveal. Had he sat down, however, to compose love-letters for any of the Abelards of history, we cannot doubt that he would have expressed the character and soul of a lover as fully as in the imaginary letters that he penned for the pagan philosopher Cleon, or the Arab doctor Karshish. His dramatic imagination could give beautiful expression to every character except his own. It is true that the famous third verse in the epilogue to *Asolando* is an exception, but for the rest his nearest self-portrait is the indirect one, " How It Strikes a Contemporary," where

" the third house from the bridge " in which the poet of the poem lived is very like a reminiscence of his own house by the canal in Warwick Crescent, though he did not actually move there till years later.

Two little sketches of his father and hers are worth detaching. Speaking of his father, Browning wrote : " When walking with me when a child, I remember, he bade a little urchin whom we found fishing with a stick and a string for sticklebacks in a ditch, ' to mind that he brought any sturgeon he might catch to the king.' " It is a charming glimpse of a lovable personality. There is not this humour in Miss Barrett's anecdote : " I surprised everybody in this house by consenting to see you Then, when you came, you never went away. I mean I had a sense of your presence constantly. . . . I said to Papa in my unconsciousness next morning : ' It is most extraordinary how the idea of Mr. Browning does beset me—I suppose it is not being used to see strangers, in some degree ; but it haunts me—it is a persecution.' On which he smiled and said that ' it was not grateful to my friend to use such a word.' "

Looking back on those early meetings, she declared that Browning had come with the intention to love whatever he should find. He denied the intention but not the presentiment. One of her greatest charms for him was her unconsciousness of her own attractiveness. To this simplicity her new tendency to analyse the progress of their affection seemed in his eyes profane. " If you let me, love, I ask not again, ever again to consider how it came, and whence, and when, so curiously, so pryingly, but believe that it was always so." He sent her a sprig of hawthorn to bear witness to the arrival of Spring, and learnt in answer that, carefully cloaked, she had descended to the drawing-room to the astonishment of Henrietta, who detained her that she might not miss the great sight of Captain Surtees Cook, fresh from the

Palace, in full regimentals. The adventure was a success, for Elizabeth walked upstairs too, as if she were a Hercules. The mention of the regimentals led Browning to confess his love for bright colours and his delight in such words as vermilion. He asks if she has read Nat Lee's tragedies. "In one of them a man angry with a Cardinal cries:

> Stand back, and let me mow this poppy down,
> This rank red weed that spoils the Churches' corn;

is not that good?"

IX

By March she has determined to suspend decisions no longer: "Either we will live on as we are until an obstacle arises, . . . or I will be yours in the obvious way to go out of England the next half hour if possible. . . . Virtually the evil is the same all round whatever we do." Now that she was near the sticking point, little anxieties and alarms began to crowd upon her, and indeed it was not till they threatened to involve her removal with her family to the country that her mind was made up at last. For instance, Mr. Barrett began to take notice, a sign sufficiently alarming in itself: "Dearest (she wrote) it was plain to me yesterday evening when he came into this room for a moment at seven o'clock, before going to his own to dress for dinner, plain that he was not altogether pleased at finding you here in the morning. There was no pretext for objecting gravely, but it was plain he was not pleased. Do not let this make you uncomfortable, he will forget all about it, and I was not *scolded*, do you understand. It was more manner, but my sisters thought as I did of the significance :—and it was enough to prove to me (if

I had not known) what a desperate game we should be playing if we depended on a yielding nerve there."

This roused Browning to the only anger he had ever shown. In one of his very long sentences, in which the indignation tumbles over the syntax like a storm-filled stream over rocks, he vented his feelings :

> That a father choosing to give out of his whole day some five minutes to a daughter, supposed to be prevented from participating in what he, probably, in common with the whole world of sensible men, as distinguished from poets and dreamers, consider every pleasure of life, by a complete fore-going of society—that he, after the Pisa business and the enforced continuance, and as he must believe, permanence of this state in which any other human being would go mad—I do dare say for the justification of God, who gave the mind to be used in this world, where it saves us, we are taught, or destroys us—and not to be sunk quietly, overlooked, and forgotten; that, under these circumstances, finding . . . what, you say, unless he thinks he does find, he would close the door of his house instantly; a mere sympathising man, of the same literary tastes, who comes good-naturedly, on a proper and unexceptionable introduction, to chat with and amuse that invalid daughter, once a month, so far as is known, for an hour perhaps,—that such a father should show himself " *not pleased* plainly " at such a circumstance—my Ba, it is SHOCKING.

For the rest, he begged her to get well, to keep as well that next autumn " you reiterate your demand to go and save your life in Italy." The issue shall hinge on that, when Browning will make her his wife formally. Still desiring to defend her parent, she attempts to excuse him on the ground that his faults are of " the intellect not of the heart," and repeats that she could never raise the question of Italy again, that there is plenty of time to consider, that " to make one's head swim with leaning over a precipice is not wise." Nothing that Browning can do " shall hinder my being torn to pieces by most of the particularly affectionate friends I have in the world. Which I do not think of much, any more than of Italy.

You will be mad, and I shall be bad—and that will be the effect of being poets." The fear of the gossip that their marriage must arouse was brought home to her by the news that one of her sister's friends had been asking, "What is this about Ba and her literary friendship?" In all this he wisely saw nothing but a further argument against delay. He kept her to the level with religious care. Her walks and drives and outings are encouraged in every way, and when one is omitted, in the tenderest way he made her feel that it was serious. The curious may be reminded that this point concludes the first volume of the letters.

One could dip assiduously into the second volume for flashes of gaiety, of feeling, of examples of these two contrasting styles, but the situation is most interesting in the beginnings, and by the end of March 1846 the matter of their marriage has become only a question of time. The fire of their affection was now burning at its brightest, half-flame, half-glow, which no misunderstanding or untoward circumstance could quench. Like a miser he tots up the fifty-four visits he has paid, and the hundred and thirty-seven letters he has received from her. "Now I know life from death," she told him, and into the detailed intimacies of that new life and knowledge we need not enter here.

A new event was that Papa had given up visiting her in the evening. He had definitely placed himself at Pisa-distance from her heart. To her the future beckoned more and more imperiously, and her prayer was that "we will live the real answer, will we not, dearest, (to) all the stupidity against genius." She was much concerned that no one should be told: not her family, for fear of involving them in responsibility, not Mr. Kenyon even, not Browning's own father and mother, of whom, she said, she felt afraid. He would not hear of this, could not bear to wound to the heart those who were so devoted to him. By the summer he is in a state of " hardly endurable anxiety and irritation, to say the least; and the thought of another year's intervention of hope deferred—altogether intolerable." Her reply to such statements in June was still, though more faintly, procrastinating: "For me I agree with your view—I never once thought of proposing a delay on my own account. We are standing on hot scythes, and because we do not burn in the feet, by a miracle, we have no right to count on the miracle's prolongation. Then nothing is to be gained, and everything may be lost, and the sense of mask-wearing for another year would be suffocating. This for me. And for yourself, I shall not be much younger or better otherwise, I suppose, next year. I make no motion, then, for a delay, further than we have talked of—to the summer's end."

Her health continued to improve. She went out shopping and bought a bonnet; she talked of taking her own letters to him to the post. She not only drove in Regent's Park, but left the carriage, had the strange feeling of standing on the grass, and committed a felony by plucking a spray of laburnum. It was a great day when she went walking for the first time out of doors, a great day when she went out twice.

A queer character flits through a few of these letters, an old retainer of the family, who had nursed Mr. Barrett on her knees. Miss Trepsack, or Treppy, as she was called, seems to have represented one of the influences which had made Mr. Barrett what he was. How could a man live in the atmosphere which she breathed contentedly without imagining arbitrary authority over other human beings his prescriptive, natural, right? Miss Barrett described her to Browning as follows:

Treppy is a Creole—she would say so as if she said she was a Roman. She lived, as an adopted favourite, in the house of my great grandfather in Jamaica for years, and talks to the delight of my brothers, of that " dear man " who, with fifty thousand a year, wore patches at his knees and elbows, upon principle. Then there are infinite traditions of the great great grandfather, who flogged his slaves like a divinity : and upon the beatitude of slaves as slaves, let no one presume to doubt, before Treppy. If ever she sighs over the slaves, it is to think of their emancipation. Poor creatures, to be emancipated.

She extended her drives to Hampstead, she wrote a letter, for the first time for five years, out of her own room; she was pressed to say whether the poet might begin to count by months or even weeks. One day a man in the omnibus which took Browning back to Greenwich lent forward and said, " Your forehead and eye interest me very much, phrenologist that I am." Amused and delighted, she confessed, " Eyes calm and serene, which was what struck me first of all in the look of them—was it ever observed before, I wonder. The most serene spiritual eyes I ever saw—I thought *that* the first day I saw *you*." She went on to criticize severely a portrait of Browning by Mr. Howitt, which in the very early days she had fastened into her copy of *Paracelsus* for a frontispiece. Beneath the rippling surface of minor interests like these, Browning continued to press her to fix a date. He would fall in with any plan so long as they were formally married, even to continue their present existence provided that the performance of the ceremony should give him the right if difficulties thickened to be by her bedside. She pointed out that such a plan, if it was to be of any use, would have to be revealed, whereupon she would be " thrown out of the window."

Meantime no one must be told, certainly not dear Mr. Kenyon. " I know Mr. Kenyon, and I know perfectly that either he would be unhappy himself, or he would make us so. He never could bear the sense of

responsibility.   Then, as he told me to-day, and as long
ago I knew, he is 'irresolute,' timid in deciding.   Then
he shrinks before the dæmon of the world—and 'what
may be said' is louder to him than thunder."   There is
scarcely any of the people whom she mentions in this
correspondence who do not live the livelier for us from
her keen yet kindly criticisms.   If these people had
known it, to be mentioned in her letters was to be remembered, not as a name but as a person, for at least a
hundred years.   We may regret therefore that Browning's plans for introducing his sister, and for inviting
Elizabeth to visit his people at New Cross, were gently
but firmly declined.   She would have alluded to them
in her letters, and given us thumbnail sketches which it
is our loss to be without.   Her excuse was that his family
would be blamed if they were in any way privy to the
secret marriage.   She did not want any of the mud to
splash those dear to him, and was especially shy of any
member of his family.   To him this seemed hard, and
her argument not well founded : " People are not quite
so tolerant of other people's preposterousness (he wrote).
. . . What possible harm can follow from their knowing ?
Why should I wound them to the very soul and for
ever, by as gratuitous a piece of unkindness as if ;—no,
there is no comparison will do !   Because since I was a
child I never looked for the least or greatest thing within
the compass of their means to give, but given' it was ;—
nor for liberty but it was conceded, nor confidence but
it was bestowed.   I dare say they would break their
hearts at such an end of all.   For in any case they will
take my feeling for their own with implicit trust—and if
I brought them a beggar, or a famous actress even, they
would believe in her because of me."   The contrast
between the Barrett and the Browning parents was
extreme, and only in a passage such as this can we gain
a glimpse of the good fairy to set against her several

sketches of the ogre. It is also odd to remember that her plight and that of the elder Mr. Browning in his youth was much the same. It tempts one to believe that the children of the slave-owners suffered as much in their way as the slaves.

He persisted that the only excuse for blame could be the supposed insufficiency of his income. He repeated his belief that an application to such a friend as Lord Monteagle would produce either a pension equal to Tennyson's or an official post, that he had no fear of men's gossip, and that the fear itself was fear of " a monstrous tyranny " against which it was a right to revolt. She still insisted that the circumstances of any marriage that they could arrange must be mortifying to the pride of his family, that on no account must he sacrifice his leisure for poetry to the imaginary need of maintaining herself, that a post given to him would probably be in Russia, a country to which she could not go; and, lastly, that she could not survive an open conversation with her father. This was her real reason, and a very natural one, as everyone will know who has had to do with a parent in the least resembling Mr. Barrett. Not only women will respond when she says : " You said once that women were as strong as men, unless in the concurrence of physical force. Which is a mistake. I would rather be kicked with a foot (I, for one woman !) than be overcome by a loud voice speaking cruel words. I would not yield before such words—I would not give you up if they were said, but being a woman and a very weak one (in more senses than the bodily), they would act on me as a dagger would. I could not help *dropping*, dying before them." Of course he told her that she must never run the risk of such an interview, " and so let us quietly go away."

Now that he began to speak of decision, of imminent action, her courage quailed. She even asked to be released from her promise.   As the final hour approached, she realized that her life had been passed in dreaming, and shrank from taking a step which would involve her in a turmoil and, as she feared, be as harmful to him as it was odious to herself.   No position is more pitiful than that of the dreamer forced to act and to decide.   The greater the need, the greater the paralysis of initiative. He entreated her to remember that their good was now one, and not " to introduce an element of restlessness and uncertainty " into this the two-hundredth of her letters.   She felt the reasonableness of this, and her spirits revived enough to begin discussing the most convenient home for them in Italy.   She continued to go out, and even called upon Mr. Boyd at his house in St. John's Wood, and accepted an invitation to see the artistic treasures at Mr. Rogers'.   The interior of his house is vividly described.   Another shock to her was the unexpected suicide of her acquaintance Benjamin Haydon, who had left some of his possessions and MSS. in her charge.   At first she believed that she was intended to undertake the onerous task of editing his journals.

X

As June wore toward its end, Browning reminded her that it would not be long to autumn, and that she must decide at any rate the month for their marriage.   August was considered too soon, October rather reluctantly too late, so September was vaguely chosen, but she was still loath to forgo a last loophole for delay.   There is not much talk of public affairs in this correspondence, but " Peel's speech and farewell " led Browning to define the function of the poets.   It was, he said in effect, " to influence the influencers, playing the Bentham to Cobden," as he put it politically.   He is cheered to learn that her drives were lengthening, that she had gone as

far as Highgate, later as far as Finchley, and that he had
a sly counsellor in Elizabeth's sister Arabel. The pair
were on their way to Mr. Boyd's, when Elizabeth's signs
of nervousness made Arabel exclaim without warning,
"Oh, Ba, such a coward as *you* are never will be married
while the world lasts." This, the victim wrote, " made
me laugh if it did not make me persevere—for you see by
it what her notion is of an heroic deed ! " He replied
that the cure for such nervousness was to continue to
go out, and agreed with her that they shall part rather
than " lead the abominable lives of ' married people,' "
and that " when your name sounds in my ear like any
other name, your voice like other voices, when we wisely
cease to interfere with each other's pursuits—respect
differences of taste, etc., all will be over *then*." So far as
they could judge, their intimacy was a security for the
future; even a lovers' quarrel had not occurred. Elizabeth wisely declared that there was nothing not ominous
in such quarrels. It was a ghastly conspiracy of guilty
elders that made them seem not so. She recounted also
a childish anecdote : " When I was a child I heard two
married women talking. One said to the other : ' The
most painful part of marriage is the first year, when the
lover changes into the husband by slow degrees.' The
other woman agreed, as a matter of fact is agreed to. I
listened with my eyes and ears, and never forgot it, as
you observe. It seemed to me, child as I was, a dreadful
thing to have a husband by such a process. Now it
seems to me more dreadful."

The dog Flush appears here and there in the letters :
not always as the darling of his mistress or as the particular prey of thieves, but as the dog who snapped at
Robert Browning, and repeated this behaviour when the
poet appeared with an umbrella. On the other hand,
Mr. Barrett made a pleasant allusion or two to " the man
of the pomegranates," which forced Elizabeth to exclaim,

" Anything but his kindness I can bear now." Was it loyalty, for we do make allowances for our kindred that we would make for no one else, or the habit of forty years of obedience, that made her still anxious to find excuses for her father? " His hand would not lie so heavily, without a pulse in it. . . . He might have been king and father over me to the end, if he had thought it worth while to love me openly enough." Then came the queer thought that had he so loved her, he would have had her confidence, and unless that love had changed his nature, he would therefore have shut the door on Robert Browning before the poet's affection for his daughter had been proved. To confide now, she wrote on July 17th, would be to be " separated from that moment, hindered from writing, hindered from meeting, I could evade nothing as I am. . . . Then the positive disobedience might be a greater offence than the unauthorised act. I shut my eyes in terror some times."

Among her friends and remoter relations, such as uncles, there was a vague notion that somehow Elizabeth had set her mind on Italy, and both friends and uncles encouraged her to contrive it, if she could. She told her uncle Hedley, who had begged her to call on him in Paris if she passed that way, that when that day arrived he might be inclined to cast her off. Astonished and indignant, he asked her what she meant, and then added laughing : " Because you will be a rebel and a runaway ? No, no I won't cast you off, I promise you—only I hope that you will be able to manage it quietly ! " So she had a gleam of comfort there. She reflected that members of a family have almost as partial a knowledge of each other as the outside world. George Sand delighted her by saying that " the souls of blood relations seldom touch except at one or two points." The genial Mr. Kenyon continued to call, but now used to say with

a smile that he was no longer of use, since Browning had
taken his place.

In one of his letters the poet confessed to a 'weakness' which shows him carrying his reserve even into
his own home. " I shall begin by begging a separate
room from yours. . . . I could not I am sure take off
my coat before you now—why should I ever ? The
kitchen is an unknown horror to me. I come to the
dining-room for whatever repast there may be, nor
willingly stay too long there, and on the day when poor
Countess Peppa taught me how macaroni is made,—
then began a quiet revolution (indeed a rapid one)
against tagliolini, fettuce, lasagne, etc.—typical, typical ! "
With a present of cakes Browning tried to win the regard
of Flush, but in vain, and his mistress nearly ordered a
muzzle for him. She also allowed him to be slapped
by her maid Wilson, who " of all the people who are
not in our confidence, has the most certain knowledge
of the truth." Wilson was devoted to Miss Barrett,
had a great desire to travel, and had said that she would
accompany her lady anywhither in the world. Another
sympathizer was Capt. Surtees Cook, who wrote to Henrietta, " I hope that poor Ba will have courage to the
end." Plainly the open secret could not now be maintained indefinitely. Sometimes Browning would ask her
what she was writing beside her letters, for her general
correspondence was still large. She would not say, but
on July 22 she hinted. " You shall see some day at
Pisa what I will not show you now. Does not Solomon
say that ' there is a time to read what is written ' ? "
This must have referred to the *Sonnets from the Portuguese.*

The discussion of the simple household that he wanted,
and she was ready to hand it over to him lest in her
utter inexperience she should make a mistake, was succeeded by a proposal for the journey that seemed to bring
the date of it within sight. She asked that she might be

o

allowed to take Wilson with her, a prop and stay that her sisters deemed essential. Wilson, however, was " an expensive servant—she has sixteen pounds a year " —a sum perhaps equal to sixty at the present time. It is typical of her habitual dependence on the whims and the wishes of other people that no sooner had she made this proposal than she was seriously alarmed. A letter from him was late, and she began to imagine that she had caused him displeasure. In a panic she withdraws at once : " I shall manage perfectly. Observe how I pinned your coat, miraculously pricking you at the same moment." He complained indignantly that he was not to be expected to sulk or to be huffy should she have an opinion of her own, and that, in the matter of Wilson, " I could no more take you away without such assistance than desire you to perform the passage of the Mont Cenis on foot." All this seemed to her, in the light of her past experience, miraculous generosity on his part.

The Italian project continued to engage Elizabeth's friends, including Mr. Kenyon, who discussed with her sisters Mrs. Jameson's suggestion that she should accompany Elizabeth. Mindful of the occurrences of the previous year, and believing that Mr. Barrett would cast off his daughter if she ventured to go, Mr. Kenyon with his usual caution, and with the best intentions, did all he could to banish the idea from Mrs. Jameson's kind head. He asked Henrietta if Ba was still dwelling upon Italy. Henrietta said Yes. " But she cannot go to Italy by herself. Then *how* ? " " She has great determination of character," Henrietta continued. " She will surprise everybody some day." Mr. Kenyon looked very uneasy, and Elizabeth, hearing of it, thought that her secret was out. While she was agitated over the best means of thanking Mrs. Jameson for her project and of declining it without explaining why, Browning pointed out that " the ground is crumbling beneath our feet," and that the great day really could not be postponed beyond a few weeks from the end of July in which he was writing. She must realize that it had become a matter of weeks, not of months any longer! She replied: "Take September," to add immediately that there was no need to specify the exact time. Luckily, his patience with her was inexhaustible.

She now became afraid that Mr. Kenyon, who, according to Browning, had guessed the truth, would speak to him, for Kenyon apparently had a way of thinking it his duty to separate any lovers whom he liked. He did it, as he had explained to her, with tact, a tact that seemed to her infernal from one example that Kenyon repeated to her himself. She found in this another reason for not confiding in Mr. Kenyon, who "just in proportion to the affection he bears each of us would labour to drive us apart." Once they shall have married, they will "stand on the sunshiny side of his philosophy," since he was a man to make the best of facts, but to be irresolute and hesitant in action. Once more, it is a charm in her letters to unveil the mixed qualities of her friends. In a final sentence she pins him: "Observe of dear Mr. Kenyon, that, generous and noble as he is, he *fears like a mere man of the world.*"

Her growing activity carried her to Westminster Abbey, but her nerves quailed at the sight of the organ, which frightened her as much as a thunder-cloud. Indeed music made her cry because her nerves, which she could not "help," were too weak for the stress of its emotions. She lingered in Poets' Corner, and noted Spenser's epitaph, the burning words in which seemed to her beyond the audacity of the present day. "We should say—the author of such a book—at most!" What a promise of companionship this must have held to Browning! as he thought of all that they had to see in Italy together.

Saturday, August 2nd, was a trying day for her. There was a storm, and Mr. Barrett appeared in her room about seven, looking "a little as if the thunder had passed into him." She was in her dressing-gown because of the heat, and he asked, "Has this been your costume since the morning, pray?" Browning had stayed with her later than usual and, knowing that her father was downstairs, she 'saw' his face through the floor while her lover was sitting opposite her. When Mr. Barrett appeared he was looking displeased, and after commenting on her wrap, he looked more so. "It appears, Ba, that *that man* has spent the whole day with you." Almost breathless with alarm, she endeavoured to explain that the rain had kept her visitor. Papa had previously been "peremptory" with her sister Arabel for allowing "only Mr. Browning in the room" at a time when his daughter might be ill with fear of the thunder. As if this was not enough Mr. Kenyon arrived, full of questions, and spectacles in hand, but luckily they were broken. Had Browning been there yesterday? She nodded. "I thought it probable that he would be here, and so I stayed away." Then, without preface: "Is there an attachment between your sister Henrietta and Capt. Cook?" Elizabeth was badly scared, for what ensuing question might he not be leading up to? As it was, the conversation turned, and she escaped.

Browning was at pains to disabuse her notion that he had fixed habits which might suffer by a marriage. He described his aims: "I want to be a Poet—to read books which make wise in their various ways, to see just so much of nature and the ways of men as seems necessary —and having done this already in some degree, I can easily and cheerfully afford to go without any or all of it for the future if called upon—and so live on, and use up my past acquisitions such as they are. I will go to Pisa and learn, or stay here and learn in another way—

putting, as I always have done, my whole pride, if that is the proper name, in the being able to work with the least possible materials." The news of Mr. Kenyon's implied knowledge made it, Browning thought, very natural to remark that the Havre packets left now at an hour later than hitherto. He also had the presentiment that Elizabeth would be whisked off to Devonshire at a moment's notice, and begged her to be prepared for such an event.

Browning too was beginning to feel the strain, and once or twice left early to spare her the possibility of any scene. There is dignity in his attitude, as he makes it clear that he was not thus careful to save himself. " There is no unstable footing for me in the whole world except just in your house—which is not yours. I ought not to be in that one place—all I could do in any circumstances (were a meeting to happen) would be wrong, unfortunate. The certainty of misconception would spoil everything—so much of gentleness as is included in *gentle*manliness would pass for a very different quality —and the *manliness* which one observes there too would look like what it is farthest from." He needed to know, he explained, the extent of her resources, what would be available for her in Italy as much as at her home. " My notion of the perfection of money arrangements is that of a fairy purse which every day should hold so much, and there an end of trouble." To the end of his life he hated even the smallest bills, and never let any outstand beyond the following Saturday.

The custom of slurring over money matters in biography is foolish, for any freaks of character as well as of event turn upon them. Where would these two have been without the " eight thousand pounds in the funds " that she reported, or how would Browning's life have run had he ever had to do commercial work for his living ? Their problem would have been different, his life much other than it was, for we may share his own belief that he could have been also, if he had liked, a man of action. The interest on her money, she said, amounted to about £160 a year, and she had beside " a little under £200 a year " from what she called " ship money," apparently shares in some mercantile marine. She told him not to be frightened, but that she spent her £40 a quarter. What might have frightened him was that she could not explain how ! It was not on dresses, not apparently upon herself: " My greatest personal expense lately has been the *morphine*." Probably she gave it away. Certainly no one could have been less experienced in housekeeping, a disability that might have proved serious to a wife who had enjoyed the invisible expenditure of a comfortable and well-appointed house. Browning was to borrow £100 from his father for the expenses of their journey, but there seems to be no record of his resources at this time, nor whether, after his marriage, he received assistance from his father, since the income from his poetry was a small matter for many years. His main eye was upon her health, and an instance of his attention is the sentence: " I seem to notice that you do not leave the house quite so often as, say, a month ago; and that you are not the better for it." He had possibly put down her condition to a want of fresh air, even from the first.

A great sight she had when Mr. Kenyon drove her to Paddington, where seats were reserved, for the spectacle of the train coming in, a monster of noise and smoke which was almost too much for her to bear. Browning was busy with time-tables and steamship lines, while even by the middle of August she remained vague about the approaching date. Yet the house became more and more uncomfortable as everyone except its master, whom none would inform, began to put two and two together. Even Treppy began to boast of the secrets that she was

discovering. Arabel had asked Treppy if she thought
that Elizabeth would go to Italy. " There is only one
way for her to go," was the disconcerting reply, " but she
may go that way. If she marries, she may go." " And
would you not be surprised ? " Arabel asked. " I ! not
in the least—I am never surprised, because I always see
things from the beginning." However, no danger was
apprehended from Treppy, so that affection for Elizabeth
was a stronger motive with the Creole than loyalty to
Mr. Barrett after all. Yet it was important that Treppy
might be able to deny personal knowledge, for, as
Elizabeth put it, " to occasion a schism between her
and this house would be to embitter the remainder of
her days."

We have already noticed that the one lack which
Browning had felt in his own home, despite the cultivated interests of his father and even the latter's special
interest in his poems, was a community of taste. It
sounds paradoxical, but he explained the matter as
follows : " There was always a great delight to me in this
prolonged relation of childhood almost, nay altogether,
with all here. My father and I have not one taste in
common, one artistic taste ; in pictures he goes, ' souls
away,' to Brauwer, Ostade, Teniers ; he would turn from
the Sistine altar-piece to these. In music he desiderates
a tune ' that has a story connected with it,' whether
Charles II's favourite dance of ' Brose and butter,' or,
no matter, what I mean is that the sympathy has not
been an intellectual one." In music, to which Browning
was devoted, as many of his poems remind us, Beethoven
was one of his favourite composers, and probably
Beethoven seemed as noisy and obscure to his father as
Browning's own poems, in which his interest was less
artistic than paternal. Thus the encouragement that he
gave to his son, for whose early publications he paid,
was pure generosity.

Another diviner of the state of her heart, though he could not see with his sightless eyes the flush of health that proclaimed it, was Mr. Boyd, and Browning was delighted to learn that, when informed of her proposed disobedience, Boyd exhorted her to stand fast in it. Indeed, Mr. Boyd " triumphed inwardly in the idea of a chain being broken which he has so often denounced in words that pained and vexed me ; and then last year's affair about Italy made him furious." Thus encouraged, she began to dream of seeing Athens, the Nile, the Pyramids : " all of it is more possible now than walking up this street seemed to me last year." Her amusing account of a visit to a large family at Finchley, where the eldest of five was five years old and the income as small as the smallest, reminds him of an illustration in Quarles' *Emblems* which was his ' childhood's pet book,' and he took her eagerness to travel as a sign of common desires : " What other woman in the whole world and Finchley (a spot of an enormous size in the Quarles-print) would propose to go to Egypt instead of Belgravia ? " Whenever she could indulge her imagination, she soared freely ; whenever she had to act herself she clung to excuses for delay.

Mrs. Jameson came to inquire about her plans and wrung from Elizabeth that the plan might be carried out, without fuss, next month. Her comment on the news was : " Very sudden then it is to be. In fact there is only an elopement for you," at which Elizabeth felt obliged to laugh. Mrs. Jameson refused to believe that the circumstances were desperate, and declared, " When I hear people say that circumstances are against them, I always retort : ' You mean that your will is not with you ! I believe in the will, I have faith in it.' " Before the 10th of September Mrs. Jameson was to be in Paris, on her way to Orleans and Italy, and as she told Elizabeth this her face held out an evident invitation. Meantime

Arabel reported that her brother Stormie had suddenly inquired of her : " Is it true that there is an engagement between Mr. Browning and Ba ? " Elizabeth was trembling that he would ask her himself, but she talked so fast when he came to her room that he had no chance. Mr. Boyd continued to encourage, and said that nothing would make him gladder than " our having gone and escaped the storms." Browning felt that with the Wimpole Street house astir with such inquiries, it was rash of him to maintain his frequent visits ; for at all costs he was anxious to spare her the possibility of a scene, and a scene in advance would imperil a secret marriage. He dreaded " a lacerated thing," only reaching his arms to sink there.

The mother of Browning was unwell, and this again made Elizabeth hesitate on the plea that Mrs. Browning could not be left. Her name entered his own letters chiefly in relation to the news that he had told her, and to the help that he was asking toward the expenses of the journey. Turning to his past life at home, Browning wrote : " As I never calculated on such a change in my life, I had the less repugnance to my father's generosity, that I knew that an effort at some time or other might furnish me with a few hundred pounds which would soon cover my very simple expenses." He went on to describe how his father had returned in horror from the plantations, thrown up his post there, and had since " consumed his life after a fashion he always detested " rather than be rich by such means. Browning, who had told his mother of the impending marriage, assured Elizabeth that " if you care for any love, purely love, you will have theirs." He was sure that he could repay the £100 that he had borrowed, and that his parents had wanted to give, in a couple of years, from which we may infer how modest were the returns from his poetry at this time. In reply she urged a quick trip through

France, and added pathetically: "May your father indeed be able to love me a little, for *my* father will never love me again."

In explanation of the affection and generosity of his parents, Browning related the only incident that has survived of his father's experiences in the West Indies. "My father is tender-hearted to a fault. I have never known more of the circumstances of his youth than I told you, in consequence of his invincible repugnance to allude to the matter—and I have a fancy, to account for some peculiarities in him, which connects them with some abominable early experience. Thus, if you question him about it, he shuts his eyes involuntarily and shows exactly the same marks of loathing that may be noticed while a piece of cruelty is mentioned . . . and the word blood even makes him change colour. To all women and children he is 'chivalrous' as you called his unworthy son. There is no service which the ugliest, oldest, crossest woman in the world might not exact of him."

XI

At the end of August Browning increasingly feared that, her obedience seeming to have been complete, Mr. Barrett would announce some morning that he had arranged for her to depart to Madeira, with which she had once been threatened, or to Palermo. When Mr. Barrett came to her room one day, and the aunt who came with him asked if he did not think his daughter much better, he replied: "I don't know. She is mumpish, I think." It was plain to Elizabeth that she was under his displeasure still, and that he "seems to have no more idea of my living beyond these four walls than of a journey to Lapland." Yet she sat as still as ever, and found it necessary to repeat: "I don't want to make unnecessary delays." She shrank, she added, from her father's eye, and began to tremble when talking to her brothers, but none the less she looked, slept, felt better than she had ever done. Doubtless the miracle of so much happiness in her situation, as it still was, seemed sufficient and more than sufficient to her nervousness. Browning warned her not to stand shivering on the brink, and asked her "to show one good reason, or show of reason, why we gain anything by deferring our departure till next week instead of to-morrow." He put it stronger: "If you find yourself unable or unwilling to make this effort, tell me so and plainly and at once; I will not offer a word in objection." He expressly added that he had not the slightest wish to frighten her into compliance, but that the days were slipping by, and that he could never forgive himself for letting the summer pass and so involving her in risks, that might be serious, of travelling in the worst of the year. This, written on August 31st, was the most urgent of his letters. She pleaded in reply that she was not holding back, and would be ready, with a week's notice, for any date that he chose. She could not, however, sail from London, because the boat left early, and her sister Arabel, who slept on a sofa in her room, was seldom out of it before nine in the morning. She therefore proposed to take the train to Southampton and to sail from there.

An unexpected and inconvenient drain upon her purse was a ransom of several guineas that she had to pay to some dog-thieves who snatched Flush from under the wheels of the carriage, plunged him into a bag, and carried him off. Apparently it was a regular London business, and the thieves had no fear of prosecution. The legend was that, if you refused to pay, you received your dog's head in a parcel. Browning had agreed that Flush must accompany them to Italy, and his statement that he would now leave immediate decisions to her, that he would attempt to decide for her no longer, produced the feminine reproach that she did not know what would become of her if he did ! In a highly characteristic letter of September 3rd Browning explained that he would never compound with the dog-stealers, but, with more insight than the energetic who are not poets generally display, he added : " This course ought not to be yours, Ba, because it would not suit your other qualities." She joined issue at once in one of the most entertaining illustrations in her letters : " Your theory is far too good not to fall to pieces in practice. A man may love justice intensely; but the love of an abstract principle is not the strongest love, now is it ? . . . Do you mean to say that if the banditti came down on us in Italy and carried me off to the mountains, and, sending to you one of my ears to show you my probable fate if you did not let them have—how much may I venture to say I am worth ? five or six scudi (is that reasonable at all ?) would your answer be ' Not so many crazie '; and would you wait, poised upon abstract principles, for the other ear, and the catastrophe, as was done in Spain not long ago ? Would you, dearest ? Because it is as well to know beforehand, perhaps." He replied that he would pay every farthing he had in the world, but—that he would shoot with his own hand the receiver of it afterwards. The subject is not irrelevant. It was used by Browning to stiffen her against the oppression that she had grown accustomed to endure.

For the first time since their friendship began they did not meet for a whole week at the opening of September. It was a precaution. She was being visited by others, but was resolved, he reminded her, to leave " at the end of the month." She had an unexpected reason for agreeing in that his headaches suddenly increased. They even drove him to bed with the sacrifice of a journey to her. She began to see that "going to Italy, that travelling, and putting an end to all the annoyances" was the best remedy for these headaches of his. Moreover, he proved to be right in his alarming prophecy that the family, including Elizabeth, was to be hurried out of town. Dover, Reigate, Tonbridge were possible destinations. She was "embarrassed to the utmost degree," and even talked of making her exit after this holiday, and not before. To start at once appeared to her to be "too soon and too sudden." With unswerving self-control he wrote: "I will not add one word to those spoken yesterday about the extreme perilousness of delay. You *give* me yourself. Hitherto, from the very first till this moment, the giving hand has been advancing steadily—it is not for me to grasp it lest it stop within an inch or two of my forehead with its crown." Her latest news produced a postscript which must have brought a sense of her procrastination to her heart: "Then I understand you are in earnest. If you *do* go on Monday, our marriage will be impossible for another year—the misery! You see what we have gained by waiting. We must be *married directly* and go to Italy. I will go for a licence to-day (Thursday, September 10th), and we can be married on Saturday. . . . I enclose the ring or a substitute—I have not a minute to spare for the post."

In another letter written the same afternoon he pointed out that, once they were married, the day of their departure could depend upon her family's movements, and that the general packing would give an opportunity for her own. "Now your part must begin," he insisted, and he would visit her the next day, Friday, to explain the arrangements that he had made. She still begged him not to be precipitate, for the country house had not been chosen yet. Then, overcome with fatigue and anxiety, she added: "Will not this dream break on a sudden? Now is the moment for the breaking of it surely."

Friday arrived with a clear field for the lovers, since her family were on a picnic at Richmond. On Saturday morning, attended by the faithful Wilson, Miss Barrett, after a restless night and a call at the chemist's on her way, arrived at St. Pancras Church, Marylebone. Here she was met by Browning and his cousin, James Silverthorne, who with Wilson was the only witness. When the ceremony was over and the register signed, she drove to Mr. Boyd, who was in the secret, and sipped some of his Cyprus wine. Wilson was sent home. At Mr. Boyd's Elizabeth was joined by her sisters, who arrived with "grave faces." Missing her and Wilson "they had taken fright," and she trembled with every glance they gave her. To complete the programme she drove with them to Hampstead. It had been a hard moment to take the ring from off her hand, but somehow she managed to keep up till the end of the day. Her return must have been as severe a strain as her departure.

Browning, who could not bring himself to ask for her under a false name, never revisited her again in Wimpole Street, so that we have a few more letters to tell us how she passed her final week at home. Writing the next day, Sunday, she told him: "In the emotion and confusion of yesterday morning there was yet room in me for one thought which was not a feeling—for I thought that, of the many, many women who have stood where I stood, and to the same end, not one of them all perhaps, since that building was a church, has had reasons as strong as mine for an absolute trust and devotion towards the man she married. And then I thought and felt that it was only just for them, those women who were less happy, to have that affectionate sympathy and support and presence of their nearest relations, parent or sister, which failed to *me*, needing it less through

being happier." It is plain what she felt. Sunday was
an ordeal, for the family was noisily discussing the
holiday she would not share, and Treppy was present,
and bells began to ring which Henrietta said were those
of Marylebone church. Then she was interrupted by
Mr. Kenyon, wearing his spectacles, and " looking as if
his eyes reached to their rim all the way round." " When
did you see Browning ? " he asked, but she had enough
presence of mind to reply : " ' He was here on Friday,'
Dearest, he saw something, but not all." She was very
agitated and felt as if she had slipped down over the wall
into somebody's garden, she said.

He wrote that her love had been proved by this great
effort, and that his was to be proved in the years ahead.
He would first do whatever lay in his power, whether
submission or sacrifice, to preserve, for her, the affection
of her family. He did not think that the news of their
marriage would leak into the papers, or that reporters
had the habit of consulting the registers in vestries. As
soon as the date of their departure was determined, an
undated advertisement would be published by themselves. The fact, the fact, was enough for him at last.
She would be killed, she wrote, if anyone was informed
before she was out of England. Even the thought of
writing to her father was too much : " I am paralysed
when I think of having to write such words as—Papa, I
am married." She would " entreat him to pardon the
happiness which has come at last." Her husband's idea
that they must get away by the end of the week alarmed
her, with the letters to be written and the things to be
done. The few days remaining, he said, gave time
enough for epics, whereas so soon as she took her pen
in her hand she began to cry.

Her family was leaving for the country on the following
Monday, September 21st, and she even thought it might
be advisable for her to follow them there, though the

place was six miles from a station! Of necessity he replied, " The way will be to leave at once."   Therefore, after some muddles about times and trains and routes, it was decided that she and Wilson should leave Wimpole Street on Saturday afternoon and meet him at Hodgson's, the bookseller's, between half-past three and four.   Her luggage was sent the previous evening to the station at Vauxhall, from which they were to start.   Her state of panic is shown by her saying, in the very last letter of all, " By to-morrow at this time, I shall have *you* only to love me, my beloved."   It was " dreadful, dreadful to have to give pain here by a voluntary act—for the first time in my life."   Her father, irreconcilable to the last, never answered her letters or mentioned her in his will. He later told Mr. Kenyon, who confessed that he could not understand such hostility to the marriage: " I have no objection to the young man, but my daughter should have been thinking of another world."

It was another world and another life that Elizabeth Barrett found when at last she became the wife of Robert Browning.

CHAPTER FIVE

MARRIED LIFE, HER POEMS, IN ITALY (1846–61)

I

HITHERTO we have followed the story of their engagement in the love-letters, and therefore from the point of view of the lovers themselves. Now that their marriage was an accomplished fact, it is well to remember how hazardous an undertaking it was. If Mrs. Browning's health had broken down, as seemed almost certain to everybody but the poet himself, Browning would have been condemned for wanton rashness which no self-styled affection could excuse. He would have become a byword for selfish imprudence in the eye of the world, and stood for posterity in a most unsympathetic light. All the probabilities were against him. Only his own faith was on the other side. Thus his recent anxiety over his wife's powers of endurance under the emotional strain of her secret marriage, of her week's subsequent and anomalous return home, of her flight with him on the following Saturday, already great, must have been extreme during the journey to Southampton, the voyage to France, the weary hours of fatigue in the diligence between Rouen and Paris. At any moment she might have succumbed, and, if she had, the risk to herself and possibly to her life would have been serious. Their first and long-anticipated hours together must have been as near distress as it was possible for them to feel in each other's company.

Mrs. Orr tells us that Elizabeth's brothers at first

shared Mr. Barrett's indignation, and that Browning's own parents, who apparently were privy to the engagement alone, were shocked and even alarmed. If his wife had become seriously ill, everyone would have held him to be culpably responsible. Moreover, as events proved, her remarkable recovery was precarious, and her fragility compromised in some degree her power to share her husband's active life, so that their companionship, exquisite as it was, had to suffer a cramping of energy on his part, a resigned acquiescence on hers. During the winters of her last years, indeed, her life, except in its happiness, was not very different outwardly from the life that she now had left. It was a life largely confined to one room, chiefly conspicuous for the comfort of its long chair and the huge proportions of its sofa. Their love triumphed, but its chief blessing was that Mrs. Browning survived the preliminary strain of her long, adventurous journey. The pair had also sympathisers. Mr. Kenyon, doubtless after the news of their safe arrival in Paris had reached him, declared them "justified to the uttermost. I considered that you had imperilled your life upon this undertaking, and I still thought you had done wisely." These were generous words, but uttered when the immediate peril was past.

Once arrived in Paris, safe but exhausted, however, it was plain that Browning's rash judgment had been right. He deserved that it should prove so; he probably had made it so himself, for, had he been less solicitous and considerate, had he given his bride the smallest reason to fear that her estimate of his goodness had been exaggerated, it is nearly certain that this misgiving would have destroyed her constitution with her hopes. One is inclined to say that with almost any other husband she would have collapsed, and so justified the world. The love that never fails was his. On it was founded the faith that removed this great mountain of anxiety. In Paris they remained a week to rest, and ran across Mrs. Jameson, whose amazement was " almost comical." With her they arranged to travel toward Italy, and a great help she must have been.   On the way south they stopped at Orleans and Avignon, whence they visited Vaucluse, sacred to Petrarch, and there Browning carried his wife in his arms into the middle of the stream, and sat her upon a rock with Flush barking at his heels in alarm for her safety.   Mrs. Jameson too said that they had been wise and not imprudent, and with her niece was able to provide every additional care.   The weather was excellent, and Mrs. Browning enjoyed the sea-trip from Marseilles, by way of Genoa, to Leghorn, the port from which they reached Pisa.   There, early in October, they took three good bedrooms and a sitting-room near the leaning tower in the Collegio Ferdinando.   The long journey ended with Mrs. Jameson's joyful admission that the invalid was not so much improved as transformed.

The story of their married life is contained in Mrs. Browning's copious and lively letters to her friends, especially to Miss Mitford.   Indeed one of the difficulties of relating it is the amount of detail that has survived.   She was an excellent letter-writer, but as we have dipped freely into the most significant and moving part of her correspondence, the story must here be presented in a more or less continuous whole.   It is a story of happy detail, of wanderings from one Italian scene to another, of few great joys or troubles, of serene, delightful, scholarly and active days.   It really needs the rambling chronicle which she provided in her own letters, not the formality of an ordered narrative.   In fact none of the biographical chapters that have dealt with it fail to be rather dry, for the mood is constant, the details repeat themselves in one pleasant place after another, and the effect of reducing these rambles to order is to turn a delightful holiday into a tour conducted by a guide. By selecting freely, and touching lightly on matters of fact, something may be preserved of the irresponsible happiness of the travellers.

At Pisa the life of quiet and exclusive companionship for which both of them had prayed began. He had none but her; she none but him, and, for once, the result was not disastrous. Their sole acquaintance at Pisa was an Italian professor of the University. They talked, and read, and wrote, and strolled in and out of museums and churches, and took drives. As she was perfectly happy, and the only flaw was the icy silence maintained by her father, to whom she wrote in vain, Browning found in her content the very joy which he had foretasted. The dream that is so often indulged, so rarely realized, was fulfilled for this pair, and it is idle to attempt to communicate their possession. It makes us realize afresh how exceptional is such mutual affection, how rare a fit marriage like theirs.

The housekeeping was Browning's responsibility. With her money reinvested to much advantage in English railways, though, on his insistence, to return to her family at his death, and their dinner arriving unordered in its details from the nearest restaurant every day, they managed well. Weekly bills were the longest he would tolerate, and, while his own poems were beginning to pay for themselves, hers already brought a return which made him write to his publisher: " There, as in all else, she is as high above me as I would have her." We should have seen more of their existence through his eyes if he had not, in later years, and before leaving 19 Warwick Crescent, destroyed all his family letters. In any marriage, however, in which the man is the moving spirit and the necessary foundation of both lives, the wife's experience becomes the more valuable. In an early letter she was able to say : " The intellect is little in comparison to all the rest—to the womanly tenderness, the inexhaustible goodness, the high and noble aspiration of every hour. Temper, spirits, manners—there is not a flaw anywhere."

It was their custom to separate after breakfast : she to her room upstairs, he to his desk in the dining-room, when both would write or read till luncheon appeared. One morning, according to the received story which Sir Edmund Gosse had from the poet himself, Mrs. Browning left the room as usual while the poet stood at the window waiting for the crockery to be cleared away. While in this attitude, and with the servant gone away, he felt someone enter behind him. Hands were laid on his shoulders to prevent him from turning round, and a parcel was slipped into his pocket. His wife's voice told him not to look at it until she had gone, and then, if he did not like it, to destroy it. The packet proved to be the Sonnets that she had been writing during their engagement, which she had never shown to him till now. The title was his invention, though the idea of a supposed translation was hers. He said that they should be called *Sonnets from the Portuguese*, because they might have been written by " Catarina to Camoens." Miss Lilian Whiting, on the authority of Browning's son, says that the poet did not receive the gift until 1849, when they were staying at Bagni di Lucca. The time and place, however, is not the most important thing about them. The Sonnets were the poetry of those moods which we have been following in her love-letters. With those letters fresh in mind, it is convenient to consider the Sonnets here.

II

The *Sonnets from the Portuguese* are forty-four in number, and more truthfully a cycle than others of their kind.

They tell the same emotional story as the love-letters, and unless one is bound to prefer poetry to prose, it is hard to say which is more characteristic of the writer. The sonnets rehearse the tale of her rescue, her conquest, her admiration, her scruples, her surrender. If ever we have in verse the true record of a true love-story, it is here. If ever there was a sonnet-cycle with a proper beginning, a middle, and an end, it is in this. Here is the very poetry of love, because the love that the Sonnets celebrate was fulfilled and no illusion. Perhaps with Petrarch in her mind, she chose the sonnet, and when she came to consider the sonnet-cycles that had been written by such lovers as Petrarch, Michael Angelo, and Shakespeare, her opportunity for originality was clear. All these writers were the lovers, not the loved; all were men. Was not the opportunity waiting for a Laura and a Beatrice to give, if she happened to be a poet, the woman's, the beloved's, response? It was long overdue, for one of the crowning defects of love-poetry written by women is their unreal habit of writing as if they were men. The lover's urgency we know, for, through her unavowed encouragement, the man, as a rule, apparently takes the initiative. From women, however subtly they may be the real instigators, it is the response that we wish to hear. Elizabeth Barrett happened to be the responsive person in her own experience, and it is this response that the *Sonnets from the Portuguese* reveal. In them was no conventional exercise, no fiction, and it is not too much to say that in reality of permanent feeling, in unity of aim, in simplicity of speech, they stand apart.

Her choice of the sonnet was fortunate for her in two ways. With Laura and Catarina in mind, it suggested the point of view of a woman, though this, we may be sure, was entirely and instinctively hers. In the second place, it dictated a strict metrical scheme, and this gave to the writer the discipline that she most required. She had previously written a few sonnets, but had not been completely at home in the form. Even in her best there is a suggestion of metrical discomfort. Always loyal to her ideals, she chose the Petrarchan form, and kept it strictly, so that her rhymes, even her ear, seemed to improve. The discipline that she embraced was abundantly rewarded. Technically they are nearly faultless, and in this form technical mastery and ease necessarily give a peculiar pleasure. It is as delightful as it is uncommon in English to find a sonnet on the Italian model which reads spontaneously, and as if the words had fallen into their proper places not by cunning but by grace. The only prosaic pleasure to be compared with it is a perfect conversational cadence in dramatic dialogue. The exquisite accent in the idiom of Congreve or of Gay is its equivalent in prose, where we find sentence after sentence that seems as if it could not be spoken wrongly. The majority of the *Sonnets from the Portuguese* have a virtue of a similar kind.

In the first she tells how Browning came, and how, until he came, she had thought herself to be in the arms of death, when " a voice said in mastery," a word that she always applied to him, " not death but love." Only God, her lover, and herself heard this revelation, and at first she was unable to believe, so that, had she died at the moment when her lover first avowed his feelings, she would have died unaware of the love standing at her side. So soon as she had become conscious of the possibility, she was abashed by the difference between them : he with his genius and the outer world at hand, she " a poor, tired, wandering singer," apparently near the end of her life. She bade him to observe her desolation and to escape from it ; if he stays, the ashes of her burnt-out life will ' scorch ' his hands. The next phase is her command that he shall go, while she

will live in his shadow, in her memory of the man she
has refused, though now as much a part of her as her
own shadow. He feeds her dreams, and she is content
that her dream-life shall be lived with him. The seventh
sonnet records how her life was transformed under his
influence. He had given "a new rhythm" to her
existence, and she was distressed because she felt unable
to make any adequate return. Her poverty, not her
gratitude, is at fault.

Having countenanced thus far his feelings, she resolves
to offer whatever she may possess, though

> I own, and grieve,
> That givers of such gifts as mine are, must
> Be counted with the ungenerous.

She will love him, but not give her love as a possession
barren to himself. Still love is love, and 'love is fine,'
and God does not disdain the meanest. Therefore she,
as a loving soul, is not so far unworthy. Transfigured
by love, she herself is enhanced by the gift. He has
been her teacher, and in loving she is following his
example. Her feeling is too deep to find expression in
words. Her silence must speak for her, since if she
speaks at all it will be to utter the grief of her condition,
not the joy of her discovery through him. Then, in
the fine fourteenth sonnet, the one that everyone knows,
beginning " If thou must love me," she puts into verse
his own convincing assertion that he loves for no reason
but love's own. The 'irrational reason' that they had
discussed in their letters was to her the only guarantee
of permanency. It is a perfect sonnet. Its list of the
reasons which do not suffice for love may be compared
with another, its peer and pair, the sonnet last but one,
wherein she tries to find a similar list of the limitless
ways in which she loves him. An ensuing sonnet
declares that he must not be over-influenced by pity;

this has been a fear to her from the very first.   She goes
on to plead excuse for seeming calm or sad when he is
with her, since sorrow has shut her within his love and
to attempt much joy would be to fail.   Nevertheless it
is his confidence which sustains her, his faith that masters
her weakness and its fears :

> Conquering
> May prove as lordly and complete a thing
> In lifting upward, as in crushing low.

In the sixteenth sonnet she says that if he will command
she is able to obey.   Her heart has openly surrendered.
Then follows a pathetic and lovely sonnet on the possibility of her being of any use to him, the great poet, so
far above her :

> How, dearest, wilt thou have me for most use ?
> A hope to sing by, gladly ? . . . or a fine
> Sad memory, with thy songs to interfuse ?
> A shade in which to sing . . . of palm or pine ?
> A grave, in which to rest from singing ? . . . Choose.

The next records her gift of a lock of her hair, and thus,
if we care to study them, the date or particular emotion
under which each poem was written can be gathered
by reference to her love-letters.   She " thought the
funeral shears would take this first, but love is justified,"
and he will find on this tress the kiss that her mother
had left.   The nineteenth celebrates the exchange on
which she insisted, and it stands lower than the rest
because of the rhetorical line with which it opens.

This line, " The soul's Rialto hath its merchandise,"
is valuable as an unintended point of reference, however,
for here she is deserted by the simplicity which elsewhere
makes the sequence beautiful and true.   The conventional note, the sophisticated image, with its unreal and
literary air, are intruders.   Her lapse sets the purity of
feeling and speech throughout in a sudden light, as a

small passing cloud will intensify our sense of a summer morning. The twentieth sonnet is a retrospect of wonder: that, a year ago, she, with the dullness of an atheist, had not divined the existence of the lover whom she has now seen. She begs him to be the cuckoo of his affection, to repeat the news over and over again, so long as he will not forget to love her in silence also. Now that their love is equal, the famous sonnet number twenty-two, no harm can come to them. The angels may drop music into their silence, but it is better to stay on earth in the lovely isolation of two souls who, intent upon each other, are allowed by the rest to remain undisturbed till death.

One of the charms of these sonnets is their variety of mood, which gives a freshness of motive beyond contrivance. It is high praise to say that they resemble letters in verse. Not one of them reads as if written to fit into a sequence, and since the number is not round, a fact worth notice, it is likely, even with Petrarch in mind, that they grew one after another like flowers, and that their cycle became, as it were, a discovery. They have the immediacy of her letters with the beauty of her best verse. Some word of his, as often as some thought of her own, suggested them. The next is a meditation on his saying how thin his life would be without her. It was not an artificial wonder. His life necessarily appeared to be already rich, both in gifts and in experience to herself:

> I marvelled, my Beloved, when I read
> Thy thought so in the letter. I am thine—
> But *so* much to thee?

We seem to overhear the tones of her voice, as we had caught them in those characteristic expressions of her letters: the " indeed indeed " and the question that brims over many sentences, like a trill, " do you understand ? " With a novel image, in this connection, she concludes this sonnet, the twenty-third; as brighter ladies have given up broad acres for love, she will resign the grave on the edge of which she stands because of him.

> I yield the grave for thy sake, and exchange
> My near sweet view of Heaven, for earth with thee !

The talk that their marriage will excite is the subject of the next (number twenty-four) : " God only, who made us rich, can make us poor." Her courage of soul is nearly complete, and it is no contradiction in her that she shrank so long from action. These verses show her soul, but, as some wise man once noticed, style is taken too easily for evidence of strength, and a courageous imagination does not necessarily correspond with intrepidity before immediate difficulties. It is on her lover that she draws both for courage and repose. To him her heart gravitates

> as a thing
> Which its own nature doth precipitate,
> While thine doth close above it, mediating
> Betwixt the stars and the unaccomplished fate.

She had lived, she continues, in her dreams until Browning appeared to become their reality with his presence,

> Because God's gifts put man's best dreams to shame.

His love has retrieved the sorrow of her past life, as if she were now looking back from heaven without grief upon her days on earth. The twenty-eighth sonnet is a charming meditation upon the letters that she has received from him, a meditation in which she re-counts every major step in their intimacy from his first desire to see her until the avowal of his heart. She prefers his presence now to any thoughts, and has become so much absorbed that she cannot think of him detachedly at all.

> I do not think of thee—I am too near thee.

As she is overcome by the intensity of her experience, her tears fall, but as the tears succeed the joy so will her light return when she next shall greet him :

> Ah, keep near and close,
> Thou dovelike help ! and, when my fears would rise,
> With thy broad heart serenely interpose.

This recalls her early fear that his love had grown too quickly, but this was an injustice to him, since, if he is the master, he can draw music from an instrument imperfect and worn.   She celebrates the occasion when he first used her pet name, the Ba of her childhood, and she welcomes him as the heir to those, now dead, to whose call she would answer most quickly when a little girl.   The thirty-fifth sonnet arises from her nervousness as the hour for her final decision draws near.

> If I leave all for thee, wilt thou exchange
> And be all to me ?   Shall I never miss
> Home-talk and blessing and the common kiss
> That comes to each in turn, nor count it strange,
> When I look up, to drop on a new range
> Of walls and floors. . . . another home than this ?
> Nay wilt thou fill that place by me which is
> Filled by dead eyes too tender to know change ?

A woman who could be so deeply devoted to her brother must have had a capacity for love that might have wrecked her life if she had chosen amiss in her marriage. Even yet the fear remains in her wonder whether his affection will endure, for what if he remains loyal and true by the sacrifice of even one of the joys to which he was otherwise destined ?   It is the years before she knew him that excite such questions and make her distort the quality of his love, a distortion for which she finds a rather laboured and artificial image, here again.

So far, we have had the emotions rather than the passion of love described for us, if indeed emotion of this intensity is not the sovereign passion after all. Her whole life was in this experience, and the whole must include its two halves. Patmore once said that a poet should use the interest and not the capital of the passions, and the restraint of simple speech, which rules these sonnets, is very moving in sonnet thirty-eight, where she distinguishes the first three of his kisses with a simplicity that shames the common record of such things. The pity that he repudiated was the equivalent, she tells us, of the gratitude in her that tormented him. The thirty-ninth sonnet is a song of gratitude, very touching to those who have read her love-letters first. Contrasting, as it deserved, this love of theirs with that which passes for love every day in the world, she wrote what proved to be true :

> Thou art not such
> A lover, my Beloved ! thou canst wait
> Through sorrow and sickness, to bring souls to touch,
> And think it soon when others cry " Too late."

An exceptionally fine sonnet is the forty-first, which may be quoted :

> I thank all who have loved me in their hearts,
> With thanks and love from mine. Deep thanks to all
> Who paused a little near the prison-wall,
> To hear my music in its louder parts,
> Ere they went onward, each one to the mart's
> Or temple's occupation, beyond call.
> But thou, who, in my voice's sink and fall,
> When the sob took it, thy divinest Art's
> Own instrument didst drop down at thy foot,
> To hearken what I said between my tears, . . .
> Instruct me how to thank thee !—Oh, to shoot
> My soul's full meaning into future years,
> That *they* should lend it utterance, and salute
> Love that endures from Life that disappears !

In this mood she renounced one of her previous beliefs, the belief that " My future will not copy my fair past," the very sonnet of which Browning had written to her his admiration. The gift of the future has been the greatest of his gifts, and she will be content never to turn back to the pages of memory on which she had been accustomed to linger.

Two sonnets complete the series. The last asks him to accept and preserve the thoughts in these poems as she has taken and tended his flowers. The penultimate, really the conclusion but for the final postscript just mentioned, gives the breadth and the substance of her devotion. Though familiar it should be quoted, for the best she had to give :

> How do I love thee ?   Let me count the ways.
> I love thee to the depth and breadth and height
> My soul can reach, when feeling out of sight
> For the ends of Being and ideal Grace.
> I love thee to the level of every day's
> Most quiet need, by sun and candlelight.
> I love thee freely, as men strive for Right;
> I love thee purely, as they turn from Praise.
> I love thee with the passion put to use
> In my old griefs, and with my childhood's faith.
> I love thee with a love I seemed to lose
> With my lost saints,—I love thee with the breath,
> Smiles, tears, of all my life !—and, if God choose,
> I shall but love thee better after death.

It is the heart of her, and the unforgettable eighth line is as an image of silver to reburnish our dull conception of all that purity means.

Now the quality of this cycle of sonnets which makes it rare among the few of its kind, and unique as the record of a woman's heart by a woman, is its truth. The series tells a story of true experience, not merely the aspiration of a warm and imaginative heart. The beautiful clarity of the language, its chastened expression, the fineness of its response, were not only, not mainly, an imaginative thing. All poets who write of love know the possibilities which beckon, but Elizabeth Barrett knew also its fruits, and for her its promises were performed. Consequently, with the evidence of her letters and the experience of her married life before us, we can say that she tasted the reality which most other people but divine. Therefore among the wealth of English love-poetry, her *Sonnets from the Portuguese* have not only beauty of form but the authority of a fact. If we want to know what human love can be and do, and what poetry this experience contains, we have her verses. They come from the heart and return to it, without embroidery or make-believe. If they are rare, it is as much because the fullness of her experience is exceptional as because she brought exceptional art or skill to making it known.

For this reason the transparent simplicity of their language is a precious thing. The style is as simple as the feeling is sincere. The words are almost as unfaltering in their order as the constancy of her heart. In this kind, this simplicity, only a few, for example Christina Rossetti's beginning "Remember me," equal the best here. It is rare, even in our best sonnets, to discover the same spontaneous flow o. English idiom in the same cramping and imported form. When we find it, we notice time after time that the words are almost wholly words of one syllable, as if the word love gave the key to the whole. We can imagine how Browning, with his own oblique imagination, had an artist's envy for this directness of speech, how he must have felt the sole person able to judge of their veracity, how they must have seemed to him the finest proof of the height which he had claimed for her powers. It was equally natural that she should not exaggerate her gift, and remind him that competent judges had declared the dramatic to be the highest form of poetry. Her two short poems, "Question and Answer" and "Inclusions," are attached by their matter to the cycle, but what a world of difference between her at her average, as in these two lyrics, and her at her best in the Sonnets themselves. In the limited sphere of love-poetry where singleness of object, constancy of heart, and fullness of response are celebrated, there are few poets. Among these few is Elizabeth Barrett Browning.

Robert Browning, who brought so much, so nearly all, to his wife, evoked also these *Sonnets from the Portuguese*. That he lived to justify them is not the least of his honours.

III

At Pisa, where we left them, they remained for six months, hearing a sung Mass in the Campo Santo, a friar preach in the cathedral, and regularly throughout the day the church bells. With thoughts of Byron, always dear to Browning, they visited the Lanfranchi Palace, and delighted in the natural life about them. He was attracted by the lizards, she by the orange-trees, for these at first are better evidence than olives that a northerner has reached the south. The golden globes on the green trees are the first to convince us that we are in the land of the sun. Later the dusty grey of the olive leaves seems better suited to the glare, the dust, the slow carts with their wine-barrels, the fierce foreground, the blue distance, the little hills that make a castle of a crumbling village. In April 1847 they followed Mrs. Jameson to Florence, and took rooms in the Via delle Belle Donne, for which Browning hired a grand piano. Domestic life was simple with dinners sent in, or eaten out, and the very meals themselves consisted largely of fruit and iced water. As at Pisa, Mrs. Browning found that so long as she allowed herself to be carried upstairs, to be considerate enough to sit quiet on a sofa, not to step in puddles, her " duty was considered to be done." They had a terrace which "swam with moonlight in the evenings," and so she could enjoy the air without going out. For the first time she learned what the heat of an Italian summer could be, and their only disappointment was to be turned away after five days from the cool monastery at Vallambrosa—where there was much meat and no eggs and "the milk and the holy water stood confounded"—because the abbot made it clear that women were not welcome. They had intended to stay for two months. She travelled thither very early in the morning in a basket-sledge drawn by white oxen at a snail's pace, while Browning rode a horse at her side. On their return to Florence they first took rooms in the Palazzo Guidi before moving to Casa Guidi, which proved their most permanent home. It was the want of sunshine in the palace that led to this last change, a costly one, for they had already engaged the first set for six months. But the change was made, she wrote, "without a single reproach" from her husband. "Any other man, a little lower than the angels, would have stamped and sworn a little for the mere relief of the thing,—but as for his being angry with me for any cause except not eating enough dinner, the said sun would turn the wrong way first."

The new rooms, to be had for twenty-five guineas a year, were unfurnished, and so gave the poet his chance to pick up pleasant things in old shops. There was a large ante-room, which housed the piano, a small dining-room decorated with tapestry and medallions of Tennyson, Carlyle, and Browning himself, a long narrow study soon full of busts and casts, and a drawing-room for Mrs. Browning overlooking the church of good omen, San Felice. Her room contained old carved bookcases, old pictures of saints framed in black wood, Keats' death-mask, Dante's profile, portraits of friends, and

Q

large mirrors.   Mrs. Browning worked in a deep chair
covered with green velvet, and reclined on a huge sofa
of the same hue.   Beside the chair was her little writing-
table, and on others were presentation copies from
contemporary authors.   In this room, which may suggest a private museum, she began to write in 1848 her
poem on Italian aspirations, called *Casa Guidi Windows*,
after the house.   She begins that poem by protesting
against those, whether Italians or foreigners, who regard
Italy as a museum, who value its past only, to whom its
ruins are a sort of national furniture to sketch, and
acquits herself of belonging to the tribe of tourists with
nothing but Murray in their hearts or heads.   The huge
oil-jar in her bedroom was not placed there to com-
memorate the story of the Forty Thieves.   It was provided by her servant to hold the rain-water that she
preferred to use.   They were happy here, and spent
their leisure either sitting in the famous Loggia dei
Lanzi or watching the sunsets over the river along the
quays.   If Italian society was still closed to them, they
made friends with some of the English and Americans
in the place, and, as Browning would not go out in the
evenings alone and she could not accompany him, they
remained at home, sometimes welcoming a friend to
hot chestnuts and mulled wine after sunset.

The pleasures of this existence did not shut their eyes
to the events that were stirring their adopted country.
It was the time of the upheavals of 1848.   Both were
liberal in their sympathies, but he less optimistic about
men and events.   Two matters occupied him : the
preparation of a collected edition of his poems, and a
project, first recorded in the Life of his friend Lord
Houghton, for becoming secretary to the British mission
to the Vatican which was then under consideration.
This was the third and last time that Browning nearly
became a diplomat.

A plan to spend the winter in Rome was abandoned because the attractions of Florence were too strong, and on the anniversary of their wedding, which Flush commemorated by running away in the evening and staying out all night, they saw from Casa Guidi the gay procession which filled the Piazza Pitti to celebrate the beginnings of a Constitution which the Grand Duke Leopold was shortly to deny. Revolution was played at, and accomplished little more than the change of inn-signs. Browning was chilled, and Mrs. Browning near despair. A vivid account of the sights she witnessed and the hopes and the disillusion that they provoked is to be found in *Casa Guidi Windows*, of which a little more presently. Popular movements readily attracted her imagination. The idea of liberty inspired much of her verse. Browning, on the other hand, despite his great admiration for Shelley, thought freedom to be no more than a necessary condition of a man's growth. It was on the individual that he fixed his eyes, and, unlike her, he did not become a hero-worshipper of any political contemporary. Indeed his prejudices were easily aroused, and, because Mrs. Trollope had criticized adversely the poetry of Victor Hugo, he was unwilling to admit her to the house. When he yielded to his wife's persuasion and grew to like this visitor, all was well. " Blessed be the inconsistency of men " was Mrs. Browning's comment when he was liberal enough to like this opponent in spite of her crimes. It is pleasant to picture this argument; lest we might fear that they found too little to differ about. It was not until they had been in Italy for several months that they so much as glanced at a newspaper. They had discussions over books when they had found a library to supply them. These were chiefly French, and the difference in their tastes led Mrs. Browning to say that her husband " won't listen to a story for a story's sake. I can bear to be amused, you know, without a strong pull on my admiration." They were at one about Balzac, Madame Bovary, and Stendhal, but not about the current romances. He preferred the French plays and vaudevilles, of which she knew much less, for he declared that these were the happiest expression of the French school apart from the masterpieces.

Wilson had been taken with shivering fits at Pisa, and we gain a glimpse of the pair in this emergency. Mrs. Browning " learnt how it is possible (in certain conditions of the human frame) to comb out and twist up one's own hair, and lace one's very own stays, and cause hooks and eyes to meet behind one's very own back, besides making toast and water for Wilson—which last miracle, it is only just to say, was considerably assisted by Robert's counsels ' not quite to set fire to the bread while one was toasting it.' He was the best and kindest all that time, even as *he* could be, and carried the kettle when it was too heavy for me, and helped me with heart and head." Even Flush was being spoiled by her husband. She actually said that his poetry was the prose of his real self. As she still spent a good deal of time upon the sofa, and could not see nearly as much as she liked, she was in a position to judge his reserves of good nature. He had once written to her that love was always from beneath, and she wrote from Florence to Miss Mitford saying : " I personally would rather be teased a little and smoked over a good deal by a man I could look up to and be proud of, than have my feet kissed all day by a Mr. Smith in boots and a waistcoat, thereby chiefly distinguished." She had not to complain of the smoke, however, for Browning " never touches a cigar." She also found that " being too happy doesn't agree with literary activity quite as well " as she had thought. In this delightful expansion of her new existence the winter of 1847–8 in Florence whiled itself away.

Another detail of their life in Florence which is sometimes overlooked is that, unlike many of their compatriots, they never thought of leaving the country because of the disturbances of 1848. She half-believed that timidity had a little to do with Mr. Kenyon's failure to join them, as he had hoped, and twitted him with his satisfaction over the state of affairs in England. Was it not because " you have a lower idea of liberty than the French people have " ? She spoke of " our brave countrymen flying on all sides," a precaution that had no place in her own feelings for Italy. Instead, as we have seen, they took empty rooms, gradually filled them with appropriate furniture, and thus laid plans for affording the expense of future summer journeys to England out of the rent that their apartments, let furnished, would produce. Browning was always providing fresh chests of drawers when she was wanting more washing-stands, so she found something in him which needed correction after all. Mr. Boyd's death was her principal regret this summer.

They visited Fano on the coast, and found in the church the picture by Guercino commemorated in Browning's poem " The Guardian Angel." Fano proved to be " uninhabitable from the heat." It was the same at Ancona, so they passed on to Rimini and Ravenna, and home again over the Apennines from Forli, after an absence of three weeks.

On March 9, 1849, a son was born to them, and christened in the Lutheran church Robert Wiedemann Barrett Browning. Unfortunately, and within but a few days, the news came that Browning's mother had died from ' ossification of the heart.' The relief and joy of his wife's recovery, and the ardent affection that he felt for his son from first to last, suffered a sudden shock under this blow. The reaction was intense and prolonged, and his health began to give way. Mrs. Browning begged him to seek a change, but he refused to budge until, she wrote, " I had to say and swear that baby and I couldn't bear the heat, and that we must and would go away." Leaving, in the end, the child with his nurse and Wilson, the parents explored the coast to Spezzia, saw the white marble mountains of Carrara, passed through the olive forests and the vineyards, along avenues of acacia trees and chestnut woods, and many surprises of lovely scenery. It was not, however, until they paused at the highest point of Bagni di Lucca and were so much charmed as to fetch the child to join them, that Browning's health and spirits began to revive. His warm heart had not room for this conflict of emotion, and the fact of the conflict doubled his grief. The baby was a robust child, too much so, his mother would say, to seem hers, with the blue eyes often mentioned in her poems, an abundance of chins, and so like his father that she hoped for an inward similarity. Browning would be present at his bath, carry him up and down the terrace at Casa Guidi, and showed himself a father as instinctively as he was proving to be a husband.

The death of the poet's mother was one of the facts which postponed a return to England. He could not bear to revisit New Cross with its reminders, and the news of the little boy had brought no sign of relenting from Mr. Barrett, while his wife's brothers were still unreconciled, if less aloof. All that Mrs. Browning could do was to send pressing invitations to Miss Browning in the hope that she and her father would join them in Florence. Lucca was not, as Browning had expected, " a wasps' nest of scandal and gaming," and the English were nowhere to be seen. It was cool in the mountains, and the cicala and the rushing stream, by which they would sit in the moonlight, chattered all day. The child throve, even Flush grew fond of him; and Mrs. Browning was strong enough to climb the hills at her

husband's side.   The evidence of so much health was
irresistible, and the poet recovered in the clear cool air.
Politics kept everyone else away, and the only people to
be seen were an occasional ' monk girt with rope ' or
' a barefooted peasant.'   One day, mounted on donkeys,
they climbed up the water-courses five miles into the
mountains.   In spite of the precipitous ascent and return,
which no untrained animal could have accomplished,
Mrs. Browning was no more than tired out at the end of
the long day.   With her child and this proof of endurance, what must she and the poet have thought of the
change accomplished by her marriage ?

" If," Mrs. Browning wrote, " he is vain about anything in the world, it is about my improved health, and
I used to say to him, ' But you needn't talk so much to
people of how your wife walked here with you and there
with you, as if a wife with a pair of feet was a miracle
of nature.' "   But there were relapses, even in this
winter at Florence, and again at Siena in 1850, to mention but two that shortly followed these recent feats.
Back in Florence again, she was at work on the new
edition of her poems to be published in 1850, and he
upon his " Christmas Eve and Easter Day," which
appeared in the same year.   In her absence from England Mrs. Browning entrusted the poet's sister with the
conduct of her proofs, an instance of the good feeling
that she always enjoyed at the hands of her husband's
family.   They were equally interested in little Wiedemann, or Pen as he came to be called, who " laughs like
an imp when he can succeed in doing anything wrong."
Among the new friends that they cultivated was the ill-
fated Margaret Fuller, but they lived a retired life, and
" retreated from the kind advances of the English
society " in Florence.   The news that Mr. Barrett had
been unwell upset Mrs. Browning, who, in her utmost
endeavour to obtain his forgiveness, asked her father

to exclude her and hers "from every advantage he intended his other children, that, having been so just, he might afford to be merciful"; but her only consolation was that this and recent letters had not been returned. "My husband and I had talked this over again and again," and the letter eventually was written. They were starved of things to read, for few books, and no new books, were available. Even the newspapers she had to read through her husband's reports, because women were not allowed in the library where he glanced at them. It was no more than a glance, for it is amusing to learn that whenever he grew disgusted with a man or with a Government, he refused to read a word of all they said and did. His wife quoted the following examples: "Thiers is a rascal; I make a point of not reading one word said by M. Thiers; Prudhon is a madman; who cares for Prudhon? The President's an ass; he is not worth thinking of." So the amount of news which she gleaned from her husband's reports was small.

News of another kind there was, however, for in March 1850 Henrietta Barrett followed her sister's example, married Capt. Surtees Cook, and was banished from her former home. The result was the same, save so far that Mr. Barrett had been the more exasperated by the efforts to conciliate him. When the bridegroom asked for his permission, Mr. Barrett answered: "If Henrietta marries you, she turns her back on this house for ever." He also wrote a letter to the bride saying that it was an "insult" to have asked his permission for an act on which she was anyway determined, and once more he kept his word, and would not allow her name to be mentioned in his presence. Mrs. Browning was sympathetic but troubled, first for the pair who had been engaged for five years, and also because she felt sure that the effect of her sister's rebellion would be to diminish her own scanty chances of reconciliation with her father. Another event was that on the death of Wordsworth, May 1850, Mrs. Browning's name was put forward by the *Athenæum* as his successor in the laureateship with the added argument that the post would be appropriately filled by a woman under a reigning Queen. Tennyson, of course, was appointed, and no one suggested Browning.

Her illness of some weeks this summer led to their taking a villa outside Siena. Here she soon recovered during September, though much time was spent in the arm-chair that Browning had found for her in the town. The villa was high up with the winds coming in at every window. It stood in the midst of its own vines and olives, and before the month was out she was able to walk a mile again, and the child recovered from a sudden touch of the sun. " The silence that fell suddenly upon the house, without the small pattering feet and the singing voice," was further depressing from the news of the shipwreck in which Margaret Fuller, her husband and their child were drowned. That another shipwreck should rob Mrs. Browning of a dear friend, revived the saddest memory of her life. Indeed, Ossoli, the husband, had been warned to shun the sea, and the idle prophecy seemed ominous when realized because Madam Ossoli, laughing it off on the even of her departure, had told Mrs. Browning that she had found a good omen in the name of the ship, the " Elizabeth," in which they were to sail. However, their domestic troubles were over, and they descended to Siena itself to see the churches and Sodoma's pictures. It is amusing to learn that Pen was growing a precocious sight-seer, who knelt at the sound of music, and crossed himself and did other imitative things. As his parents held Tractarianism in aversion, how did they regard these signs ? Apparently with good humour, for Mrs. Browning wrote that her husband " says it is as well to have the eyeteeth and the Puseyistical crisis over together. The child is a very curious imaginative child, but too excitable for his age, that's all I complain of." He was not tall, in spite of being measured every day against the door by his father. His mother declared that he was said to grow about an inch a week, and that anyone, after hearing his father's reports, would probably cry on seeing the child, " how little he must have been to be no larger now." Mr. Kenyon had virtually made himself a father to Mrs. Browning, and, since the arrival of the child, he had insisted on the Brownings accepting a hundred a year. She records in her letters the straits in which they would sometimes have found themselves without it.

IV

For Browning the year 1850 had chiefly meant the publication of " Christmas Eve and Easter Day," the modest initial success of which was not maintained. The year 1851, however, is a milestone in their married life, for in the summer they began eighteen months of wandering in Venice, London and Paris, while Mrs. Browning's *Casa Guidi Windows* also appeared. Before following the travellers, we will glance at these works, beginning with Mrs. Browning's because it bears obvious traces of her experiences in Italy.

The two parts into which *Casa Guidi Windows* is divided do more than reflect her hopes and her disillusion upon the liberation of Italy. The first part is largely descriptive. It convinces us that the windows were provided with a pair of quick, sympathetic eyes. She was a spectator of picturesque events, and the hopes that these awakened were part of their interest and their poetry. Consequently, we are readily transported into these gay Italian scenes, in which the aspiration seems part and parcel of the processions and the sunlight. The opening lines have a pleasant happy rhythm, like the tinkle of sheep bells on a sunny morning, and contain the spirit of the poem :

> I heard last night a little child go singing
> 'Neath Casa Guidi Windows, by the church,
> O *bella libertà*, O *bella !* stringing
> The same words still on notes he went in search
> So high for, you concluded the upspringing
> Of such a nimble bird to sky from perch
> Must leave the whole bush in a tremble green,
> And that the heart of Italy must beat,
> While such a voice had leave to rise serene
> 'Twixt church and palace of a Florence street !
> A little child, too, who not long had been
> By mother's finger steadied on his feet,
> And still O *bella libertà* he sang.

Even the protest that Italy must not be regarded as a heap of lovely and historic ruins, whose great men had all died long ago, does not overweight the poetic impulse, and the descriptive scenes are as lively as their companion passages in the letters. When we come to the second part, however, not only have the hopes drooped but the impulse deadens, and there is more of exhortation and didactic assertion than her verse will bear. Didacticism is to be criticised in poetry, not because the content does not matter, but because the only thing that does matter is that part of the content which the poet's imagination has transformed. In other words, when the imagination has fused its material the question how far this is also didactic does not arise. The use of the adjective at all is superficial evidence that the teaching has overcome the poet, and that his imagination has not subdued his matter. This happened to Mrs. Browning here, and made the two parts of her poem as unequal in quality as they were opposite in mood. Though several good passages might be quoted from both parts, the second too is most happy in its opening, for the feeling that she might have been mistaken in her hopes was a quality of feeling within her poetic range :

> I wrote a meditation and a dream,
> Hearing a little child sing in the street.
> I leant upon his music as a theme,
> Till it gave way beneath my heart's full beat,
> Which tried at an exultant prophecy
> But dropped before the measure was complete. . . .

Here is unconscious, but sufficient, criticism, not so much of the accuracy of her prophecy as of the power of her imagination to fuse political ideas. Indeed wherever, in the second part, she criticizes herself, a child in these things, she is nearest to poetry. Wherever she criticizes men and events she is further from it. This said, it should be added that *Casa Guidi Windows* is the best of her political poems, and better than many of the lyrics which have been preferred to it.

Under the influence of his wife Browning had promised likewise to be outspoken. His subject was not the political movement in the streets outside, but the state of religion as this might be discerned in a dissenting chapel, in a Roman Catholic basilica, in the lecture-room of a German professor engaged upon the " high criticism " of Christian tradition and belief, with the Christ of Browning's own ideal standing in the background. To describe each attitude to the Christian religion, and to compare them with the Christ, is the subject of " Christmas Eve and Easter Day." The poet emerges, though not entirely, in the spectator of these scenes, so that he is and yet is not speaking in his own person. Like many of Browning's poems this is a feat of imagination, which every competent reader respects, which every intimate reader admires, but which requires in all a certain strain of the attention. Its.length makes it difficult to quote from and its most quotable passages are long themselves : the vision of the double rainbow, the Blake-like description of the judgment and end of the world, the wonderful description of the crowd "famishing in expectation" in St. Peter's, the vision of the face of Christ. Such a poem is either known well or unread, and criticism can form no sufficient bridge between the hesitant and the familiar reader. It can, however, attempt to show, what many good critics shirk, the reason why these two attitudes exist, and the curious mixture of qualities that explain them.

Browning, among other things, was a religious poet in the sense that Christianity was his foundation, not at all in the sense that he resembled writers of devotional poems. His strength was that religion was his foundation, not his subject, and that on this foundation all his moods were displayed. The amount of humour in "Christmas Day" is considerable. It plays over the lecture-room at Göttingen. It penetrates the little Bethel. It is as certain, but as kindly, as the light of the sun. Now this foundation of his he was anxious to proclaim and to defend, but because his descriptive powers were wonderful, because his imagination did not flag, he is not, in the dull sense, a didactic writer. Why then is our attention strained ; why do many find him tedious ; why do many shrink from reading any but his shorter poems ? To answer this question, which even this fine poem imposes, we must consider the nature of his intelligence. He had a restless curiosity of mind, and delighted in analysis. Whether it was the motive of a man in an exceptional situation, or the explanation of a certain course of conduct, the dissection is remorselessly pursued. On the subject of religion he delighted to unfold all the arguments for and against revealed truth, and it is this conduct of an argument that is fatiguing. Once the attention wanders, the

thread is lost, and the arguments have nothing fresh
about them but the vividness with which they are displayed. Unfortunately, for many readers, this vividness
is defeated by the length. You have to attend, perhaps
to think, the whole time, and very few are prepared to
pay so stiff a price for poetry. It is the length and the
amount of discussion that deprive Browning of many
readers, and, as neither quality can be explained away,
it is impossible to alter this. Either Browning's energy
and powers of attention are altogether exceptional, or
most of us are right in resenting the effort that the poet
expected. No qualified person complains that " Christmas Eve and Easter Day " has passages that the poem
would be better without. The complaint, here as elsewhere, is that the whole would be better appreciated if
it were shorter. We feel, in sum, that there is too much
reasoning in these poems, however finely put the terms
of it, that the end and not the process of an argument
should be a poet's main concern, and that both the
arguments and the end in Browning are already familiar.
He is apt to make a beautiful thing that nobody wants,
a splendid museum-piece that embarrasses the modest
householder. His own statement, in the essay to the
spurious letters of Shelley, that " the misapprehensive-
ness of his age is exactly what a poet is sent to remedy "
is true, but his method was apt to be that of an architect
who would present palaces to slum-dwellers.

As his wife once said, Browning ' saw ' everything as
passionately as other people feel, and among the things
that he saw were every detail of a scene and every
point of an argument. In a rationalistic age he would
convince men of the arguments in favour of Christianity.
" Christmas Eve and Easter Day " is as full of them as
a quiver, but few beliefs of this order are convincing
by their reasons. It is our imaginations which the
Gospels and the Church touch. The words " I am "

will bring people to their knees whom the word " because " will start laughing or yawning. This being so, Browning most infects us with his courage and belief when he writes a short lyric like the epilogue to *Asolando*. The splendid poem " Prospice " puts our fears of death to shame. It is not so when he brings all the artillery of his mind to argue us out of opposition. It is true that he makes fine verse of these arguments, but though the language is splendid, it is not the poetry of delight. I shall content myself therefore with a glimpse of the interior of St. Peter's, simply because this is one of the shortest quotable passages in the poem :

> As the swarming hollow of a hive,
> The whole Basilica alive !
> Men in the chancel, body and nave,
> Men on the pillar's architrave,
> Men on the statues, men on the tombs
> With popes and kings in their porphyry wombs,
> All famishing in expectation
> Of the main altar's consummation.
> For see, for see, the rapturous moment
> Approaches, and earth's best endowment
> Blends with heaven's ; the taper-fires
> Pant up, the winding brazen spires
> Heave loftier yet the baldachin ;
> The incense-gaspings, long kept in,
> Suspire in clouds ; the organ blatant
> Holds his breath and grovels latent,
> As if God's hushing finger grazed him,
> (Like Behemoth when he praised him)
> At the silver bell's shrill tinkling,
> Quick cold drops of terror sprinkling
> On the sudden pavement strewed
> With faces of the multitude.

In the same fashion the arguments are made alive, but people are less interested in the recesses of an argument than in the details of a building or a crowd, so that we arrive at a paradoxical conclusion. The most patient and enthusiastic readers of Browning have been those

critics, like Mr. Arthur Symons, who are most sus-
ceptible to the art of language, most appreciative of the
technical mastery, not those to whom the subject of
religion might be expected to appeal.   In what other poet
do we find this strange alliance between the presiding
spirit of beauty and the subject-spirit of controversy ?

V

About the end of May 1851 the Brownings left Florence.   Deciding that it was too late in the year to go
south to Rome and that economy was necessary, they
made for Venice.   The beauty of the place and the soft
climate suited her to perfection, but Browning, equally
responsive, became unwell.   The gondola seems the
most appropriate of all carriages for her, and during the
month of their stay she " went everywhere " in it.   The
architecture, the silence, the opera, coffee in the moonlight on the Piazza of St. Mark's every evening, united
to make her happy.   The invalids temporarily changed
places, and " out of pure humanity and sympathy " she
was " forced to be glad to go away."   They went on
to Padua, and thence drove to Arqua " for Petrarch's
sake," passed through Brescia by moonlight, and stayed
two days at Milan, where she climbed to the top of the
cathedral, and by way of the Italian lakes and Switzerland travelled straight through from Strasbourg to Paris.
There the shops, the restaurants, the sight of the President " in a cocked hat and with a train of cavalry passing
like a rocket along the boulevards " were the last of
their pleasures before arriving in England in " a puddle
and a fog."   If it had not been that she was very anxious
to see her sister Arabel again, she could scarcely have
made up her mind to revisit London.

In the two months of their stay, which lasted till the
end of September, they were in the midst of a social

racket which she found so fatiguing that the fortnight of Wilson's holiday, during which Mrs. Browning was left in sole charge of her child, was almost a rest. The obduracy of her father made her cling closer to Browning, of whom she wrote to Mrs. Martin : " Husband, lover, nurse—not one of these has Robert been to me, but all three together." Her brothers thawed, came to see her, and made friends. The affection of both sisters was never clouded. Against the advice of Mr. Kenyon, she wrote to tell her father of her arrival in England. So that no injustice may be done to Mr. Barrett, the sequel shall be given in his daughter's own words :

> I could not leave England without trying the possibility of his seeing me once, of his consenting to kiss my child once. So I wrote, and Robert wrote. A manly, true, straightforward letter his was, yet in some parts so touching to me and so generous and conciliating everywhere, that I could scarcely believe in the probability of its being read in vain.
>
> In reply he had a very violent and unsparing letter, with all the letters I had written to papa through these five years sent back unopened, the seals unbroken. What went most to my heart was that some of the seals were black with black-edged envelopes; so that he might have thought my child or husband dead, yet never cared to solve the doubt by breaking the seal. He said he regretted to have been forced to keep them by him until now, through his ignorance of where he should send them. So there's the end. I cannot, of course, write again. God takes it all into His own hands, and I wait.

If Mr. Barrett had been sincere when he told Mr. Kenyon that he had " no objection to the young man," why should he have written to *him* a violent letter ? Should not Mr. Barrett as well as his daughter " have been thinking of another world " ? His implacability is the more remarkable because he was the father of one of the most affectionate daughters who ever lived. Even now, reduced to silence, she hoped still, and we cannot

R

think that many husbands as clear-eyed as Browning
would have consented to invite this final and "unsparing"
rebuff.   He had promised, five years before, to spare no
sacrifice, and he kept his word.

After Browning had recovered from an attack of
influenza, they returned to Paris at the end of September
and prolonged their stay for about nine months.   Once
more, they were in an atmosphere of revolution, for on
December 20th, 1851, Louis Napoleon assumed power.
This, later, provoked her husband's character-study of
the man in the poem, " Prince Hohenstiel-Schwangau."
For the rest Browning was as sorry to leave England
and his family as his wife was glad and relieved.   The
circumstances made them feel differently.   In Paris both
could be content.   Carlyle travelled thither with them,
and they made many friends.   Madame Mohl, whose
evening receptions introduced them then and later to
French society, and Joseph Milsand, who had just made
Browning known in France and to whom the poet
dedicated many of his later poems, were among them.
He wanted to meet Victor Hugo, and Mrs. Browning
to set eyes on George Sand.   Disappointed in his wish,
he reluctantly followed his wife to the lady's reception,
but her queer set of " the ragged Red diluted with the
lower theatrical " was not congenial, and even Mrs.
Browning felt that she herself had never penetrated her
heroine's outer mask.   There were closer pleasures.
Mr. Browning and his daughter paid the poets a visit,
and became devoted to Penini, who had already begun
to draw.   These details blend with her hopes and fears
for France, and we see her in her letters giving not only
vivid pictures but explanations designed to overcome the
timidity of her friends in England.   One of them is
worth quoting : " Constitutional forms and essential
principles of liberty are so associated in England that
they are apt to be confounded, and are, in fact, con-

stantly confounded." However impulsive her feelings, you are never safe from illuminating observations of this kind.

At the end of June 1852 they were in London again. Mrs. Browning declared in a letter, " The only excitement and fatigue which does me not harm, but good, is travelling." This was a year of travel. The principal writing that appeared during these months was Browning's essay on Shelley, a sound but detached criticism on its rather limited lines. The poet who is a seer, whose apprehensions are " seeds of creation lying burningly on the Divine hand," is given the pre-eminence, and Shelley is said to have grown to his stature when he ceased to attack abuses and learned that " innumerable negative effects are produced by the upholding of one positive principle." There are, however, two ways of upholding : to show the beauty of the idea upheld, and to produce the arguments in its favour. As we have seen, Browning was far from always content with the first. They went to see Mr. Kenyon at Wimbledon and found Landor there " full of life and passionate energy." Mazzini was brought to their rooms in Welbeck Street by Mrs. Carlyle, a lady who proved more congenial to Mrs. Browning than to her husband. Crystal-gazing was coming into fashion, and Mrs. Browning was attracted at once : " It was very curious altogether to my mind, as a sign of the times, if in no other respect of philosophy. But I love the marvellous." Invitations poured upon them, and they were beckoned to the country from eight houses at once. Browning was unable to leave town, so they limited themselves to a couple of days at Farnham, where they met Charles Kingsley, and to such new friends as they made, Ruskin, and, according to his brother, Dante Rossetti. Our detestable weather was too much for its old victim, and by September Mrs. Browning was glad to be in Paris once more. " How the sun shines " is almost the opening phrase of her first letter from France.

VI

The next three years, 1852–55, were spent in Italy, and Florence, after the recent excitement of the inauguration of the Second Empire in Paris, seemed dull at first. A new edition of her poems was called for in 1853, and Browning was at work on the pieces which composed the two volumes of *Men and Women* on their first appearance in 1855. In 1853, however, he was gratified by the production of *Colombe's Birthday* at the Haymarket with Miss Faucit (Lady Martin) in the principal part. His wife was about to begin *Aurora Leigh*, and to become more and more interested, to Browning's regret, in spiritualism. She fell a victim to a vogue which professed to satisfy her cravings, or, as she put it, to extend the possibilities of human nature. The main point now of this tendency of hers is that, however much Browning might disapprove of some of the people with whom his wife was brought in contact, it did not seriously disturb the harmony of their marriage. He could be irritated by opinions that he did not share. He could not be irritated with herself. " You know (she wrote) I am rather a visionary, and inclined to knock round at all the doors of the present world to try to get out, so that I listen with interest to every goblin story of the kind," and the air was thick with them in the 'fifties. She was dangerously elated rather than obsessed, and her old interests were not extinguished : " Robert has just been reading . . . *Diane de Lys*, and throws it down with— ' You must read that, Ba—it is clever—only outrageous as to morals.' Just what I should expect from Alexandre Dumas, fils. I have a tenderness for the whole family, you see."

The winter was passed happily once she had recovered from the attack that befel her from having insisted on travelling by the Mont Cenis route to Genoa. Her letters are even more full of life than usual, and they give us an idea of the different way in which she and Browning were reacting to the political ferment in France and the prostration of Italy under Austrian bayonets. Both situations seemed to her deliberately misrepresented in England, the insular complacency of which irritated her much. "I always tell Robert (she wrote) that his patriotism grows and deepens in exact proportion as he goes away from England. As for me, it is not so with me. I am very cosmopolitan, and am considerably tired of the self-deification of the English nation at the expense of all others. . . . I have continually maintained the non-representativeness of our ' representative system '; and socially speaking we are much behind hand with most foreign peoples." It was not only that her outlook was generous. She was well informed because she was capable of absorbing the facts that she learnt readily in her travels. It was over the table-rapping that she was apt to be credulous. Though she admitted frauds, she put down many trivialities to the undeveloped beginnings of a new knowledge. The main "fact" she thought to have been established, because she hoped intensely that communications might exist. When they later witnessed the proceedings of the American medium Home, Browning was convinced that he was a charlatan, while his wife did not at first recognize the imposture. As everyone knows, the main interest of "Mr. Sludge the Medium," which appeared among *Dramatis Personæ* in 1864, is the portrait of a weak character under temptation too strong for it. Condemnation falls equally on the impostor and on those whose credulity actively encouraged him step by step in degradation. As Edward Dowden said, the subject is "exhausted to the dregs," and it is marvellous how the poet made a poem, so colloquial in its language, out of the mud that was under everyone's feet. There is more modernity and more poetry in the dissection of Mr. Sludge than in *Aurora Leigh*, because, apart from the difference in quality of the two poets, Mr. Sludge is really modern, whereas Miss Leigh is the phantom of a romantic imagination in spite of wearing modern clothes. Browning's poem is very long because its treatment is over-thorough. *Aurora Leigh* is expanded to the size of an epic because Mrs. Browning blew into it as into a big toy balloon. On Mr. Sludge everything pertinent is said. Half as much would have doubled the number of its readers.

From July to October 1853 the Brownings were once more at Bagni di Lucca, in the company of the American sculptor Story, and Robert Lytton, and here " By the Fireside " and " In a Balcony " were composed. " We are doing a little work, both of us. Robert is working at a volume of lyrics, of which I have seen but a few, and those seemed to me as fine as anything he has done. We neither of us show our work to one another till it is finished. An artist must, I fancy, either find or make a solitude to work in, if it is to be good work at all." This for the consolation of bachelors. Nevertheless she saw as much society about this time as ever in her life, and a small circle near at hand suited both of them better than numerous acquaintances and formal gatherings. She was a keen observer of character and physiognomy, and hated, she said, every sign of age because it was a screen. Whatever men's age, the inner sense of feeling as young as ever is general. She had a similar hatred for graves and cemeteries, for everything connected with the physical side of age and death. Though Browning must have been well aware of the intensity with which she clung to her familiar impressions, without warning he appeared shaved on their arrival in Rome, and she was " horror-struck." Moreover, when his beard had grown again it was streaked with grey. Luckily, for once, this sign of time seemed to his wife to give a touch of " elevation " to his appearance.

They had arrived in Rome after a brief return from Lucca to Florence, and their entry was unpropitious in other ways. One of the Storys' children was suddenly seized with convulsions and died the same day; two other children fell ill, and for a time there were fears that little Pen would not escape. Indeed Browning declared that his wife lost her head for the moment, and perhaps these shocks had something to do with her dislike of Rome, in spite of the society of artists that soon gathered round them. Browning, Pen, and his mother were all painted. She complained of having " almost too many visitors." Thackeray was near by, Fanny Kemble and Lockhart were regular comers. It was Lockhart who said : " I like Browning, he isn't at all like a damned literary man." This circle and its doings, which included Gibson's tinted Venus, is preserved for us in Henry James's life of Story, the least familiar perhaps of the novelist's works.

By May 1854 they were back in Florence, and their only regret was to be unable to escape the heat in the hills or to afford a summer visit to England. They occupied themselves with *Aurora Leigh* and the completion of *Men and Women*, and contributed, at the request of Browning's sister, two poems, jointly published under their respective initials, for a bazaar on behalf of the Ragged Schools of London. Mrs. Browning's is called " A Plea," and her husband's " The Twins." The last is surely the wittiest and most delicious lyric that a begging has yet inspired. During the summer Mr. Barrett met with an accident that left him lame, and he suffered afterwards from want of exercise. With what Mr. Kenyon called " the Barrett obstinacy," he refused even to take drives, and once more sent no answer to his daughter's note of sympathy. She herself was far from well in the autumn " with the worst attack on the chest I ever suffered from in Italy." With her fever and cough Browning had sleepless nights, keeping the fires going and making coffee for her. Indeed she wrote, " Except for love's sake it wouldn't be worth while to live on at the expense of doing so much harm," and he was driven " almost frantic " by the news of the sufferings of the troops in the Crimea. Responsibility seemed to her to rest on " the most corrupt system in Europe." She thought the sense of shame in England to be a deserved reward for the national habit of claiming " moral superiority." Of Florence Nightingale, who had called and left flowers on her when last in London, Mrs. Browning wrote : " She is an earnest noble woman, and has fulfilled her woman's duty where many men have failed." It is worth adding that Mrs. Browning did not think that Florence Nightingale would have been equally acclaimed if, instead of binding wounds, she had stirred an inch as a thinker or an artist. " I do not consider the best use to which we can put a gifted and accomplished woman is to make her a hospital nurse." A wider comment follows : " We are oligarchic in all things, from our parliament to our army. Individual interests are admitted as obstacles to the general prosperity. This plague runs through all things with us." It was then the army. It is now coal. Such instances of her judgment are apt to be overlooked among the stream of personal observations in her letters.

With the turn of the year she lost her old friend, Miss Mitford, who died in January 1855 and had long been forgiven for the pain she had caused by referring to the death of Mrs. Browning's brother in her *Memoirs*. In

April, after a wonderful recovery, she wrote of her husband dictating four hours a day to a transcriber, and of her own untranscribed six or seven thousand lines.

VII

By midsummer 1855 they were back in London and their second absence from Italy occurred. His *Men and Women* was passed through the press after their arrival, but *Aurora Leigh* did not appear until 1856. For the rest their experiences and their worries tended to repeat themselves. Henrietta was living in Somerset and too hard up to come to town, while the household at Wimpole Street was again convulsed by matrimony. The offender this time was Mrs. Browning's brother Alfred, " the third exile," who, however, escaped a scene, as if Mr. Barrett was learning from experience of their inefficacy. Alfred " had written to my father nine or ten days before the ceremony, received no answer, and followed up the silence rather briskly by another letter to announce his marriage." The phrase ' rather briskly ' is good. The number of people who wished to see the poets proved rather overwhelming, and as usual Mrs. Browning began to sigh for the quiet of Florence. They had brought a piece of Italy with them in the person of Ferdinando Romagnoli, a Florentine whom the faithful Wilson had married. He and she remained in the service of Penini till their deaths, so it is clear that Wilson never regretted her desire to travel.

Among the pleasures of this distracting summer were an evening with Ruskin, to whom Browning introduced Leighton on a subsequent visit, and another that Tennyson, whose *Maud* had just had a great success, spent in their rooms in Dorset Street. He " dined with us, smoked with us, opened his heart to us (and the second bottle of port) and ended by reading *Maud* through from end to end, and going away at half-past two in the morning. If I had had a heart to spare, certainly he would have won mine. He is captivating with his frankness, confidingness, and unexampled *naïveté* ! Think of his stopping in *Maud* every now and then—' There's a wonderful touch ! That's very tender. How beautiful that is ! ' Yes, and it *was* wonderful, tender, beautiful, and he read exquisitely in a voice like an organ, rather music than speech." Another listener was Dante Rossetti, who made a surreptitious drawing of the poet while he was reading. The painter-poet told Hall Caine that Browning followed with a reading of his " Fra Lippo Lippi," a reading as various and spirited as Tennyson's was sonorous and sustained.

They had resolved to winter in Paris. By trusting to a misguided friend they found themselves in unsuitable rooms which involved a search of six weeks before they discovered a pleasant and warm apartment in the Rue du Colisée. Mrs. Browning was very poorly before the change was made. She told Mrs. Jameson how " that darling Robert carried me into the carriage, swathed past possible breathing, over face and respirator in woollen shawls. No, he wouldn't set me down even to walk up the fiacre steps, but shoved me in upside down in a struggling bundle." Once settled, she recovered in the mild weather and worked hard at the completion of *Aurora Leigh*, while Browning began his (discarded) task of re-writing *Sordello* for the benefit of the average reader. That he abandoned his attempt is evidence not only, as he put it in his dedication to Milsand, that he had imagined another thing at first, but also that, as he had told his wife before their marriage, the form and treatment of his poems fixed themselves at the first draft. Indeed, as we read, we can feel him thinking, see the work grow from line to line. Its beauty and its difficulty arise alike from the method natural to him. He had always been fond of playing the piano, and of improvising or playing upon the organ in an empty Italian church. Now, unhappy with his attempt at revision, he started once more to draw. Later, under the stimulus of his friend Story, he was to devote much time to modelling, and it is interesting to remember that his robust vitality found expression in three arts, so that he was, to some extent, what he seemed, a rich personality of the type familiar at the Renaissance. One is convinced that the chief limitation upon him was the age in which he lived, for noble achievements in art are unnatural to an industrial society. The spirit of the two is opposed. Consequently, over-much of Browning's energy was spent in the attempt to find a form for the contradiction, to impose a rhythm upon it, to mould an obstinate material, to wring beauty and harmony out of confusion and grit. It is to his honour that he never turned his back on the confusion, but the sense of confusion is obstinately present in his work. How far is the awkwardness a failure of his form, how far is it a quality of his material? So responsive an imagination could not be at rest in a restless world. The world would not let him alone, so he rarely spoke out of his own heart. The temptation to define its points of view, to depict its innumerable attitudes, was irresistible.

Mrs. Browning was working in ' a sort of furia ' at her poem during this winter, and interested to hear that Mrs. Trollope had thrown over the medium Home " from some failure in his moral character." Florence was agog on the subject, and Mrs. Browning's comment suggests the situation afterward depicted by her husband in " Mr. Sludge." She wrote : " I have no doubt that the young man, who is weak and vain, and was exposed to gross flatteries from the various unwise coteries at Florence who took him up, deserves to be thrown over." She believed, however, that his ' physical faculty ' was 'undisproved.' Spiritualism and mesmerism were still popularly associated. She herself was too busy finishing *Aurora Leigh* to have much time even for writing letters, and was still too tired to go out except for a drive. Browning, in spite of his drawing, had time upon his hands, which he did not like, and his principal distraction was a visit to the theatre to see Ristori, and a dinner with Monckton Milnes at which Mignet, Cavour, and George Sand, crowned with a wreath of ivy, were present. He was also worried by the illness of Mr. Kenyon, and very nearly decided to return to England to see how his old friend really was. They had to be in England before the end of June to deliver *Aurora Leigh* to the publishers in time for its appearance in the autumn.

Mr. Kenyon, who was seeking convalescence in the Isle of Wight, lent the Brownings his house in Devonshire Place during their stay. Anxiety for him hung over them, and Mr. Barrett was equal to the occasion by sending Mrs. Browning's favourite sister Arabel out of London almost as soon as Mrs. Browning had arrived. Luckily the sister was also in the Isle, so in September the Brownings followed and saw her and Mr. Kenyon there. Even Pen had begun to observe. "It has naturally (wrote his mother) begun to dawn upon my child that I have done something very wicked to make my father what he is. . . . In fact the position is perfectly hopeless—perfectly." Pen, however, won the heart of his uncles, who were also with Arabel in the island. These small mercies were welcome, for Mr. Kenyon was plainly in his last illness. In December, some six weeks after Mrs. Browning had left England for the last time, he died. His last act of generosity toward them in his will only deepened their sense of loss, and the immediate success of *Aurora Leigh*, which had appeared at the time of their departure, was blunted for Mrs. Browning by the grief that followed.

VIII

Aurora Leigh is a novel in verse consisting of nine books and telling a rather wild and melodramatic story. Mrs. Browning, who had admitted that she was naturally headlong, meant when she called this poem her most ' mature ' work that she had deliberately let herself go. It is a work of impulsiveness rather than of imagination, and the story which made it popular on its appearance is less attractive to us to-day than the flashes of poetry by which it is lightened here and there.   The temper of the work is nearer that of Tennyson's narrative pieces than of any story by Browning, for the writer was less interested in the truth of her characters than in the virtue or weakness that they display.   It created some commotion in the drawing-rooms of the period because it touched on controversial themes, such as the virtue of a violated woman, the insufficiency of social philanthropy and reform, the reasonableness of a young woman living independently by her writing.   There is much of Mrs. Browning in the poem, not only in its recollections of childhood and country, but even in the heroine herself. She made an honest attempt to be absolutely modern, and the result was indeed a faithful picture of the romantic ideals of her age and her type, though not of the age itself or of actual human nature.   Though it would be too much to say that Mrs. Browning wrote under the influence of George Sand, *Aurora Leigh* makes us understand afresh the impetuous qualities in the Frenchwoman that attracted her.

A brief outline of the story is necessary, partly because it is little read to-day, partly because Mrs. Browning had ambitions which were as much a part of her as her real lyric gift.   She saw the world as a warm-hearted and generous woman sees it, and she desired that the troubles of the world should be treated in the same spirit as the troubles in private life. It is, then, the horizon not the garden of her mind that the tale of Aurora Leigh reveals.

The heroine is the child of an English landowner and an Italian mother, on whose death she is brought to her father's Herefordshire home. The house is occupied by her aunt, a correct and rather acid spinster with a contempt for Continental manners. The principal neighbour is a cousin, Romney Leigh, whom the aunt hopes that Aurora will marry. He has almost a mania for social reform, and looks askance at Aurora's devotion to poetry. This difference in their attitude to poetry leads her to refuse him. She says that he is seeking a partner, not a wife. The angry aunt tells her that if she persists in her refusal she will be penniless, because the property of her father ceased to be his to bequeath when he married a foreigner. This intensifies Aurora's determination not to " sell herself." The aunt dies and leaves her a small legacy. Aurora rejects her cousin's offer of help, establishes herself in London as an author, and has a moderate success.

Among her new acquaintances is Lady Waldemar, who confesses that she is in love with Romney, and asks Aurora to help her in preventing Romney's marriage with one of his *protégées*, Marian, a daughter of the slums. Aurora visits the girl, and forms a very high opinion of her character. This social misalliance is to be solemnized at a fashionable church to which Romney, in his anxiety to bridge the gulf between rich and poor, invites the relatives of both families. A lively scene is the strange medley that assembles : the ragged friends of the bride and the sleek supporters of the bridegroom. At the last moment Marian fails to appear. Instead she sends a letter to say that she is unequal to the match. This news produces a riot, for Marian's friends in the church suspect that the wealthy husband has attempted to deprive one of their own class of her rights.   Aurora believes that Lady Waldemar has spirited the girl away.

Book five opens with many reflections on poetry, and on women's contribution to it.   We also learn that, eighteen months after the abortive wedding, Romney and Lady Waldemar have become engaged.   On the proceeds of a book Aurora departs to Italy.   On her way through Paris she suddenly recognizes Marian in the street, and finds her living with her infant in a poor suburb.   For all her kindness Aurora cannot restrain a stream of priggish remarks, till the true story makes her ashamed, not of herself, but of her rashness.   Marian explains that it was by Lady Waldemar's influence that she wrote the letter, convinced that Romney would come to repent of his choice.   The arguments were ingenious, but accompanied by the lie that Romney was in love with Lady Waldemar.   In return for her compliance, Marian received her passage-money to Australia, to which a former servant of the lady happened also to be going. The servant proves to be a procuress; the end of the journey is a brothel, where, after being drugged, Marian was raped.   Driven almost to frenzy, she wandered across France, until a miller's wife took pity on her, and found her a place in Paris.   From this she was turned into the street when she was seen to be with child.

Aurora carries Marian to Florence, and writes the truth about her to a friend.   The news is not to be passed on to Romney if he has already married.   She also writes a private letter of denunciation to Lady Waldemar herself.   Aurora next hears that Romney has been seriously ill and that he has been nursed attentively by Waldemar.   In the eighth book, while Aurora is still in Florence, Romney suddenly appears.   He tells her that his philanthropic schemes have gone awry, that he has been pelted in the street, that Leigh Hall has been burnt to the ground. He adds that her books have taught him the weakness of his schemes, and virtually confesses that his attachment to her is as strong as ever. Supposing him to be married, Aurora grows angry, only to learn, as the reader will have suspected, that it is his turn to be annoyed. He repudiates such a wife indignantly, and hands to her a letter which Waldemar has asked him to deliver.

The ninth and last book opens with this letter, which informs us that during his illness Waldemar had heard Romney confess his love for Aurora, and that the servant's infamous treatment of Marian was not her mistress's doing. She had indeed, when she heard of it, offered to come to Marian's aid, but Romney had told her loftily that he regarded Marian as his wife, and that his wife was in no need of anyone else's help. Lady Waldemar also said that one of her reasons for preventing the marriage had been, not only her own feeling for Romney, but the knowledge that he did not really love the girl. If it had not been for Aurora, she goes on, Romney might have loved herself. With a renewed assurance of her hatred, Lady Waldemar's letter ends.

Aurora has hardly had time to realize that Romney is not married when Marian enters. She has overheard and recognized his voice, and, drawn by her old magnet, has paused to listen. When she asks him if he will really marry her, and be a father to her child, and he agrees and Aurora supports him warmly, Marian is overcome at such constancy, but refuses him. She is now but the ghost of her old self, and all her love is absorbed by the child. Marian then vanishes, and Romney declares that his last presumption was to fancy himself necessary even to Marian. He has loved and lost, and he tells Aurora that he no longer aspires to her since he himself is an object of pity. She learns that he is blind through an accident that happened at the fire.

His own loss (though his eyes do not betray themselves) has taught him not to measure others' troubles by statistics, as he used to do, but to see some compensations in them. In this deeper knowledge lies more hope for him than in any medicine. Overcome at this news, Aurora says that she loves him, and on her side has grown to repent her pride and want of generosity. She has been a proud artist, but has since learnt that " art is much, but love is more." Her eyes have been opened by the fate that has closed his. Convinced at last that more than pity prompts her, he takes her hand. They turn instinctively to the east, and looking toward the dawn resolve to build on new foundations, lit by her poetry and steadied by his practical experience, a better life for both of them and for the world.

It should be clear even from this rapid summary that *Aurora Leigh* is the work of one who cannot invent a story, but that such a tale as this gave its author many opportunities to vent her impulsive feelings. The contemporaries of Mrs. Browning were uneasy in their consciences over the convention that insisted that unmarried mothers should be treated as human filth. She approaches the question but begs it by making this unmarried mother a victim to force and not to her own choice. England had to wait nearly fifty years before " the story of a pure woman " was told, without shirking the woman's consent, by Thomas Hardy. Again, the matter of social reform was coming into fashion, and Dickens had begun to open people's eyes to the question whether, once the poor were clapped into an institution, all was really well. Mrs. Browning was content to regard evils as wholesome medicine for the soul. She gave no glimpse here of any alternative to regimentation of the poor. She is most herself when discussing women's relation to the arts, and satirizing men's condescension to their endeavours. Her blank verse, fluid

S

and reckless, is at its best in her early descriptions of the English countryside, in the happy expression of a thought, in isolated fragments. The story that she told, and the manner of its telling, were much to the taste of her day. A novel in verse receives either an immediate success or perpetual oblivion. To the early descriptive passages, already quoted in the opening chapter, we may add two examples of the verse :

> We women are too apt to look to one,
> Which proves a certain impotence in art.
> We strain our natures at doing something great,
> Far less because it's something great to do,
> Than haply that we, so, commend ourselves
> As being not small.
>   Yet how proud we are,
> In daring to look down upon ourselves.
>   (Bk. V)

>   Thus is art
> Self-magnified in magnifying a truth
> Which, fully recognized, would change the world
> And shift its morals. If a man could feel,
> Not one day, in the artist's ecstasy,
> But every day, feast, fast, or working-day,
> The spiritual significance burn through
> The hieroglyphic of material shows,
> Henceforward he would paint the globe with wings.
>   (Bk. VII)

The opening of the sixth book contains a discerning passage on the difference between the French and the English way of looking at life. One of the main objects of the poem is to enforce the familiar lesson that nothing can be done with men except by touching their souls, and to remind her readers that poetry has this power because it is the visible beauty of religion. One is chary of making quotations, however, because their weakness is most apparent when detached. In spite of defects, the writer carries one along, and once in the stream individual lines gain something of the quality that made them living to their author. *Aurora Leigh* seemed to her the most mature of her works because she was impulsive, and to give rein to an impulse often seems to impulsive persons the deepest revelation of themselves. This is frequently a delusion, but it is inseparable from such a character. Into the personal experience enshrined in the Sonnets their author's imagination poured. In *Aurora Leigh* it overflowed in all directions, and the result is not to be compared either with the beautiful strictness of her sonnets or with the freely ranging letters. Her prose could be free and fluid, whereas her verse very easily ran wild.

IX

An unusually cold winter tied Mrs. Browning to her room in Florence, where her husband, she wrote, was more delighted over the success of her poem than if it related to a book of his own. She herself only protested that the inner meaning was overlooked. The blindness of Romney had been necessary in order that he might be taught to see, and the degradation of Marian's circumstances that she might reach the ' sentiment of personal dignity.' It is because the circumstances and their purport are imperfectly united in poor verse that the poem fails, as a tract will fail that preaches without convincing the imagination. These reflections upon the criticism that her work was receiving are accompanied by a lively description of the Carnival, for which Penini was provided with a domino. Mrs. Browning herself attended with her husband the masked ball at the opera, and was delighted with the universal gaiety, courtesy, and the fusion of classes that she observed. She loved to see all characteristic social things, and was tempted to risk her social reputation by a visit to the Bal de l'Opéra at Paris. With the warmer weather she resumed her drives and acquaintances, which now included the celebrated Mrs. Beecher Stowe, who was unspoiled by the vogue of *Uncle Tom's Cabin*. It was part of Mrs. Browning's pride that here was a woman who had succeeded in moving the world. In another public direction Mrs. Browning also pushed forward.

She had been reading Victor Hugo's *Contemplations*, and, moved by her admiration for Napoleon III, she drafted a letter to the emperor, praying that he would recall the poet from exile. It was never sent, but it is still a moving and generous document, and it possesses that quality of directness that her verse, similarly inspired, would often miss.

In April Mr. Barrett died, and his death showed that his own pride was no stronger than his daughter's affection. He could not be softened, and she could not grow cold, not even after his recent refusal to give the address of Henrietta to Mr. Kenyon's executor, though the request was made in order that a small legacy might be paid to her. He had also affirmed that his married daughters had " disgraced the family," and his profession of having " forgiven " them produced no sign. Browning wrote to Mrs. Martin : " There must have been something in the organization, or education at least, that would account for and extenuate all this ; but it has caused grief enough, I know ; and now here is a new grief not likely to subside very soon." The year was anxious in other ways. During their summer holiday at the Bagni di Lucca their guest, Robert Lytton, fell ill and Browning took a strenuous share in nursing him. He bathed in the mountain stream, and rode with Pen, whom his mother called " a rose possessed by a fairy." The boy, however, soon fell ill with the same gastric fever, and, though he made a good recovery, these trials left their mark on Mrs. Browning's health.

An exceptionally cold winter did not improve matters, and in the spring of 1858 she was still having to complain somewhat of her chest and her cough. She occupied herself with German romances and with teaching German to Pen, who " reads German, French, and, of course, Italian, and plays on the piano remarkably well, for which Robert deserves the chief credit."

About this time Home, the medium, visited Florence, and the impatience that Browning showed at the manifestations led Home's followers to declare that Browning was jealous because a floating crown alighted on his wife's head instead of on his own ! Knowing his exaggerated opinion of her poetry, the really astonishing generosity that he showed for the work of anyone but himself, this explanation seems a perfect index of the type of mind from which it came. No shot could have been more unlucky, but the incident evokes the circle into which Browning was compelled to accompany his wife, where her presence seemed to him a profanation of her. More welcome arrivals included Hawthorne, who described Mrs. Browning and her boy as hardly belonging to this world. Indeed at his touch both seem to blend into the texture of his own novels. His sketch of Browning is vivid, for the host at Casa Guidi is described as being " in all parts of the room and in every group at the same moment," quick-thoughted and commonsensical, and effervescing with nonsense " of genuine and excellent quality."

The summer of 1858 was spent in France, and at Paris, where Mr. and Miss Browning awaited them. Mrs. Browning compared her " weakness " for France with her " passion " for Italy. If only Paris had been a little nearer the sun, she could have lived there content. Its boulevards were looking " more splendid than ever," and everything from its costumes to its cutlets delighted her. Napoleon III, she wrote, " I think the only great

man of his age " among the public men in whom she
was interested.   She had found the journey by express
train a luxury and a repose.   To be " shut in a carriage "
was a delightful protection after the diligence and the
ship.   The thought of a heaven " where there shall be
no more sea " seemed to her an inspired description.
They arrived on Mr. Browning's birthday and found
him looking ten years younger, and radiant at meeting
his son, and his grandson, again.   The new buildings in
Paris were a sight worth coming to see even from Italy.
" The architectural beauty is wonderful.   Give me
Venice on water, Paris on land—each in its way is a
dream city."   Florence was her " chimney-corner " still,
but Paris was " the fountain of intellectual youth " and
her heart beat quicker in its boulevards.

They made for the coast, and, after leaving some inconvenient rooms that Browning had suddenly chosen at
Étretat, installed themselves for eight weeks at Havre,
that Mrs. Browning might take baths of warm sea-water.
In October they returned to Paris, where Arabel stayed
with them, and then made their way slowly back to
Florence, when it was decided that Rome would be
better for Mrs. Browning during the winter.   Some
American friends placed a carriage at their disposal,
and a pleasant journey was enlivened by one narrow
escape from a sudden plunging of the horses and by a
fight between two oxen-drivers whose drawn knives
incited Browning to intervene.   He escaped injury
except to his trousers, though his wife and child were
' frantic with fright.'   He seems himself at such
moments, and his success in polite society shows how
adaptable he was.   His address in a Victorian drawing-
room was part of his readiness to enter every mode of
life.   With a rapier on his hip, or with the wits at the
Mermaid, he would probably have been the same.   He
chose a pair of gloves as thoughtfully as he would have

chosen a revolver, and he put them on to pay a call as gravely as for a boxing match.

X

They lodged in the Via Bocca di Leone, and found Rome very full and very cold. However, she was able to go to St. Peter's on Christmas morning to hear the silver trumpets, and " enjoyed it both æsthetically and devotionally," putting to the music her own words. *Aurora Leigh* had been thoroughly revised for its new and fourth edition, and, for their quiet selves, a good deal of entertaining was done. Browning took early walks before breakfast and returned with a vast appetite. He also " plunged into gaieties " and was out every evening for a fortnight running. The boy developed an appetite of another kind, and devoured Dumas's novels, so that his mother began to congratulate herself upon his hereditary tendencies.

We have noticed the success of Mrs. Browning's poem, and it is curious to recall the parallel position of her husband. He was becoming an influence in America and a name at least in England, but the sales of his books were disappointingly small. That he was regarded, even in official circles, however, is clear from the invitation that he received to dine with the Prince of Wales, who was then in Rome. Browning accepted and, urged by his wife, championed the cause of Italy, which was on the eve of its war of liberation against Austria. Mrs. Browning particularly warned her husband to eschew compliments at the royal table. It seemed that he had a weakness for making them, but that they were often so literal as to look like rebukes. " I had a delightful evening at your house. I never spoke to you once," is an example of a remark made to an old friend that winter. We are told that the young prince listened, but left the

political part of the conversation to his suite. Browning
sat to the young Leighton at this time, and the drawing
produced one of Mrs. Browning's acute comments. She
called it " very like, though not on the poetical side,
which is beyond Leighton."

The political situation in Italy now possessed Mrs.
Browning's thoughts, and the intervention of Napoleon
III on behalf of Italy appeared to justify her two enthu-
siasms at once. Browning was inclined to less rosy
hopes, but she was able to write : " Robert and I have
been of one mind lately in these things, which comforts
me much. But the chief comfort is the state of facts."
Because the poets did not indulge in huff or quarrel over
a difference of opinion, a wild legend has arisen that they
never differed at all. The truth is that they were human
enough to differ without quarrelling, and that this
should appear to be impossible to most people is the
really astonishing thing. Both the Brownings were
impetuous in feeling and in expression ; both had
opinions upon every subject ; and both delighted in the
discussion of ideas. One of the two things which had
annoyed Browning in his wife's love-letters was her
fleeting notion that he might sulk if she made a suggestion that he did not approve. Their harmonious relations resulted from a good temper in which many
differences had free play.

By the time that they reached Florence in May 1859
the Grand Duke had fled, and a Provisional Government
had been formed with a division of French troops to
support it. It is pleasant to read of Mrs. Browning too
much absorbed to think of departing, though her hopes
and her health suffered under the disappointment of the
truce of Villafranca. She believed that England and
not Napoleon was to blame for this check to Italian
aspirations, and was glad that Browning was coming to
accept her view. In one of her sentences which brings

us near the heart of this intimacy she wrote : " Robert has taken up the same note, which is a comfort. I would rather hear my own heart in his voice. Certainly it must be still more bitter for him than for me, seeing that he has more national predilections than I have, and has struggled longer to see differently." Browning subscribed ten scudi a month to the Italian war fund, and Pen was given pocket money when he did his lessons well for the same cause. The unity among the Italians was a welcome sign to Mrs. Browning that they had grown since the days described in *Casa Guidi Windows*. She was indignant with England because she did not understand that it was rather fear of France than want of sympathy with Italy that dictated English policy at that time. With her idealization of Napoleon such a fear would have been incomprehensible to her. The excitement that filled her was extreme, and even gave her the unusual energy to go to the theatre in order to see Salvini, whose performances in *Othello* and in *Hamlet* filled them both with admiration.

After the news of Villafranca she complained of ' a peculiar frailty ' and they sought escape from the heat at Siena. The peace with Austria fell like a human blow. She could not sleep, she was feverish and over-excited, and suffered what she called a bad attack. " Robert has been perfect to me," she wrote. He sat up with her for a fortnight, and undertook also the lessons that she had been giving to Pen during the day. She was extremely weak, and could not walk without assistance. She was haunted even by political dreams. To take any matter quietly was beyond her temperament. The strain on Browning must have been severe, and we have another example at this time of his extraordinary kindliness.

At Siena they received a visit from Landor, who had become very irascible and very old. He paid this visit because Browning had lately undertaken the management of his financial and even of his domestic affairs. Shortly before they had left Florence, the old man, whose explosiveness was proverbial, arrived at Casa Guidi. He said that he had been turned out of doors by his wife, from whose villa at Fiesole Landor had already departed three times. Browning, who often said that Landor's writings had meant more to him than those of any contemporary, visited the villa and, having convinced himself that there was no hope of a reconciliation, provided for Landor's immediate needs. Then, having enlisted the help of Landor's brothers in England, Browning undertook to manage the allowance that they provided, and made himself the " guardian " of the formidable old man. Indeed he found him a suitable apartment and Wilson was installed to look after his needs. This onerous responsibility is best described in Mrs. Browning's own words. Later in the year she wrote to Miss Browning:

> We left Mr. Landor in great comfort. . . . Wilson has thirty pounds a year for taking care of him, which sounds a good deal; but it *is* a difficult position. He has excellent, generous, affectionate impulses, but the impulses of the tiger every now and then. . . . At present Landor is very fond of Robert; but I am quite prepared for his turning against us as he has turned against Forster, who has been so devoted for years and years. Only one isn't kind for what one gets by it, or there wouldn't be much kindness in this world.

Browning, however, succeeded in appeasing Landor's real and imaginary griefs, and Mrs. Browning received reports from her husband of the ' sweetness and gentleness ' of the old man. She smiled with an overflowing heart, for such testimony, as she knew, returned to its source in her husband.

There is an ominous sentence in one of Mrs. Browning's letters from Siena: " One soul has gone from me, at least, the soul that writes letters." Of such an abundant correspondent as herself, it reads like the beginning of the end. Her capacity for friendship infected most of those she knew, and led Dr. Gregonowsky, a Prussian physician, in the absence of her own doctor, to follow her to Siena and to refuse any fee for his advice and care. Yet she grew somewhat stronger and had pleasant memories of her stay. Among them was a picture of Pen " driving in the grape-carts (exactly of the shape of the Greek chariots) with the grapes heaped up round him " and riding on his own pony " the colour of his curls." This was a present from his father, though Mrs. Browning declared that it was she, never her husband, who spoiled the lad. He must have been an amusing child, for, after helping the peasants with their cows or at the vintage, he would read aloud to them the revolutionary poems of a Venetian poet, and had already learnt to play Beethoven's seventh sonata under the tuition of his father.

She was advised to go further south than Florence for the winter, and, though both she and her husband were losing their taste for wandering, they only stopped at Florence on their way to Rome. Travelling meant that they were spending money and also interrupted their opportunities for work, especially now when most people in their neighbourhood made a point of visiting them. To be away from Florence both summer and winter deprived them of a home, and they needed a quiet home as much as they needed to live in Italy. Another risk at Florence was the proximity of Landor. It was a responsibility for Wilson which Mrs. Browning would rather not meet. If Landor did not like a dish, he would dash the plate on the floor, and, though Wilson was prepared for such things, it must have been a great change after the serenity of the Browning household. When the old man was soothed, he beguiled the time writing Latin verses against his wife and Louis Napoleon.

Browning's method with him is explained by his wife :
" He will miss Robert dreadfully.   Robert's goodness to
him has been really apostolical.   And think of the effect
of a goodness which can quote at every turn of a phrase
something from an author's book ! "   After spending
six weeks in Florence the Brownings arrived at Rome in
the beginning of December 1859.

In these days, when short skirts and sleeveless dresses
are frowned upon by the priesthood, it is curious to learn
that crinolines were forbidden in St. Peter's at the time
of the Brownings' visit.   The city was almost empty of
visitors, however, through fear of revolution or disturbances.   Mrs. Browning took advantage of this to nurse
herself after another attack and to correct the proofs of
Poems before Congress, the last volume to appear in her
lifetime.

XI

It is a slender volume of political pieces, the natural
supplement of *Casa Guidi Windows*, but written in the
light of events eleven years later.   All who have followed
the eagerness with which Mrs. Browning pursued the
fortunes of Italy during these years will have seen that
the expression of her feelings in verse was a necessity.
Moreover, she was not merely satisfying her heart by so
writing.   She hoped also to touch English folk at home
to a sense of their narrow insularity, and to do the only
act within her power that might serve the Italian cause.
The number of poems is only eight, and most of these
are anecdotal, the incidents having been chosen for the
temper of patriotism or gratitude to France that the
Italians had displayed.   But there is also a preface which
is more eloquent than any of the verse.   The pith of it
is as follows :

What I have written has simply been written because I love truth and justice *quand même*,—" more than Plato " and Plato's country, more than Dante and Dante's country, more even than Shakespeare and Shakespeare's country. And if patriotism means the flattery of one's nation in every case, then the patriot, take it as you please, is merely a courtier; which I am not, though I have written " Napoleon III in Italy." It is time to limit the significance of certain terms, or to enlarge the significance of certain things. . . . So, if patriotism be a virtue indeed, it cannot mean an exclusive devotion to one country's interests. . . . Let us put away the little Pedlingtonism unworthy of a great nation, and too prevalent among us. If a man who does not look beyond this natural life is of a somewhat narrow order, what must be the man who does not look beyond his own frontier or his own sea ?

I confess that I dream of the day when an English statesman shall arise with a heart too large for England, having courage in the face of his countrymen to assert of some suggested policy,—" This is good for your trade : this is necessary for your domination; but it will vex a people hard by; it will hurt a people farther off; it will profit nothing to the general humanity : therefore away with it !—it is not for you or for me."

Life would be a miserable place without such dreams, and all decencies were dreams once, and without the poets we should despair of the human sty as for ever uncleansable by the practical. Is it significant that this faith which was preached by a woman poet in 1860 was died for by another woman during the late War, and that the one phrase which lingers among the cries of those four years is Edith Cavell's ? " Patriotism is not enough," she said, and the faith for which she died was the faith also of Mrs. Browning. She made us feel that she possessed it, though not by the beauty of her verse. It is not the less convincing because it was the substance of her character. At this time of day it may be worth while to recall that the Congress mentioned in the title had nothing to do with the United States. The only one of the eight poems that did not refer to Italy was called

" A Curse for a Nation " and denounced slavery in America. "Oh, the dreadful curses!" her sister wrote.

This poem was misunderstood as an attack on England, and Browning was furious over the treatment of his wife in the *Athenæum*. Commenting on his anger, Mrs. Browning wrote : " I complain more about Robert, only he does not hear me complain. . . . The blindness, deafness, and stupidity of the English public to Robert are amazing. Of course Milsand (the Frenchman !) had ' heard his name ' ! Well, the contrary would have been strange. Robert *is*. All England can't prevent his existence, I suppose. But nobody there, except a small knot of pre-Raffaelite men, pretends to do him justice. Mr. Forster has done his best in the press. As a sort of lion, Robert has his range in society, and, for the rest, you should see Chapman's returns ; while in America he's a power, a writer, a poet. He is read—he lives in the hearts of the people. ' Browning readings ' here in Boston ; ' Browning evenings ' there. For the rest, the English hunt lions too, but their favourite lions are chosen among lords chiefly or railroad kings." Her own popularity became irksome by contrast. " English people will come and stare at *me* sometimes, but physicians, dentists, who serve me and refuse their fees, friends who give up their carriages and make other practical sacrifices, are *not English*—no—though English Woolner was generous about a bust. Let *me* be just at least."

Both poets make us realize the beauty of character, and it may be said of her, as she said of Browning, that the least important part about him was his genius. When therefore a poet appears whose character rings as true as his genius, we have an unusual opportunity. We are unexpectedly forced to set two beauties side by side, and can judge them without prejudice. In Browning we take the genius for granted and can look at the man, and the man, whose imagination has already won our homage, proves a revelation. For once, there are no buts on either side, and the effect is to make us see high character poetically. It is as if the poet had opened a new loveliness to our eyes, as if there were a new possibility of beauty for us in human relations. Art is so often our consolation that it is refreshing to be able to regard it as the grace of a life already noble. Judging by its own measure, the world has called Browning conventional. The truth is that he was whole.

Apart from the interest and criticism evoked by her poems, there were personal shadows, for Mrs. Jameson died in March and another friend, old Lady Elgin, long paralysed, passed away. It is interesting to be able to date precisely the most beautiful of Mrs. Browning's later poems, indeed her finest lyric. In a letter to Miss Isa Blagden, written from Rome in April 1860, Mrs. Browning says that she has sent " the last thing I wrote " to Thackeray for his new magazine, *The Cornhill*. This was " A Musical Instrument," which appeared in the number for July. This poem on Pan's pipes occurs in every anthology, and is, as it deserves, the most familiar of her works. Though it can be read for itself, and has a lovely metre in which the disappointment of the ear at the fourth line in each stanza is one of its delights, it is also an allegory, a symbol of her own poetic reaction to the suffering of her early years. Except in the last verse this allegorical element is well controlled, but, when we come to know her well, we accept this grain of sand as a true part of the author, and for that reason do not quarrel with an apparent flaw. The poem is more musical than anything else of hers, and the check in the middle of its rhythm is like an eddy upon running water. In this sudden return from the horizon to the sanctuary of her heart, from political to personal sympathies, she recovered her inspiration in one breath, and the seven stanzas in the poem are so equal and knit so closely that to quote one would be to hack Pan's reed without making it an instrument of music. It was included by Browning in the volume of *Last Poems* that he published, after her death, in 1862.

Napoleon's action in annexing Nice and Savoy after all he had done for Italy was a shock to her, but she believed that he had a duty to France in asking the new nation that he had helped to create to contract behind the Alps for its frontiers. Browning, who had been less enthusiastic over Napoleon, was less surprised. She wrote: " I would rather not hear Robert say, for instance: 'It was a great action; but he has taken eighteenpence for it, which is a pity.'" She thought this judgment not fair, but it was less harsh than many which reached her. Among the few interesting English in Rome during the spring of 1860 were George Eliot and Lewes. "The author of the *Mill on the Floss* is here, they say, with her elective affinity, and is seen on the Corso walking, or in the Vatican musing. Always together. They are said to visit nobody, and to be beheld only at unawares." Among those who visited the Brownings was Prinsep, the artist. He conducted Browning into the byways of the city that he might hear the improvisations of two minstrels of the populace who were urged to their best efforts by the news that a great English poet was to witness their contest. The friends also heard the forbidden Hymn to Garibaldi sung in a certain restaurant, which was invaded by the Papal police, but these walked out in silence after accepting a generous measure of wine. These amusements, very human and fascinating to him, did not occupy all of Browning's time during the winter. His wife reported that he " deserves no reproaches," since he had been working at a long poem that she had not seen, and at several lyrics which he had shown to her. The long poem is not identified. It is thought to have been either " A Death in the Desert," or possibly " Mr. Sludge." Mr. F. G. Kenyon, the editor of Mrs. Browning's letters, declares that the poem on Sludge is probable, for " Home's performances were rampant" at the time.

XII

In June 1860 they returned to Florence, where Mrs. Browning was allowed by her husband to receive the *Spiritual Magazine* from England. They found Landor well on their return, and even Wilson. She recounted that the old man had thrown his dinner out of the window only once. As in the previous year they soon passed to the Villa Alberti at Siena, but a change was beginning to be felt. Browning was putting on weight and looking more robust than ever, but Mrs. Browning was beginning to lose ground. While Pen and his father went for long rides, she could often scarcely crawl downstairs to sit under her fig-tree, and was sometimes in mysterious fits of fear. These were caused partly by the shock of learning that her sister Henrietta was mortally ill, and partly no doubt by a real decline in her own health. She had begun to age. One sign of this is to feel as if a part of us had been chipped off whenever someone near to us dies. " How (she wrote to Mrs. Martin) the spiritual world gets thronged to us with familiar faces, till at last, perhaps, the world here will seem the vague and strange world, even while we remain." The centre of gravity was shifting for her. She enjoyed the quiet of the " great lonely villa," and her great friend Isa Blagden was only a mile away. Landor too was close by but still amenable to Browning's kindness. " The office (Mrs. Browning wrote) is hard, and I tell Robert that he must be prepared

T

for the consequences : an outbreak and a printed statement that he (Robert), instigated by his wicked wife,
had attempted to poison Landor slowly. . . . My husband manages every detail of his life, and both the
responsibility and trouble are considerable.   Still he is
a great writer."

Soon after their return to Rome in the autumn Mrs.
Surtees Cook (Henrietta) died, leaving three children
younger than Pen behind her.   It was during this winter
that Browning took seriously to modelling under his
friend Story.   He spent six hours a day copying busts,
and was usually out somewhere in the evenings.   Mrs.
Browning was feeling so languid that she abetted these
amusements to dispel the gloom that would otherwise
have surrounded him, she said.   He probably thought
that solitude was good for her at this time, and she said
herself that she was grateful to him for keeping out
intrusive visitors.   Her state of mind can be judged
from a remark referring to her boy : " For the first time
I have had pain in looking into his face lately."   As he
was well, the anxiety that this implies must have sprung
from the growing weakness that *she* felt.   She endeavoured to distract her thoughts by gathering all the news
she could concerning the panic in England which led to
the formation of the volunteers, the growing tension in
America between the North and South, and of course
the progress of Italian aspirations.   There was also her
continued interest in Spiritualism, on which, after all,
she never wholly lost her head.   " As far as I am concerned (she wrote to Miss Fanny Haworth) I never
heard or read a single communication which impressed
me in the least : what does impress me is the probability
of there being communications at all."   Her hopes
were certainly aroused, and tended to expand, but at
that date mesmerism itself was supposed to be super-
natural.   Levitations and the like she believed to have

been proved, and her intense belief in personal immortality, unlike Browning's, tended to make her credulous. She was never in the dark over his precise feeling in any matter. In a revealing phrase she records that "the peculiarity of our relation is that even when he's displeased with me he thinks aloud with me and can't stop himself."

For some reason he had no inclination to work at poetry this winter, and thus he took to modelling in order to work off his superfluous energy. Without active occupation, she tells us, he would magnify a fly on the wall into a monster, which reminds us of Blake's confession that he could look at a knot in a piece of wood until he was frightened. "I know (Mrs. Browning continues) that whatever takes him out of a certain circle (where habits of introvision and analysis of fly-legs are morbidly exercised) is life and joy to him." On this ground she excused the modelling because, at that date, the poet could work only by fits and starts. She pointed out also that England gave him very little encouragement to write, so little that an Englishwoman of rank had recently shocked the American Minister by asking him if Browning were not an American author.

She was planning to spend the summer in France in order that Browning might meet his father, but already she had come to dread the fatigue of the journey. A cold May left her dispirited, though there had been no lack of vitality in her reply to the refusal by Thackeray of one of her poems. In an excellent and even admiring letter, Thackeray, as editor of *The Cornhill*, had declined "Lord Walter's Wife." He wrote: "In your poem, you know, there is an account of unlawful passion, felt by a man for a woman, and though you write pure doctrine, and real modesty, and pure ethics, I am sure our readers would make an outcry, and so I have not published this poem." In her reply she said, "From your 'Cornhill' standpoint (paterfamilias looking on) you are probably right ten times over. . . . But I am deeply convinced that the corruption of our society requires not shut doors and windows, but light and air; and that it is exactly because pure and prosperous women choose to ignore vice, that miserable women suffer wrong by it everywhere. Has paterfamilias, with his Oriental traditions and veiled female faces, very successfully dealt with a certain class of evil? What if materfamilias, with her quick sure instincts and honest innocent eyes, do more toward their expulsion by simply looking at them and calling them by their names?"

The letters are a credit to both, and hers is worth recalling because we sometimes forget she was a free spirit whose *Aurora Leigh* was thought corrupt in its day. Once again, if this letter to Thackeray be compared either with the poem that he names or with others of similar motive, we see that her prose was much more convincing on ethical and political questions than her verse. Since she wrote no prose, apart from her rather academic literary essays, her letters and her later prefaces are valuable evidence of a quality that was wasted in her verse. The letters remain, but who realized what an admirable leader-writer was being wasted?

This was almost the last spurt of her energy. She complained of being very weak before she left Rome at the beginning of June, though the development of Pen was delightful to watch. For example, when Hans Andersen called, Pen said: "He is rather like his own ugly duck, but his mind has developed into a swan." As his mother remarked, this was not bad for a boy of twelve. But her strength of body could not subsist on such delights, and her husband already saw that a journey to France was out of the question for her. She endeavoured to resist and make the effort, but he overruled her, and she reluctantly agreed that "certainly he has the right to command me away from giving him unnecessary anxieties." In her last letter, dated June 7, 1860, the day after the death of Cavour, who, she said, was worth a hundred Garibaldis, she had penned those words. She had no more strength to resist. Once arrived at Casa Guidi, she suffered a bronchial attack. Though it resembled its numerous predecessors, Browning had forebodings of alarm. He himself gave to Miss Haworth an account of the last evening. On June 28 (he wrote a month later):

> I sent the servants away and her maid to bed, so little reason for disquietude did there seem. Through the night she slept heavily and brokenly—that was the bad sign; but then she would sit up, take her medicine, say unrepeatable things to me, and sleep again. At four o'clock there were symptoms that alarmed me; I called the maid and sent for the doctor. She smiled as I proposed to bathe her feet, " Well, you *are* determined to make an exaggerated case of it!" Then came what my heart will keep till I see her again and longer—the most perfect expression of her love to me within my whole knowledge of her. Always smiling, happily, and with a face like a girl's, and in a few minutes she died in my arms, her head on my cheek.

It was on June 29, 1861, that she died. She was buried in the English cemetery at Florence, and a little later a monument was placed there designed by Leighton, her and her husband's friend. On the walls of Casa Guidi is the slab bearing the words composed by Tommasseo which the municipality placed there in her memory, and which no Englishman familiar with her life and work can see unmoved. Her son eventually bought the house which two such lives made holy, for poetry was not the only grace that abounded there.

CHAPTER SIX

MEN AND WOMEN AND *THE RING AND THE BOOK*

I

Not to overweight the story of their married life, we have confined our attention to her works, mainly, in the previous chapter. Indeed Browning was not specially productive during the years of his marriage, and, a few poems apart, the works that he composed during these fifteen years were two. " Christmas Eve and Easter Day," which derives really from his courtship, the incidental preface on Shelley, and the great series of *Men and Women* were the fruit of these years. The latter, as readers of " One Word More " will remember, originally consisted of fifty poems. They were re-arranged later, and when his collected works appeared only thirteen poems were included under this title. The name, indeed, would apply to all the dramatic lyrics and their kind, and in this chapter it is more convenient to consider the original group.

" Cleon " and " The Statue and the Bust " first appeared separately in 1855, the same year as the two volumes of *Men and Women*. It seems probable that " The Statue and the Bust," which condemns the two lovers for their procrastination even though one was already married, was coloured by Browning's memory of his own wife's hesitation to take the final step of running away. His own fears, at that time, seem to be crystallized in the judgment that he passes on his characters :

> The counter our lovers staked was lost
> As surely as if it were lawful coin :
> And the sin I impute to each frustrate ghost
>
> Is—the unlit lamp and the ungirt loin,
> Though the end in sight was a vice, I say.

Was not Elizabeth Barrett 'a frustrate ghost' in that upper room in Wimpole Street, whither, as Mr. Chesterton has put it, her father came to pray over her with 'melancholy glee'?

According to the general verdict, *Men and Women* is the enduring creation of Browning's genius. For all 'selections' this is the chief source. In this group, and in its forerunners and successors of similar titles, he perfected his method of the monologue, and composed a great gallery of character studies for the like of which, in originality of conception and in beauty of workmanship, we look in vain elsewhere. His profound but oblique dramatic gift discovered in these soliloquies the happiest ground for its exercise. Considered by themselves, they seem the creation of a born dramatist and creator of character, but the plays remain to correct this judgment. It is a master of self-revelation and the analysis of motive in an individual, not a master of characters in action, that they reveal. Moreover, very few of them suffer from the prolixity that marred some of his more ambitious efforts in this kind. Neither "Karshish" nor even "Bishop Blougram" fatigue by their length in the same way that "Prince Hohenstiel-Schwangau" or "Mr. Sludge" is apt to do. The form controls the substance and exhausts without exhausting. The smaller masterpieces of Browning are admittedly here.

A word should be said upon those poems in the group which evoke, or at least bear upon, the poet's experience of married life. In "A Woman's Last Word" he has written one of the very few poems in our language which convey the emotion peculiar to married love, an emotion different in kind, we must remember, from the emotion of courtship. This lyric takes its place with the handful of poems to which Samuel Bishop, Samuel Henley, Anne Countess of Winchelsea, and Coventry Patmore have contributed. Is the rarity of this emotion in poetry a reminder of the rarity of complete union, or is it also because it is an emotion that shrinks from utterance that Browning (who achieved it with rare fullness) was less copious than Patmore (who made it the basis of his thought)? Comparisons are to be deprecated, but, although Patmore's philosophy suffers no logical flaw from the fact that he married three times, an instinct that will not be denied tells us that Browning was more dignified in his widowerhood than Patmore who married again twice. The pathos of the latter's ode entitled " Tired Memory " arises from his own self-doubts, which we share, and the curious can compare his ode with Browning's " Any Wife to Any Husband." Whatever the respective value of the poetry that these two poets made of their parallel experience, only Browning's proved to be stronger than death, and irreplaceable on this side of the grave. With the poems that touch upon such love, " By the Fireside " belongs. It declares truly that Browning's love, triumphant over a circumstance of secrecy odious to his open nature, was the central fact of his life, and the test of his character :

> I am named and known by that moment's feat;
>   There took my station and degree;
> So grew my own small life complete,
>   As nature obtained her best of me—
> One born to love you, sweet.
> And to watch you sink by the fire-side now
>   Back again, as you mutely sit
> Musing by fire-light, that great brow
>   And the spirit-small hand propping it,
> Yonder, my heart knows how !

It is trite but wonderful that no other love of which we have record surpasses, if it equals, the love celebrated here. Her memory haunts the poems that were written years after her death. It inspired some of the loveliest of the love-lyrics that he wrote, with the freshness of youth upon them, in extreme old age. We also owe to it the marvellous poem on death, for " Prospice " was composed in the autumn of 1861 a few months after she died. Meantime, the famous conclusion to the series of *Men and Women* is " One Word More," which was Browning's answer to the *Sonnets from the Portuguese*. It is rhymeless, but its trochaics have the very pulse of a beating heart :

> I stand on my attainment.
> This of verse alone, one life allows me ;
> Verse and nothing else have I to give you.
> Other heights in other lives, God willing :
> All the gifts from all the heights, your own, Love !

Like the moon of which he writes, he shows to the world the other side of him :

> Side unseen of herdsman, huntsman, steersman—
> Blank to Zoroaster on his terrace,
> Blind to Galileo on his turret,
> Dumb to Homer, dumb to Keats—him, even !

How the conversational cadence of the last phrase suggests the intimacy, the daily open secret, of his love for her !

There is his statement, as we have seen, of the poet's function in his own day, as he conceived it, in " How it Strikes a Contemporary," his own response to the arts of music and painting in " A Toccata of Galuppi's," " Master Hughes," " Andrea del Sarto " and " Fra Lippo Lippi." Good poems upon music are rare, and even in famous ones musicians will complain that they find but rhapsodies without knowledge, except in

Browning's, where the very score can be read, the
keyboard and the pedals be felt. His own tribute to
Keats in " Memorabilia " is as fine as the better known
and grotesquely concluding stanzas to Shelley entitled
" Popularity."

It is sometimes forgotten that Browning was not
only fond of grotesque rhymes. One of his chief claims
to greatness was his humour, his mastery of the grotesque
convention, and he stands above his contemporaries of
the Victorian age, as Shakespeare by virtue of creating
Falstaff overtops the Elizabethans, by possessing this
quality. It saved him from the sentimentality and
sloppiness which was one of the weaknesses of the
period, since an age will have its failings no less peculiar
to it than the creations of beauty we prefer to recall.
" Caliban upon Setebos," a creation to set beside Shakespeare's, is a familiar instance. One example of this,
the grotesque at its most romantic, is the weirdly beautiful " Childe Roland." Nothing, in a sense, is less like
Browning than this beautiful poem. The romantic
horror of landscape has been rendered so faultlessly that
romantic readers have searched for an allegory where
none was intended. As we shall see, there is a kind of
allegory in their wasted search, for a great deal of energy
has been misspent upon the search for a philosophy in
Browning's poems. He was, in truth, half a Christian,
though hardly assignable to any of the Christian sects,
and his philosophy was no more than the vivid expression of a vital temper and a courageous heart. To him,
as to all sincere Christians, life was a period of probation,
the result of which testing would determine the destiny
of the soul in a future life. Nothing could be simpler,
nothing more thorough, nothing more clear.

The reason why so much has been written about
Browning's work, however, is worth explaining. The
philosophy is never obscure, passages in the individual

poems often. This is not due to the complexity or profundity of their thought. It arises from the involved, elusive, condensed and crowded style to be found at its worst in his prose. (In the plays and pseudo-plays, by the way, the prose is better than in the preface on Shelley or in the Letters.) A commentary is often necessary to explain the purport of a passage, and the rhymes, when there are any, are often a hindrance, not a help. The unit lies in the argument, and that unit may extend over twenty or more lines, packed with parentheses. The criticism to which this mode of writing lies open is this. The unit of idea and the rhythmical unit do not tally. Consequently, when following the track of the matter, we read for sense not sound, and the music is lost. If we read for the unit of sound, the matter becomes unintelligible. Browning is frequently hard to remember by heart. Even a poem like " The Bishop Orders his Tomb " is not easy to read aloud. Many a good actor would baulk at the task of reciting it, because the unit of sense and the unit of sound stand in each other's way. There is excellent excuse for Browning primers, to explain the drift of individual poems. There is no good excuse for long disquisitions upon their philosophy. There is plenty of room for literary criticism, but this room is not proportional to the bulk of his work. The kernel of the whole is the series of *Men and Women*. The rest, as we shall see, multiply examples of his art, but the later poems do not add proportionally to its surprises, modifications or development.

Browning conceived it to be part of his function to record the movements of his time. Indeed the day may come when he will be consulted as a valuable index, not merely of English idiom in his century, but of many of its intellectual moods. His vocabulary was enormous, enough on which to base the reputation of a great writer. His eye was acute for current controversies, though these are necessarily prosaic in substance and more fit to be expounded in prose. Yet his literary power could make the verse containing them as wonderful, in its way, as the poetic substance was weak. The poetry that he offers is often the poetry that we do not want, but the verse is frequently fascinating even when one happens to be bored. He was so thoroughly a poet that prose was not at his disposal, and even when the reader rejects a poem there is something splendid in this spectacle. Every movement of his mind insisted on running into verse. He did not always make fine poetry of his thinking, but he could not think in prose, and so his verse has always some quality. The tendency of his arguments, none of which is new, is to draw from the old difficulties inferences in support of revealed truth. The effect is to convince us that no argument meets the case, that, as theologians maintain, the foundation of belief in God, in personal immortality,[1] in the Christian dogmas, is an act of faith sustained by the authority of the witness that Christ left behind Him. For the same arguments can be used impartially to infer and to deny the fact of revelation. Therefore, it is when Browning touches our hearts, and forgets our heads for a moment, that he conquers. The famous lines in " Bishop Blougram's Apology " come home to us all, though the experience is interpreted in diverse fashions :

> Just when we're safest, there's a sunset-touch,
> A fancy from a flower-bell, some one's death,

---

[1] Cf. Mrs. Orr's Life : " The arguments, in great part negative, set forth in *La Saisiaz* for the immortality of the soul, leave no place for the idea, however indefinite, of a Christian revelation on the subject. Christ remains for Mr. Browning a mystery and a message of Divine Love, but no messenger of Divine intention towards mankind."

> A chorus-ending from Euripides,—
> And that's enough for fifty hopes and fears
> As old and new at once as nature's self,
> To rap and knock and enter in our soul,
> Take hands and dance there, a fantastic ring
> Round the ancient idol on his base again,—
> The grand Perhaps.

The only less-known description of Death touching the actor who had been playing his part on the stage, is a stroke of grotesque that might, in this very modern poem, have come out of the Middle Ages. It was but a step to pass to Mesmerism. His own observation of Spiritualism was to be treated later.

The two epistles from Cleon and Karshish, describing how Christianity struck the best Roman and Semitic minds on its appearance, have their sting in the tails of both. The poems are complementary. They also interest through the historical imagination which evokes types still with us. The local decay of Christian belief may prove the local return of Paganism; and the world which Browning knew, that industrial corner which we inhabit, has lost its faith in Christianity. The attitude of Cleon,

> And (as I gathered from a bystander)
> Their doctrine could be held by no sane man,

is the attitude of the modern sceptic. The attitude of Karshish is the dawn of the Christian hope, of Rabbi Ben Ezra, in effect, its twilight. People lose the faith but hope to retain the emotions it created. Then they try, like Browning, to re-build with these emotions the structure they have pulled down. They may partially succeed for themselves; Browning did; but this house on the sands crumbles for their successors. These have to choose between more solid foundations. Faith is one, materialism another, to one of which the struggling compromise of creative evolution generally reverts.

Browning's Men and Women belong to all times and are drawn from all periods. The human nature common to them is most conspicuous when their changing situations are reviewed. The poems not touched on here contain most of the favourite lyrics, and those tiny stories, like " Before " and " After " (the duel), which seem like etchings. A volume of representative Selections from Browning would make a book of fine poetry equal in size to the complete work of many poets. It is probably true that only a selection from such a Selection is widely familiar. Seen in perspective, however, *Men and Women* is but one of at least four groups of kindred poems.

II

Roughly speaking, the mass of Browning's writings is divisible into three parts, though rather for convenience than accuracy. The first begins with *Pauline* and concludes in 1846 with *Bells and Pomegranates*. The second includes *Men and Women* and culminates in 1868 in *The Ring and the Book*. The third contains the works written between 1870 and his death in 1889; *Fifine*, *Red Cotton Night-Cap Country*, the translations from Euripides and Aeschylus, *Jocoseria*, *La Saisiaz*, *The Inn Album*, the *Parleyings*, *Ferishtah's Fancies*, and *Asolando*.

With the exception of *Dramatis Personæ*, published in 1864, a series similar to *Men and Women*, *The Ring and the Book* was the first great work that Browning produced after the death of his wife. There can be little doubt that he needed an arduous task to occupy his energies, and, once she had passed from him, he worked more regularly than before. He had invented a method, the dramatic soliloquy, and had applied it, as it could be best applied, to comparatively brief poems. He was now to take this method, and to multiply his speakers by ten, in order that the point of view of every prominent actor might be used to convey the story in which each took part. It seems a marvellous, and scarcely promising, procedure, for it involves two difficulties, one of which is fundamental. Any story told ten times over might seem doomed to pall, and is it told if every version is different? Secondly, if multiplication is to be indulged, why stop at ten? There is no answer to these objections, except the illogical answer that, for those who can read Browning at all, *The Ring and the Book* does not pall, and, for the minor point, one must stop somewhere. No one regrets, however, that Browning has founded no school of soliloquists, that he displayed a new method and kept it his own. He remains a storyteller whom no one has ventured to imitate.

The second fact to note about *The Ring and the Book* is that it differs from traditional epics in eschewing an heroic hero and an heroic story: of course there are novels in verse that receive the courtesy title. The murder of Pompilia by her husband is a common murder, concerning ordinary folk, and the poem is a masterpiece for the intense and various interest that is squeezed out of an old piece of police-court news. There are villains and noble people in the tale, but there are no monsters and no Titans. Browning stretches out his hand, like God in the fresco of Michael Angelo, grips a group of common humanity, and wrings it like a sponge. Blood, tears, humour, pedantry, hate, endurance, loyalty, love and judgment drip upon the ground. The poetic feat is comparable to the painting of a vast ceiling, and just as we may feel the strain of upgazing at that ceiling so may the attention quail before the study of twenty thousand lines. As a matter of fact, of Browning's long poems, *The Ring and the Book* is easily the least tedious.

The commonplace incident and people involved are suggestive, for Browning was a man of genius without eccentricity. He was a normal man with an imagination of the highest. It was natural that he should take an ordinary story and lavish his utmost art upon it. Since he could communicate his abounding interest in the subject, this should be the measure of a healthy one. Therefore, to some extent, our criticism of Browning's demands upon our powers of attention is a criticism of our capacity to attend. With abnormal geniuses we are properly chary of such an argument. Before a poet like Browning we are less unwilling to admit our inferiority. It was part of this sanity to eschew an extraordinary subject. The genius appeared in making it variously and vividly alive.

This he did by the variety of his nine characters— Guido speaks twice—and the different tones that modulate the very rhythm of their speeches. The child-like simplicity of Pompilia, which fills the most popular of the twelve books, is a welcome relief after the sophisticated persons who precede her; and who but Browning would have added a Tertium Quid after the pros and cons of Roman gossip, or exploited the pedantry of the lawyers on both sides? The inexhaustible energy of this performance might have sufficed for two ordinary poets. The interest gradually rises till the speech of Caponsacchi, and Pompilia carries it beyond even him. Then the lawyers provide an anticlimax. The pedantry of learning or the opportunity of eloquence is all it means to them. We are in the dusty court among the professionals. The Pope lifts the theme as high as human wisdom can carry it, before the agony of the condemned criminal produces Guido's frantic plea. This, the most dramatic speech, fills the eleventh book. In the last Browning completes the cycle that he had opened in the introduction. The more we consider it, the riper seems his art.

With every speaker the interest takes fresh life. I think too that this treatment of the story comes as near as possible to the heart of things. The characters reveal themselves even more than what they did. For the blow struck, the word spoken, the silence kept : what are they but the ripples of the tide that swells below them in darkness ? The surge of conflicting impulse and emotion but half-understood by ourselves is the living truth of existence. To present this confusion is to re-create the story, and ten versions of it preserve the conflict more livingly, because less finally, than one. A court of law endeavours to sift the facts, but the life of the facts lies in the contradictions of the different witnesses.

The passages most suitable for quotation are to be found at the conclusion of the more important books ; and the final words of Guido, of the Pope, of Pompilia, have been quoted in most criticisms. At the end of Book I occurs the famous apostrophe to the poet's wife, but it is not always noted that the opening line of this apostrophe

> O lyric Love, half-angel and half-bird

is the one weak line in an else magnificent passage. I cannot resist quoting the latter half of this address to her :

> Hail then, and hearken from the realms of help !
> Never may I commence my song, my due
> To God who best taught song by gift of thee,
> Except with bent head and beseeching hand—
> That still, despite the distance and the dark,
> What was, again may be ; some interchange
> Of grace, some splendour once thy very thought,
> Some benediction anciently thy smile :
> —Never conclude, but raising hand and head
> Thither where eyes, that cannot reach, yet yearn
> For all hope, all sustainment, all reward,
> Their upmost up and on,—so blessing back

U

In those thy realms of help, that heaven thy home,
Some whiteness which, I judge, thy face makes proud,
Some wanness where, I think, thy foot may fall!

Here, however, is the vivid account by Pompilia of the
child-marriage into which she was thrust, one of the
pieces, which are wonderful by contrast, of straightforward narrative in the poem:

However, I was hurried through a storm . . .
Into blank San Lorenzo, up the aisle,
My mother keeping hold of me so tight,
I fancied we were come to see a corpse
Before the altar which she pulled me toward.
There we found waiting an unpleasant priest
Who proved the brother, not our parish friend,
But one with mischief-making mouth and eye,
Paul, whom I know since to my cost.   And then
I heard the heavy church-door lock out help
Behind us : for the customary warmth,
Two tapers shivered on the altar.   " Quick—
Lose no time ! "—cried the priest.   And straightway down
From . . . what's behind the altar where he hid—
Hawk-nose and yellowness and bush and all,
Stepped Guido, caught my hand, and there was I
O' the chancel, and the priest had opened book,
Read here and there, made me say that and this,
And after, told me I was now a wife,
Honoured indeed, since Christ thus weds the Church,
And therefore turned he water into wine,
To show I should obey my spouse like Christ.
Then the two slipped aside and talked apart,
And I, silent and scared, got down again
And joined my mother who was weeping now.
Nobody seemed to mind us any more,
And both of us on tiptoe found our way
To the door which was unlocked by this, and wide.

But in this quality of vivid narrative, I do not think
the speech of Caponsacchi, the priest with whose aid
Pompilia escaped from her husband, can be surpassed.
If one, ignorant of the poem, and prepared to make
trial but of one speech, should ask which, it is to the

speech of Caponsacchi that one would direct him. The speeches of the two lawyers are generally considered the most easily dispensable, but they show a master at play with his art, much as we imagine the carvers to have been at play when they indulged a humorous fancy on misericords and corbels. Artists and critics rarely agree on indulgences of this kind, but can we not sympathise with an artist when he is obviously enjoying himself? It does not require much generosity to admit that the speeches of the two lawyers must have been great fun to write, whatever they may be to us who read them. Is the reader's pleasure the only one to be considered by a poet, and may he never kick his heels for his own amusement? If we will consider these two speeches and, say, the grotesque passages in *Pacchiarotto*, from the writer's not the reader's point of view, I think we shall find that Browning was giving to himself, as an artist on holiday, the same kind of pleasure that he gave to us in *The Pied Piper of Hamelin*. The "jolly learned man of middle age," Hyacinthus de Archangelis discourses on supper:

> May Gigia have remembered nothing stings
> Fried liver out of its monotony
> Of richness like a root of fennel, chopped
> Fine with the parsley: parsley-sprigs I said—
> Was there need I should say " and fennel too "?
> But no, she cannot have been so obtuse!
> To our argument! The fennel will be chopped.

The Latin tags in which his speech abounds, to make it tasty and grotesque, are not suited to quotation. Besides, in his later works, Browning was to give more grotesque expression to his humour for playing with words and rhymes than these. Only a great artist desires to play with his material; and it is a sign of academic seriousness to reject those passages in which his imagination was taking a holiday with its tools.

Sculpture has been called the noblest of the arts because its prime subject, the human body, is at its best the noblest object in nature. It is the function of sculpture to display this object in the round. From every side, from all points of view, the sculptor would display it harmoniously. If he succeeds, he succeeds on every side of it. This is the aim of the elaborate method perfected by Browning in *The Ring and the Book*. Its object is to present this story in the round, to create an epic like a piece of sculpture. The poem indeed resembles a mighty group of figures, which we see from every side as if it were a monument in marble. There is also a certain quality in Browning's style that enforces this comparison. The English language was a quarry to him, and he delighted in it as much for the native roughness that he retained as for the delicacy that he could impart to it. The glory of his language is its native idiom. Its beauty combines delicacy of handling without sacrifice of natural qualities, so that the strength balances the sweetness and the sweetness the strength.

The Ring and the Book is the only one of his long poems which is not too long, perhaps because there are twelve contributors to it. His temptation might have been to devote twenty thousand lines to one soliloquy. When his other long poems fatigue us, that is what we feel. But in his epic he enhanced one soliloquy by another, and the parts are in proportion to the whole. Moreover, the arguments of each speaker are not abstract but human. Their substance is poetic in itself. The most ambitious of his works is also the greatest. *The Ring and the Book* is his supreme thing.

The poem imposes the feeling that it must be familiar to everyone, and to extract quotations is rather like chipping fragments from a marble. The impression of the whole is what we cannot but want to convey. Here are a few of the noble lines in Pompilia's utterance:

> My boy was born,
> Born all in love, with nought to spoil the bliss
> A whole long fortnight : in a life like mine
> A fortnight filled with bliss is long and much.
> All women are not mothers of a boy . . .
> I never realized God's birth before—
> How he grew likest God in being born.
> This time I felt like Mary, had my babe
> Lying a little on my breast like hers.

Or the beautiful forgiveness of her husband Guido :

> We shall not meet in this world nor the next,
> But where will God be absent ?   In His face
> Is light, but in His shadow healing too :
> Let Guido touch the shadow and be healed !

As we know how Browning and his wife regarded what ordinarily passes for marriage, Pompilia's words may be added :

> Marriage on earth seems such a counterfeit,
> Mere imitation of the inimitable :
> In heaven we have the real and true and sure.
> 'Tis there they neither marry nor are given
> In marriage but are as the angels : right,
> Oh how right that is, how like Jesus Christ
> To say that !
>   Marriage-making for the earth,
> With gold so much,—birth, power, repute so much,
> Or beauty, youth so much, in lack of these !
> Be as the angels rather, who, apart,
> Know themselves into one, are found at length
> Married, but never marry, no, nor give
> In marriage, they are man and wife at once
> When the true time is : here we have to wait
> Not so long neither !   Could we by a wish
> Have what we will and get the future now,
> Would we wish aught done undone in the past ?
> So let *him* wait God's instant men call years;
> Meantime hold hard by truth and his great soul,
> Do out the duty !
>   Through such souls alone
> God stooping shows sufficient of His light
> For us i' the dark to rise by.   And I rise.

The word ' him ' refers to her friend and rescuer, Caponsacchi, and how beautiful are these, her final words.
Since there is no room for adequate quotation from
each book, let us conclude with a few lines from the
first and the final passage of the conclusion. Like
Guido, the poet speaks twice :

> Such, British Public, ye who like me not,
> (God love you !)—whom I yet have laboured for,
> Perchance more careful whoso runs may read
> Than erst when all, it seemed, could read who ran,—
> Perchance more careless whoso reads may praise
> Than late when he who praised and read and wrote
> Was apt to find himself the self-same me,—
> Such labour had such issue, so I wrought
> This arc, by furtherance of such alloy,
> And so, by one spurt, take away its trace
> Till, justifiably golden, rounds my ring.

It was with the publication of *Men and Women* that
the tide of his general neglect and unpopularity had
begun to ebb; but not until the publication of *The
Ring and the Book*, in 1868, was his greatness recognized,
so there was excuse for this irony still. As he laid his
great task aside completed, he took farewell of his reader
by justifying the method that he had perfected in this
poem, and turning again to the thought of her, which
never left him :

> Why take the artistic way to prove so much ?
> Because it is the glory and good of Art,
> That Art remains the one way possible
> Of speaking truth. . . .
>   Art may tell a truth
> Obliquely, do the thing shall breed the thought,
> Nor wrong the thought, missing the mediate word. . . .
>
> So write a book shall mean, beyond the facts,
> Suffice the eye and save the soul beside.
>
> And save the soul !   If this intent save mine,—
> If the rough ore be rounded to a ring,

Render all duty which good ring should do,
And, failing grace, succeed in guardianship,—
Might mine but lie outside thine, Lyric Love,
Thy rare gold ring of verse (the poet praised)
Linking our England to his Italy.

The link between her and himself remained unworn till the end of his life; and, whether we pursue it during his twenty-five years in London, or in the poems that he was to write after her death, that great memory is constant. In Pompilia Mrs. Orr believes there were many traces of her influence, in the mother's utterances and in her ideal affection for Caponsacchi most of all.

CHAPTER SEVEN

HIS WIDOWED YEARS AND LATER POEMS

I

The death of Mrs. Browning was a blow that cut the life of the poet into two unequal halves, and, though his robust temperament gradually survived the shock of a loss that was present to him till the end, from this time forward we have to think of him as a widower who worked and travelled and overlooked the education of his son, as a man performing a duty the inspiring motive of which had now vanished. For three weeks he seemed inconsolable, and his good friend and neighbour Miss Isa Blagden, who persuaded him to join her with Penini at her villa at Bellosguardo, called this her 'apocalyptic month' because of the poetic grief that alternated with his frequent cry "I want her, I want her." Discovering that he "began to go to pieces," when he lingered in the familiar house, he decided to complete the break in his life by leaving Florence for ever. "The cycle is complete," he declared; "I want my new life to resemble the last fifteen years as little as possible." He even added: "I don't mean to live with anybody, even my own family, but to occupy myself thoroughly, seeing dear friends however." It is worth noting that his most intimate friends had always been women, and it was in the main his old, and yet to be made, friends among women who consoled and lightened this last period of his life. "I

296

shall grow still, I hope," he wrote, " but my root is taken, and remains."

Sharing his wife's recoil from the " earth-side " of death, he entrusted Miss Blagden with the overseeing of the monument by Leighton that was, a little later, placed upon Mrs. Browning's grave. He himself had less than his wife's pity for the human shell, and so little feeling for the frame that the departed spirit had forsaken that he was indifferent to the associations that affect many. He said that he would like to be buried in whatever country he happened to die, but he had " no kind of concern " as to his last resting-place.

In July, with his boy, he left Italy for France, and spent two months with his father and sister near Dinard before going to London, where Arabel Barrett, his wife's favourite relative, was living. It is characteristic of his mood that, noticing Tennyson on the platform at Amiens, Browning pulled his hat over his face and avoided recognition. The first phase of his widower-hood was spent as far as possible alone. He soon discovered, however, that the lodgings on which he had insisted were unbearable, and he found himself a house, 19 Warwick Crescent, by the side of the Regent's Canal, which remained his home till the last two years of his life. The attractions of " grim London " were two-fold. Miss Barrett lived near by in Delamere Terrace, and Browning wished to give an English education to his boy. He had no wish to send Pen to an English public school, but intended to engage a tutor so that the lad might be prepared for Oxford. Browning felt that his responsibility was the greater because his wife had laid upon him no express charge. As he seems to have proved in every way an affectionate and considerate father, it is curious to hear from Mrs. Orr, his friend as well as his biographer, that he had little of the paternal instinct. If so, we cannot avoid concluding that its absence made no difference in his care. He had delighted in his infant. He grew to be loved by his son, whose success as an artist made him more proud than the fame which came to himself. Mrs. Orr implies that he was indifferent to children, but that this could not be guessed from his conduct. A good son, a good husband, a good father, can truthfully be said of him. To animals he was admittedly devoted. The garden at Warwick Crescent was soon supplied with queer pets; first a pair of geese, and then an owl, which the poet's way with odd creatures, from toads to lizards, successfully converted into responsive friends.

If there was a touch of wan beauty in the canal by the side of his house, that peculiar sadness of green leaves and soiled water which makes so pathetic a thing of a town garden or a deserted tow-path in a wilderness of brick, the ugliness of the neighbouring Harrow Road and Edgware Road must have seemed squalor to one whose home had been in Italy, one who had not spent a winter in London for fifteen years. It may have chimed with the mood of his return, and symbolized the painful years of exile on which for his son's sake he had determined, but he still hoped eventually to have done with it all when once his boy should have been started in life. At first then the poet lived alone, visiting Miss Barrett every evening and attending with her the sermons of a certain Nonconformist preacher, Thomas Jones, at Bedford Chapel, to whose addresses Browning contributed an introduction in 1884. This man, called sometimes the "Welsh poet-preacher," was of humble birth and natural eloquence, which the devout Miss Barrett and the poet equally admired.

The immediate tasks before him were to edit and publish his wife's volume of *Last Poems*, which appeared in 1862, her essay on the "Greek Christian Poets," reprinted from a newspaper in 1863, and a volume of

Selections from her verse, chosen by himself, in 1865. Secondly, he had to prepare that body of lyrics, of which his wife had spoken in Rome, which gave to the world *Dramatis Personæ* in 1864. These occupations possibly helped to decide his refusal of the editorship of the *Cornhill Magazine* which was pressed upon him on the retirement of Thackeray. He also had to stand guardian over his wife's memory from the odious attempts of various people to constitute themselves, without consulting him, Mrs. Browning's biographers, and even to publish without permission such letters of hers as had fallen into their hands. The fury which he felt with " their paws in my very bowels " was repeated at any subsequent interference with her memory. When, years later, in 1888, a reference of Edward Fitzgerald which Browning thought slighting produced the violent " Lines to Edward Fitzgerald," Browning pleaded in excuse : " I felt as if she had died yesterday." We can readily understand why at the moment he was giving nothing fresh of his own to the world.

From the public point of view there had been a long interval of silence. *Men and Women* had been published in 1855, and nine years were to pass before *Dramatis Personæ* succeeded it. None the less the tide of public disfavour had turned since 1855, for it was in 1863 that Browning was called upon to supervise the three-volume edition of his poetry, and his old and helpful friend Forster was being helped by Barry Cornwall (Procter) in preparing the first, an excellent, Selection from Browning's works. Browning also helped his friend Story, the sculptor and poet, in the revision of *Roba di Roma*. In regard to Forster's admirable selection, it must be repeated that he had been one of the few admirers of Browning's poetry who, in a position to draw attention to its quality, did not keep silence. Once, for instance, when in earlier days Carlyle had been specially enthusiastic, Browning's comment was, "If only those words had been ever repeated in public, what good they might have done me!" All this, it will be observed, was task-work, however necessary or generous the motive, and it was not until 1863 that he abandoned his seclusion, began to accept invitations, and to give up, as Sir Edmund Gosse quotes him, a morbid mode of life.

The quiet existence that he was now leading began to be diversified by annual holidays abroad, usually on the coast of France, later in Switzerland, last of all on the Italian slopes of the Alps. These holidays usually produced some poem connected with the place or district or people whose stories he encountered, and there is no doubt that so soon as he was out of England, in spite of the resources of London music, dinner-parties and visits to country houses, Browning recovered his happier mood again. In 1862 he was at Cambo, near Biarritz, with Pen and a copy of Euripides that was to bear abundant fruit a few years ahead. Meantime he was meditating the theme that he had found in the little yellow book chanced upon in a stall in the piazza at Florence during the last days that he had spent at Casa Guidi. But four years were to pass before the writing of *The Ring and the Book* was to be begun. The conception flashed upon him as he had paced his terrace on the evening of the day when he had finished the old book. He was to brood over it until 1865, when the great poem grew under his hand rapidly.

The holidays of the years 1863, 1864 and 1865 were spent in Brittany, near Pornic, from which "Gold Hair," and the details at least in "James Lee's Wife," derive. It was at Pornic that he confirmed also his new habit of regular work, the objects of which were to repay his abundant opportunities by making the most of his genius before his death, and the determination to be thoroughly occupied. The result was that he bequeathed a vast literature. Indeed the amount that he wrote, even after *The Ring and the Book*, was almost as great in volume as all he had composed before.

II

It is convenient here to consider a few points about *Dramatis Personæ* (1864) which would have interfered with the consideration of *Men and Women* and *The Ring and the Book* in the previous chapter. There we followed the perfection of a method which culminated in the great epic poem, and alluded only to *Dramatis Personæ* in passing. The two groups of shorter poems are akin, and the latter can be considered most conveniently in relation to this period in his life. The great poem on death, " Prospice," clearly looks back to Casa Guidi, and " Mr. Sludge the Medium " recalls Browning's Italian experiences of Spiritualism. " James Lee's Wife " is Browning's only experiment with a sequence of lyrics. " Abt Vogler " is a companion poem to " Master Hugues " with its musical theme. " Bishop Blougram's Apology," said to have been suggested by Cardinal Wiseman, is balanced in the new volume by the wonderful testimony of St. John in " A Death in the Desert." Those who are curious of Browning's precise relation to orthodox Christianity need only to read the speech of the Pope in *The Ring and the Book*, " A Death in the Desert," and " La Saisiaz." It comes to this. Browning had a passionate instinct for religion, and found his instinct best satisfied by the example and teachings of Christ, but his belief in the historic basis of the Christian story had been shaken, and he contented himself by saying that the truth man needs is here, whether we regard it as fact or symbol. What we have is enough. The use that we make of it is much more important than the category to which it belongs. The issue of such a point of view is expressed magnificently in what may be called the neutral terms of *Rabbi Ben Ezra*, which indeed has appealed to the religious instinct of most diversely constituted minds. This perhaps is the most famous of all the poems in *Dramatis Personæ*. A typical instance of Browning's attitude to Christianity may be seen in the final verses of " Gold Hair." Speaking in his own person, he says that he holds Christianity to be true, first because

> 'Tis the faith that launched point-blank her dart
>   At the head of a lie—taught Original Sin,
> The Corruption of Man's Heart.

No better example could be found of his attachment to its teachings. Any demur arose over its statements of historic fact.

" Caliban upon Setebos," that masterpiece of grotesque, is also here, and one line in it illustrates one of Browning's favourite theories. He had told his future wife, in one of his letters, that when a poet was seeking to convey a crude thing, its essence rather than its similitude should be rendered. What the imagination could make of it, not what the mind could remember, was to mark the poet's touch. Thus, when he wished to describe the abuse with which Caliban covered his absent master, he spoke of Caliban

> Letting the rank tongue blossom into speech.

If this be contrasted with the gutter-idiom that made some of Mr. Masefield's long poems notorious on their appearance, the opposite principle becomes plain. The reproductions of Mr. Masefield were intended to be a violent reaction from conventional poetic speech, but this is not to assume that he had any quarrel with the great speech of such a poet as Browning. Caliban is as great a creation as Mr. Sludge is a subtle piece of portraiture, and what a range from the savage in his slime to the pampered impostor of the modern drawing-rooms !

Another version of the theme of " The Statue and the Bust " is to be found in " Youth and Art," which again tells how a poor artist ' would not be rash ' enough to marry a poor singer, nor she something more than rash to screw him to the pitch. This poem is more immediate, more human in its appeal than that on the two statues. The weaklings are not judged. She confesses :

> We have not sighed deep, laughed free,
>   Starved, feasted, despaired,—been happy.

The thought of the blessing that his great risk had brought to him and his wife seems clearly present in both poems. " Confessions " and " A Likeness " are two other vivid sketches of modern life, and the latter has some of the most audacious rhyming even in Browning. " Dis Aliter Visum " is another variation on the same theme, as if to remind us that Browning was inexhaustible.

It is sometimes charged against him that his poetry lacks repose, but at his best, as in this volume, the life is so abounding that we do not feel the want. We do not feel the need for repose with the fresh breeze filling our lungs and fanning our faces. To a heart in regular pulsation repose means death, and there is a sense in which the life of Browning's poetry is like a heart beating in full vigour. Only when he becomes too argumentative do we flag, and there is never too much argumentativeness in *Dramatis Personæ*. These poems are such triumphs of their kind that it becomes impertinent to praise them. Open the volume anywhere, and one's ear and imagination are held.

No wonder the volume brought him new readers, for a second edition was necessary within a year. Browning wrote : " Chapman says ' the new orders come from Oxford and Cambridge,' and all my new cultivators are young men—more than that, I observe that some of my old friends don't like at all the irruption of outsiders who rescue me from their sober and private approval, and take those words out of their mouths ' which they always meant to say ' and never did." We must remember that Elizabeth Barrett had been one of the few influential writers who had praised his work when it had few supporters, so that even here she held a place apart for him. There is excuse, if no justification, for his estimate of their relative poetic powers. His most vivid expression of it was as follows : disputing the preference for his own poetry shown by his old friend Madame du Quaire, formerly Miss Blackett, he said :

> You are wrong—quite wrong—she has genius; I am only a painstaking fellow. Can't you imagine a clever sort of angel who plots and plans, and tries to build up something —he wants to make you see it as he sees it—shows you one point of view, carries you off to another, hammering into your head the thing he wants you to understand; and whilst this bother is going on God Almighty turns you off a little star—that's the difference between us. The true creative power is hers, not mine.

While it is natural that he should have admired the spontaneity of his wife, it is odd that he should not have felt his own superabundant powers of creation, and acknowledged that Mrs. Browning was at her best when she had taken most pains and refused, as in the *Sonnets*, to let the pen run away with her. He combined indeed creativeness with powers of mental concentration, and the latter, it is true, tended to an argumentativeness in verse that was sometimes more ' painstaking ' than beautiful. We may believe that he read most of her poems for the character that they revealed and that he had come to worship, that this was already the case before he had seen her, and, with her writings before us, it is not hard to see how this might have occurred. But there was in him, too, a fountain of pure lyricism, and the world is so far at one with his judgment as to have given the popular pre-eminence to his shortest songs. It is needless to repeat that only one of her lyrics can justly compare with them.

III

This record of quiet work and holidays in France was marred in 1866 by the death of Browning's father. The last glimpse of Mr. Browning is a vivid picture of a delightful man, who perhaps only lacked ambition to have his qualities more widely acknowledged. Browning wrote :

> He retained all his faculties to the last—was utterly indiffer-ent to death—asking with surprise what it was we were affected about since he was perfectly happy ?—and kept his own strange sweetness of soul to the end—nearly his last words to me, as I was fanning him, were, " I am so afraid that I fatigue you, dear ! " this, while his sufferings were great. . . . As it is, he was known by half-a-dozen friends. He was worthy of being Ba's father—out of the whole world only he, so far as my experience goes. She loved him,—and *he* said, very recently, while gazing at her portrait, that only that picture had put into his head that there might be such a thing as the worship of the images of saints. My sister will come and live with me henceforth. You see what she loses.

Mr. Browning had lived to be eighty-five, and for the past seventeen years the poet's sister Sarianna had taken care of him. Now she became the inseparable companion of her brother, with whom she left Paris,

x

where she and her father had lately made their home,
for Brittany. Le Croisic, where they spent this and the
following summer, gave occasion to two of Browning's
well-known poems, " The Two Poets of Croisic " and
" Hervé Riel." Two years later, in 1868, Miss Arabel
Barrett died, the last close link with his wife, and the
subject of a strange coincidence. Five years before,
Browning had recorded a dream that Arabel had told
to him. In this she had asked her sister, knowing that
she was dead, " When shall I be with you ? " and Elizabeth had answered, " Dearest, in five years." Browning
reported this to Miss Blagden, adding, " You know I
am not superstitious . . . only a coincidence, but notice-
able." Had this coincidence befallen his wife, we can
guess the anxiety, and the hopes, that she would have
founded upon it.

This year, 1868, was remarkable in other ways.
Browning, who had been consulting Jowett at Oxford
upon the education of his son, and had been made an
honorary Fellow of Balliol in 1867, began to associate
with both universities, and kindred honours to be
showered upon him. An edition of his works in six
volumes was published this year. Jowett, now a warm
friend, but a qualified admirer of the poetry, said of
Browning : " I had no idea that there was a perfectly
sensible poet in the world, entirely free from vanity,
jealousy, or any other littleness, and thinking no more
of himself than any ordinary man." Browning declined
the offer, though he was certain of election, of the Lord
Rectorship of the University of St. Andrews, vacant by
the death of John Stuart Mill, but the year was famous
with the publication of the first two volumes of *The
Ring and the Book*.

The appearance of this great work was the crest in
more senses than one of Browning's career as a man of
letters. Not only did this mighty poem pass quickly

into a second edition, but the decade that its publication opened was the fullest in the poet's life. The public had admitted his quality; the Universities were proud to honour him, and Society, following at his heels, sought him out in town and country. On every prominent occasion in the musical, artistic, and learned worlds he had the opportunity of being present, and he repaid these invitations with characteristic generosity, for he held it his duty to indulge those who entertained him with the social gifts and lively conversation that had won him many friends in the past. Except in his refusal to make public speeches, he set himself out to please, and no great man perhaps has ever been more approachable, or less self-conscious. In private houses, at good concerts, at private views, at University dinners, Browning was generally to be seen, and on these occasions he bore out Jowett's testimony to his simplicity. At the same time he never degenerated into a diner-out or social figure, but he worked harder than before. During this decade indeed he wrote and published nine volumes of poetry. The dates are: *Balaustion's Adventure*, including a version of the *Alcestis*, 1871; *Aristophanes' Apology* (the last adventure of Balaustion), 1875; the *Agamemnon* of Aeschylus " transcribed," 1877; *Prince Hohenstiel-Schwangau*, 1871; *Fifine at the Fair*, 1872; *Red Cotton Night-Cap Country*, 1873; *La Saisiaz*, 1878; *The Inn Album*, 1875; *Pacchiarotto, and How he Worked in Distemper*, 1876. This list is not given in order of date, so as to group the poems by subject so far as is possible. We have three on classical themes, four on subjects concerning France or Switzerland; the inn stories are English in their setting, and *Pacchiarotto* returns to Italy though the poet himself is turning upon his critics at home. We shall deal with these later, only recalling here that the *Pacchiarotto* volume contains among its shorter pieces some of his famous things.

What a product for ten years apparently spent on the amusements of cultivated society !

On his annual holidays he would generally seek recreation in some quiet spot abroad, but in 1869 he and his sister joined his old friends the Storys in Scotland. The three following summers were spent in Normandy at the fishing village of Saint-Aubin, which became doubly attractive to the poet from the presence there of his intimate friend Joseph Milsand. The two lived in a pair of primitive cottages within a stone's throw of one another, and Browning delighted in being " thoroughly washed by the sea-air from all quarters " in this wild and exposed corner of France. A precious memory of the past also came to him from across the sea.

> Exactly opposite this house (he wrote to Miss Blagden), just over the water, shines every night the light-house of Havre, a place I know well and love very moderately : but it always gives me a thrill as I see afar, *exactly* a particular spot which I was at along with her. At this moment, I see the white streak of the phare in the sun, from the window where I write and I *think*.

It was August of the year 1870, and the Prussian war-cloud over France had burst. The next year was to produce the imaginary apology that Browning put into the mouth of the fallen Napoleon III, but at the moment he was warned by Milsand to hasten home if he was to escape the war-fever that converted every foreigner into a suspected spy. The ordinary Channel steamers were no longer running, and with great difficulty Browning and his sister reached Honfleur, where they were thankful to find a cattle-boat willing to embark them for England.

IV

It was for the benefit of sufferers in Paris that Browning, who rarely published his poems in periodicals except to do someone a good turn, sold his famous ballad " Hervé Riel " to the *Cornhill*, and he was pleased when he was able to send a hundred guineas as the " product of a poem " to France.   The facts of this act of French heroism had been forgotten at St. Malo, but when the archives of the French Admiralty were examined it was found that Browning was correct, except that Hervé Riel had asked, not for a day's holiday with his wife, but for a lifetime.   His discharge from the service was to be his reward.

This is a convenient place to mention the few sonnets that Browning, as occasional pieces, wrote during his life.   The three that are chiefly quoted find no place in his collected works.   There is the straightforward sonnet in answer to the question " Why am I a liberal ? " the happy sonnet called " Helen's Tower " evoked by the memorial which Lord Dufferin erected to the memory of his mother, and the beautiful sonnet to Goldoni, penned while the messenger was waiting at the door. The two first are contained in William Sharp's *Sonnets of the Century*, and that to Goldoni is given in Mrs. Orr's Life of the poet.   Its own beauty, the hurried circumstance of its composition, and the rarity of the sonnet-form in Browning's work, justify its reproduction here :

> Goldoni,—good, gay, sunniest of souls,—
>   Glassing half Venice in that verse of thine,—
>   What though it just reflect the shade and shine
> Of common life, nor render, as it rolls,
> Grandeur and gloom ?   Sufficient for thy shoals
>   Was Carnival : Parini's depths enshrine
>   Secrets unsuited to that opaline
> Surface of things which laughs along thy scrolls.

There throng the people : how they come and go,
  Lisp the soft language, flaunt the bright garb,—see
On Piazza, Calle, under Portico
  And over Bridge !   Dear king of Comedy,
Be honoured !   Thou that didst love Venice so,
  Venice, and we who love her, all love thee !

Beneath the bright surface critical appreciations dart
like gold-fish in a little bowl, but we feel that the form
was too narrow for the poet to move freely.   It had
fitted Mrs. Browning exactly; she had been all her
previous life in prison, like a pet gold-fish in her father's
house, and her desire to range in wider forms of verse
was not unlike the startled rushes of a creature suddenly
finding itself free.

The chief events of 1871 were the publication of
Balaustion's Adventure and *Prince Hohenstiel-Schwangau*.
The latter poem was written in Scotland, while Browning's sister was the guest of the Milsands at Saint-Aubin.
The next year saw the publication of *Fifine at the Fair*,
a poem which has caused more heartsearchings to some
of the poet's admirers than any other.   It has been
thought to contain a plea for self-indulgence, and many
surmises have been made upon the condition of Browning's feelings at the date of its composition.   Even Mrs.
Orr says : " Some leaven of bitterness must have been
working within him, or he never could have produced
that perplexing piece of cynicism, *Fifine at the Fair*."
" We may even fancy (she remarks, though with a
caution) we read into the letters of 1870 that eerie,
haunting sadness of a cherished memory from which,
in spite of ourselves, life is bearing us away."   Yet the
evidence of the later poems, right up to the last volume
of *Asolando*, bears abundant proof that the ' cherished
memory ' had not faded, and that the subject of *Fifine*
cannot be traced to any change of heart in Browning
himself.   Defending him from ridiculous insinuations,

Mrs. Orr ingeniously suggests that the enjoyment coming to him now that he had left his seclusion appeared to his imagination a kind of disloyalty to his old allegiance, and that his imagination dramatised this into the " cynical mood of fancy " manifest in *Fifine at the Fair*. " The present," writes Mrs. Orr, " came to him with friendly greeting. He was unconsciously, perhaps inevitably, unjust to what it brought." This suggestion, a good instance of Mrs. Orr's revealing criticism, is so interesting that we are almost tempted to be grateful for the foolish remarks which gave it rise. We may also note how inevitably, as death, which now took away Isa Blagden, removed one dear friend after another, Browning replaced his women friends. He instinctively embodied Dr. Johnson's dictum and ' kept his friendships in repair.' Women must have felt extraordinarily happy and safe with him. Indeed we may wonder whether he realized how devoted to him some of these women came to be. No man was more sympathetic to women; no man more devoted to a single love.

An account of the summer holiday spent at Saint-Aubin in 1872 has survived in *Records of Tennyson, Ruskin and Browning* by Annie Ritchie, Thackeray's daughter. Noticing the white cotton caps that were worn in this part of France, she suggested the title for *Red Cotton Night-Cap Country*, which was dedicated to herself. Since no one has seen in this story a defence of suicide, may we not infer that *Fifine* too was an exploration of psychology ? It was not new for Browning to like the analysis of " indefensible " principles or ugly growths. After all, two early poems, " Porphyria's Lover " and the magnificent " Johannes Agricola," had depicted the points of view of two monsters, and the pair were grouped originally under the common title of " Mad-house Cells." Mr. Sludge and to some extent Bishop Blougram were morbid characters. Cali-

ban had been allowed to confess what religion meant to
him.   Prince Hohenstiel-Schwangau had had his say in
defence of opportunism.   Aristophanes likewise maintained the right of Comedy to tickle the groundlings with
licentiousness.   Was there really more in these later
and longer poems than the same imaginative curiosity,
and have they not seemed more important because
Browning's tendency to prolixity grew upon him with
age, so that we may argue a significance where we should
infer no more than the garrulity of advancing years?
Like all artists who have perfected a method, Browning
was naturally tempted at last to show how much he
could wring from apparently unpromising themes.   We
feel, in short, that a method so rich was not being spent
on subjects entirely worthy of it, for we want more than
a display of virtuosity from a poet of Browning's powers.
The tale unfolded in *Red Cotton Night-Cap Country* had
taken place near Saint-Aubin between 1870 and 1872.
We know that Browning was attracted by workaday
stories, and those grotesque glimpses of life that occur
in police-court happenings.   It is too much to expect
that even he could make a poem like *The Ring and the
Book* out of every instance that beguiled him.

   With the various scenes that compose *The Inn Album*
we return to England.   That this poem is succinct in
form, and not at all casuistical in substance, reminds us
how dangerous it is to assert that Browning was weaken-
ing, or becoming the slave of a method even.   It is at
least equally true that he wrote too much, and that the
world at large grows weary of too many examples from
the same hand.   In music Bach, in painting Rubens,
are examples of great artists the extent of whose work
is too vast for the appetites of ordinary men.   Humanity
prefers to sigh over the unfulfilled promise of a Chatter-
ton, a Shelley, or a Keats.   The great men who lived
long enough to work out everything that was in them

create a surfeit, which would no doubt remain a surfeit even if it was limited to masterpieces. Those of us who have a preference for a certain vintage of Bordeaux, or for one of the great white Burgundies, and have been enabled to indulge it for a long time from a well-stocked cellar, sigh eventually for a change. A taste that is not mechanical must become dulled to a similar stimulus, and this perhaps is peculiarly true of the exciting flavour of Browning's poems. At first it carries us away. Then we grow to enjoy its presence in the less immediately attractive forms. At last curiosity over its fine shades is satisfied. The poetry which has become a part of ourselves is now a possession. You cannot enjoy the wine that was drunk yesterday, even though a great memory remains. Through having become Browningised you have ceased to be a Browningite. All that you could take from him is yours.

V

The years between 1873 and 1878, which produced the classical poems, *The Inn Album* and *Pacchiarotto*, were also busy years of social life. Browning now was regularly in request, and took a peculiar delight in his visits to Oxford and Cambridge. In Society scholastic leisure, with its traditional graces, was what he specially enjoyed, and a college dinner, even one keeping the diners for five hours at table, while the wine passed and speeches succeeded, was scarcely too long for him. He was enjoying in his age the society that he had missed in his youth, and perhaps he was better suited to the high table in his seat of honour than he would have been below the daïs with undergraduate friends, though it is hard to fancy that he would not have made himself at home in any company. It had been the society of the rough crews that he had appreciated on his early voyages to Italy. In that country he had immersed himself in the arts of poetry, painting and sculpture, but had had to satisfy his love of music by solitary improvisations on the organs that he would find in the churches. In Florence he had made the acquaintance of Miss Egerton-Smith, and it so happened that she also had made her home in London. Music was a passion with her, and she also lived in a quiet corner. She must have been one of the few women who were newspaper proprietors then or now. It became her habit to call for him in her brougham and to carry him off to every concert worth attending.

The result of these activities was to leave him physically exhausted at the end of every London season, and he shunned the idea of an English holiday perhaps because this suggested more of the life in country houses of which he had had enough. He wanted repose, but lacked the energy to move, and the consequence was that the arrangements for his holiday were usually made at the last moment in a hurry. Italy was too far away then for a brief visit, and the North of France had already been explored. In August 1874 Miss Egerton-Smith came to the rescue by proposing that she should meet the Brownings at Mers, near Tréport; and, as she had proved a welcome companion on earlier occasions in England, the plan was tried. It was so successful, that the friends went to Normandy in 1875, to the Isle of Arran in 1876, and to La Saisiaz, near Geneva, in 1877. The product of this first holiday, in 1874, was *Aristophanes' Apology*, which he brought back nearly finished in November, after having extended his travels to Antwerp where his son, now a man, was studying painting under Heyermans. It is wonderful that a man of Browning's age should have worked so hard during these holidays, but he nearly always took repose in some change of occupation, and no doubt the quiet room by the sea, with the great wind for a companion on his walks along the coast, was a mental rest after the concerts and social evenings of London. There is little to be said of his holidays at Villers, 1875, and at Arran in the following year, except that the proofs of *The Inn Album* were corrected at the former.

When he arrived at La Saisiaz in 1877, he was unusually depressed and fatigued. Was he missing the sea, and finding, as Mrs. Orr suggests, the Alpine valley oppressive, or was he, as he came to fancy, under the shadow of a coming blow? Miss Egerton-Smith was an eager companion in the rambles of the Brownings, and used to devise excursions with the same ingenuity as she found holiday haunts for them. One day, on the eve of starting for one of these excursions, she died, without warning or previous apparent sign of illness. It was a sudden shock, and once more moved the poet to consider, as he took alone the walk on which she was to have accompanied him, whether they would meet again, or whether all of her was lying in the narrow grave at Collonge. It had been part of his joy in her friendship to have penetrated a manner that had seemed to others cold; to have recognized the quality that was as much unseen by the world as had been his own father's :

Disembosomed, re-embosomed,—must one memory suffice,
Prove I knew an Alpine rose which all beside named Edelweiss ?

Browning discusses the question of immortality, arguing that if this life be accepted as a place of probation only, the evil things of life fall into their due place; and, alternately, that, if this hypothesis be not granted, the hope of immortality will not be denied, and this hope is supported by the fact that assurance would rob us of personal responsibility. It is curious that he and his generation do not seem to have considered that the individual has racial instincts no less than private ones, and that a belief in a future life so strong as to be an assurance may derive as much from this racial consciousness as from personal desire. Whether it be the physical tie that unites us to our ancestors or the seed of future generations that lies in us all, there is at least a physical basis for the dream of personal immortality. Whether it be a recollection of pre-natal life in the womb or the promise of paternity, our sense of a personal existence beyond our own life has a physical foundation. Its loftier aspiration is also grounded in the racial consciousness that is latent in all, and inevitably vivid in the poets and mystics. It is true that such facts are no sufficient substitute for the craving that some profess for the survival of personal identity after death, but on the other hand it is impossible to set limits to the depths of this perfectly natural consciousness in those who possess it at all. The material foundation of these hopes is better understood than it was in Browning's day. If there is still no rational justification for their ultimate demands, there is at least much stronger warrant for their existence. The more material we make our evidence, the further from crude Materialism are we carried.

Browning returned from La Saisiaz to write *The Two Poets of Croisic*, which is notable for one of his shortest and most lovely lyrics, the prologue, and for the charming " pretty tale " of the cricket and the minstrel with which it ends. In the last volumes we are never safe from beauties that make the strictures to which they incline us look ridiculous. Indeed the six volumes which came from him during the closing eleven years of his life abound once more in lyrical pieces, including some of his most famous love-songs. They suggest that his imagination could never grow old.

With that sudden turning away from past haunts, and occupations no longer congenial when the companion with whom he had enjoyed them was dead, after the loss of Miss Egerton-Smith Browning abandoned the concert-room as decisively as he had abandoned Florence after his wife's funeral. Moreover, the death of this friend was a break in his habits in other ways. It closed the long series of autumn holidays on the fringes of France. There was no friend now to beckon him and his sister to some spot which they had not yet explored in the North, and with old age coming on he needed to be beckoned. Where was warmth to be found, where a spot in itself sufficient to summon him ? Inevitably the thought of Italy reawoke. Pen was now launched as an artist, and was certain to be drawn to Italy again. Browning's sister had never visited it. There was sun and warmth and beauty, to which perhaps he would have yielded earlier if his friends, from the Milsands to Miss Egerton-Smith, had not kept him this side of the Alps. For seventeen years he had had Northern holidays. He was now ripe for Italy again.

VI

With the natural tendency to revisit his earliest glimpses of its beauties, the choice seemed to lie between Asolo and Naples. Florence was not to be thought of. Rome also he knew too well. He was drawn toward Asolo and Venice, and at the end of August 1878 he left with his sister for the summit of the Splügen Pass. There they paused before making a leisurely descent into Lombardy. It was amusing to watch the travellers come and go, to have the sense of companionship without society. The mountain air and long walks, sometimes extending to five hours, intensified his natural vigour, and it was here that he produced many of the poems soon to form the collection called *Dramatic Idylls.* " Donald," that terrible picture of a sportsman, and the grim story of " Ivan Ivanovitch " seem to have been written with great rapidity at this time. As his way was, when in a productive mood, stories that had long lain at the back of his mind half forgotten would well up in his imagination unsummoned. "Donald " was a memory of something that he had heard more than forty years before. He believed that his best things came to him in this fashion, but " Donald " is not his " best."

The friend that he was soon to make in Venice, the characteristic friend of this Venetian sunset of his life, Mrs. Bronson, records that he had used to see Asolo in his dreams with the cry " Do let us go there ! " only to be hurried out of its sight by some mysterious stranger who accompanied him. With his arrival in the little city, not greatly changed from his early memories of it nearly half a century before, the dream, having been fulfilled, no longer troubled him. He found no exaggerations in his memories of the place, and even the echo that he had once located, in a particular corner of ruined castle above the town, returned his greeting. Some children playing near when he was repeating his old experiment tried it themselves, but, not having his secret of the precise angle from which to call, received no answer. " Perhaps the mighty secret will die with me," the poet said. He missed, it is true, the little inn at which he had once stayed, but found instead another like it with " primitive arrangements and unsophisticated ways ; but there is cleanliness, abundance of good will, and the sweet Italian smile at every mistake." He loved the Italians, and the chiselled features that he often noticed in the workmen about a house would remind him, but for their want of regal robes, of some magnifico in Tintoretto's pictures. The primitive inn at Asolo was soon exchanged for a quieter and more comfortable hotel in Venice, and he did not quite " renew his ancient rapture " in Asolo until a year or two later when he stayed at Asolo under Mrs. Bronson's care.

There were interruptions to these Italian holidays, however, and sometimes the illness of his sister or, in 1882, a flood at Verona and a severe chill caught at St. Pierre de Chartreuse prevented him from reaching Venice. In 1884 his sister was not strong enough to go further than St. Moritz, and two years later the same cause kept them to this country. They stayed in Wales at Llangollen, not far from their friends Sir Theodore and Lady Martin, who had a country house at Brintysilio. The latter, when Miss Helen Faucit, had taken the parts of Lady Carlisle and Columbe in Browning's early plays. In a late letter to her he recalled the Vale of Llangollen and " delightful weeks, each tipped with a sweet starry Sunday at the little church " where he would attend the afternoon service. This was at the parish church at Llantysilio, in which his friend later placed a memorial tablet on the wall near where he used to sit. He was never a regular church-goer, but he was drawn to the chapels of the University colleges on his visits to Balliol, and Trinity College, Cambridge, and he responded to the little country churches or town chapels " where the worshippers are few " and sincere. Even in Venice, Mrs. Bronson tells us, he discovered a Waldensian chapel where an eloquent pastor preached. The atmosphere of ancient learning and of simple faith appealed to two inherited strains in his own nature, and where either spirit was in the background he preferred to stay away.

On his way to Venice, where he spent seven of the last eleven autumns of his life, he liked to break the journey at some spot in the mountains for the sake of the exhilarating air, the long walks, and the uninterrupted life which the cosmopolitan visitors to Venice made difficult for him. Twice he loitered at Saint-

Pierre la Chartreuse, often visiting the monastery and staying once to hear the midnight Mass. Twice he stopped at Gressoney Saint-Jean, finding its view of Monte Rosa worth the strenuous climb on mule-back up the mountain, but Gressoney became too difficult of access for his sister after the second year. She must also have been vigorous, however, for on leaving the place, in 1885, she was his companion on the long trudge down to San Martino d'Aosta, which took them seven hours without rest or refreshment by the way.

The most important to him of these visits to Venice was the one that took place in 1880, for it was on this occasion that the Storys introduced him to Mrs. Bronson, who did much to make his holidays delightful in that and subsequent years. He had made his quarters at a quiet hotel, the dilapidated home of an Italian family in difficulties. When their fortunes had ebbed beyond repair, Mrs. Bronson, a hospitable American, placed at Browning's disposal a set of rooms in an annex to the Palazzo Giustiniani, her own home. The Brownings enjoyed these comfortable quarters again in 1885, and three years later Mrs. Bronson insisted that they should lodge under her own roof. While she respected his desire for repose, she entertained various distinguished people, and Browning would sometimes appear at her receptions in the evenings. For the most part his growing love of unvarying daily habits followed him to Venice, which he loved to explore on foot. The gondola was chiefly used to take him to the Lido for other walks on its quieter shore. From his walks in the city he would often bring back either news of some historic fact or site that he believed had been overlooked, or else some object that he had found in an old shop. He had always had some difficulty in restraining his collective propensities. In the evening there were Venetian comedies to hear by Gallini or Goldoni, and these years have an air of peace and splendour as if to symbolize the sunset glories of the poet's life.

He seemed, indeed, to be taking root in the city when his son came to live there in 1885. Partly to please the young man, Browning endeavoured to purchase the Palazzo Manzoni, which he considered the most beautiful house in Venice, but the negotiations broke down at the last moment. Two years later, however, Pen married Miss Fannie Coddington and soon afterwards bought the Palazzo Rezzonico, " a stately gem of the rococo " in Henry James's words. Browning thought that his son had made the necessary alterations with good taste, and was glad to see him happy in the sunshine in a place that offered him also an alternative Italian home. The Palazzo Rezzonico shortly became transformed into a sort of Browning shrine. The chapel was restored in memory of his mother by the young artist, and the father was surprised to find the rooms not only splendid but comfortable.

VII

The distinction with which Browning was being received in Venice was the social reflection of the influence that he was exerting in England. Such long poems as *Balaustion's Adventure* sold in some thousands within a few months of their publication, and new volumes of Selections continued to appear. He admitted himself that Tennyson and he were dividing the honours of poetry. There was, indeed, a kind of conservative reaction from the vast shock to traditional beliefs excited by Darwin's book a quarter of a century before. Browning came to be regarded as its natural point of rally : the poet who had survived it undismayed, and who still held many of the traditional beliefs after giving weight to objections and discussing the arguments based upon

Y

them. From this point of view he seemed to be a teacher worth study, and as many of his poems were difficult, these two motives readily combined. They suddenly inspired Dr. Furnival and Miss E. H. Hickey to found the Browning Society, which took shape in 1881. It was a singular, if embarrassing, honour to be paid to a poet in his lifetime; but the later Victorians took the arts gravely, and a Ruskin Society was also formed. The poet first treated the project as a joke, and then did not oppose it. Indeed it is a tribute to his good sense that though the society aroused some ridicule in England, where intellectual movements are thought ridiculous, and they rarely seem at home in English life, this ridicule spared Browning. In public he left the society to itself, though he was patient in answering questions by private inquiry from its members. It is also the English way to reserve a place, perhaps two places, for ' grand old men ' in the arts as in politics, and thus to make amends to those who have survived long years of neglect. When once we had stopped Hardy from writing further novels, there was no limit to the adulation which we paid to his less disturbing poems. When Browning continued to write in his own way, heedless of our neglect, right into his seventh decade, we capitulated. A younger generation was doing all it could to repair the neglect of its elders, and a new succession of volumes stimulated the interest now widely awakened by the old.

In 1879 and 1880 two series of *Dramatic Idylls* appeared. Both collections may be described briefly as short stories in verse. They concern mainly the lives of humble people, for a change, and tragedy, humour, legend, are prominent in the first, as grotesque (particularly in " Pietro of Abano ") is in the second volume. Action, in the crisis of soul which a sudden decision may reveal, is the hub of both series. His love of animals inspired the fine story of a horse in " Muleykeh," and his hatred of indiscriminate vivisection the story of the dog " Tray," a kind of companion to that on the treachery that lurks in sportsmen, the ballad of " Donald," contained in the next volume, of 1883, *Jocoseria*. This is chiefly noteworthy for containing " Never the Time and the Place " and " Wanting is—What ? " which everyone, knowing them from anthologies, scarcely remembers to have been the product of Browning's old age. Here too is that little pungent scene, " Adam, Lilith, and Eve," not unlike one of Hardy's lyrics, only more human in its immediate irony. In the following year, 1884, appeared *Ferishtah's Fancies*, twelve parables in which Browning, easily recognizable in his Persian robes, gives his convictions on such subjects as prayer, the meaning of pain and evil, punishment present and to come, and the value of the little pleasures of the senses, for instance eating cherries. In spite of their merits, they seem to me to have more ethical than poetic interest, though, as if prepared for such an opinion, Browning interleaved his parables with some exquisite little songs. These contain the perfume as the Fancies were to comprise the flower. The epilogue is particularly beautiful.

Two more volumes were to complete his legacy to the world. In the *Parleyings with Certain People of Importance in their Day*, published in 1887, the monologue becomes a colloquy, but on the whole there is more abstract discussion than human personality in the book. Bernard de Mandeville (whose " Fable of the Bees " to illustrate his famous fallacy that private vices are public benefits has lately been reprinted) is invoked to prove that evil is the servant of good in the world; Daniel Bartoli to illustrate how much more moving is the true story of the duke and the heroic daughter of the druggist than a pious fable; Christopher Smart to explain the one great moment of poetic impulse in his

life; Bubb Dodington to expound the higher roguery
of democratic politics, possibly with Gladstone, from
whom Browning had recoiled over the Irish question,
in the poet's mind; Furini man, artist and priest, to
discourse superbly on art and the study of the nude as
its chief glory, and at length upon the subject of evolution. Gerard de Lairesse takes up the theme of landscape art, and this parleying contains some of Browning's
most splendid poetic landscape-pictures; Charles Avison,
the organist of Newcastle, evokes a disquisition on
music, and Browning adds a chorus of the train-bands
to the air of the composer's march.

The immense treasures of Browning's learning and
imagination are lavished on this volume, in which, however, for many people philosophic discussion occupies
too large a place. We are compelled to ask if poetry
should be set to glorify the solid materials of prose,
and it is one of the paradoxes of Browning's temperament that he was, in person, both a poet and a scholarly
man of the world, and, in poetry, a critic of ideas and
systems, no less than a lyrical singer; as curious of the
human heart and mind, as if he were only a story-teller,
as noble a song-maker of love and death and natural
beauty as if he had no more prosaic interests at all.
The *Parleyings* comprise a kind of epitome of all these
preoccupations, and, as if to leave nothing out, the
epilogue to the book debates the advantages and abuses
of the invention of printing.[1] With a genial tilt and
unabated vigour the whole globe seems made to spin
on the point of the poet's pen. It is difficult to judge
how much our confusion is due to the poet's excess
and how much to our own abasement before his evident
superiority. *Asolando*, light and lovely by contrast, was
published on the day of his death.

[1] The concluding paper, on "The Effect of Printing on
Literature," in *Critical Essays* was written, as the curious may
discover, independently of this poem.

VIII

In June 1887 Browning moved from Warwick Crescent to a more commodious house in De Vere Gardens, which enabled him at last to unpack his father's curious library and to display the treasures that he had collected in Italy for many years. He was as fond of old furniture as his father had been of old books, and he had discovered, after long waiting, a house fitted to accommodate them. Yet, under the surface of almost his usual activity, he gave signs, to his friends if not to himself, that he was at last growing old. In the new house were written some of the shorter poems included in his last volume, *Asolando* ; and, during the year 1888, he was busy revising the last, uniform edition of his works to be published in his lifetime. The summer of 1887 he spent with his sister at St. Moritz, at the villa of one of his American friends. The winter proved trying for his strength, and with the task of revision behind him, he was glad to start for Italy, in August 1888, resting at Primiero, near Feltre, before descending to Venice. When he returned in the following February, his health seemed to be restored, but the journeys both ways had proved so exhausting that he had said he did not expect to return to Italy again. The English climate, however, has arguments which no one who is not a prisoner can resist, and the weather was so abominable in August that he was glad to make the attempt again. Moreover, Mrs. Bronson had invited him to stay with her at Asolo, where she had made for herself a house on the edge of one of the old walls of the little city.

Browning was near by, and unfortunately he lingered through October in rooms that had no fire-places. He was strangely blind to the need for taking care, and even attributed his breathlessness to the ' mountain ' air of

Asolo. He seems to have been not well, as he thought, but in a state of nervous excitement. His brain teemed with the historical associations of the spots about him, and his imagination was almost feverishly responsive to the beauty under his eyes. All that had delighted him in earlier years drew him with a new, intense pleasure. On his walks, Mrs. Orr tells us, " he would peer into the hedges for what living things were to be found there. He would whistle softly to the lizards basking on the low walls which border the roads, to try his old power of attracting them." He even proposed to buy a ruined house in Asolo, to rebuild it and call it Pippa's Tower, but the negotiations were not finished until he reached Venice, and permission for the sale was not finally granted until the day of his death.

His evenings were spent with music or reading, and when he read aloud his own poems, with dramatic emphasis as was his wont, it is interesting to learn that they always seemed perfectly clear to his listeners. English, not being an inflected or even a grammatical language, is not precise. The meaning of a sentence often depends upon the order of the words and the accent given temporarily to one of them. In poetry, where inversions are allowed, the meaning is often obscure until the grammatical order and the intended emphasis have been guessed. Perhaps the chief criticism to which Browning's magnificently idiomatic style lies open is that it imposes too much guesswork on the reader, especially, of course, when the sentences are parenthetically prolonged. To minimize this Browning, latterly and under the advice of Milsand, took great pains with his punctuation, but, to take a ready example, there are people who find the meaning of the first two verses of the famous epilogue to *Asolando* not at once clear. From the point of view of a schoolmaster, these stanzas would be an amusing exercise for boys to parse.

They are the most familiar example from Browning of the inconvenience of a language with no genders, no inflections, few tenses, and the fewest rules. To have heard Browning read one of his obscure passages must often have been a revelation, and since he wrote by ear, for sense if not for sound so much, doubtless he was honestly puzzled that he should be a puzzle to others. His method of reading aloud, always contrasted with the sonorous chant of Tennyson, gives a hint of value on the nature of his style. Its appeal is to the ear, but rather as the actor or conversationalist uses it than as the musician, though, of course, Browning is full of music too. The epilogue to *Asolando* is a very musical piece of verse, but it is the paradox of this manner of writing that the mind's ear and the body's do not seem mutually satisfied, as they finally are in these stanzas, until a flash of divination has taken place. The sound is " an echo of the sense " only after the sense has been fully grasped. In the epilogue to *Asolando*, who is " you " ?

IX

At the end of October, 1889, he left Asolo for the last time, and joined his son and daughter-in-law in their palatial home in Venice. He was constantly thinking of a tragedy that he hoped would surpass his previous works, and when honours and medals came to his son at exhibitions he was as much pleased as he had been over the admiration that had been given to his wife. A complete edition of her writings was also being issued at this time. The curious exaltation in which he was living is shown by a little incident. At a dinner party Browning met a London doctor, and in proof of his good health offered him his pulse to feel. The doctor drew an exactly opposite conclusion, but doubtless kept this to himself. So the daily walks in all weathers were continued until one foggy day he returned from the Lido with a bronchial cold. He refused to go to bed, and on November 29th he even talked of travelling in a few days to England, " though scarcely fit," he wrote, for the fatigue. The next evening he was worse, and on the following day an Italian doctor was summoned and saw that the condition was grave. His heart was showing signs of exhaustion. Despite an apparent rally during the early days of December, his doctors thought recovery unlikely, and on Thursday, December 12th, he became much weaker. At five o'clock that afternoon he said to one of his nurses, " I feel much worse. I now know that I must die," and at ten o'clock he was dead. " His death," one of the doctors remarked to his son, " was what death ought to be, but rarely is." On the same day his publisher had telegraphed to him the welcome extended to his last volume, *Asolando*, which had appeared that morning, and its concluding lines have become sacred from this association as seeming to be the fittest epitaph we could compose.

The English cemetery at Florence in which Mrs. Browning had been buried was now closed, and while the family were endeavouring to have the ban on further interments lifted, the offer came from England of burial in Westminster Abbey. According to the Venetian custom the body had to be removed within a short time to the mortuary island of San Michele, and its passage in the municipal barge was made the occasion of a public funeral. Venice bore the great poet with honour to his rest, and placed a tablet on the walls of the Rezzonico Palace recording his residence there. The inscription concluded with two of his own lines :

> Open my heart and you will see
> Graved inside of it " Italy."

Asolo placed a similar tablet on the house he had in-
habited in the little city.   On December 31st, 1889, he
was buried in Poets' Corner.   His wife would have been
buried with him had sentiment allowed her coffin to be
disturbed, but verses from her poem " The Sleep " were
sung over him, and at the Abbey funeral they were not
divided.

CHAPTER EIGHT

CONCLUSIONS

MR. W. B. YEATS once called William Morris " the happiest of the poets " because there was a depth of lazy summer sunshine in his verses and the dreamy content of tilth and orchard and happy labour in his style. With Browning we have the same thing with a difference, the full, vivid life of a poet who was also a man of the world. The tone in Browning is that of the city and the salon, where the life of art and intelligence, restless and curious, replaces the dreamy content of the fields. When we think of his gifts and his opportunities, Browning seems one of the luckiest of men. His home was a very happy one. He never had to work for hire. No obstacles stood in the way of the poetry to which he devoted himself. In love he was equally fortunate. After waiting many years he found the woman whom he had begun to despair of finding, and the strange obstacles in the way of their union were overcome in a little less than two years. The great responsibility that he then undertook was successfully shouldered, and he enjoyed fifteen unclouded years of married life. With her beside him, he did not find it hard to wait for other recognition, and from the first he was valued by a few. Before he had earned an income from his poetry he and his wife were left a fortune by a friend, and during his life he scarcely had a day's illness. He lived to be nearly eighty and his powers of production did not flag.

For the last twelve years of his life he shared with Tennyson the highest honours in his own country and was also famous in Italy, his second home. He had a son to whom he was devoted, and whose success as a painter was the pride of his old age, and, for a final touch, he died in his son's palace on the Grand Canal at Venice on the very day when the most popular of his works appeared.

As man and artist he was masculine to the core. There was no eccentricity or want of balance in his genius. His life and work prove that the supposed alliance of great wits to madness is not essential. In everything but his magnificent endowment he was an ordinary being, and he used his imagination so plentifully that his works form a literature in themselves. He had an immense capacity for affection, and this capacity was equalled by his wife. The only circumstance that hit him to the heart was her death when both were only middle-aged. In gifts, in love, in fortune Fate played into his hands. If this world had been his main concern, he would have had almost everything, but he looked beyond it, and the great question What lay beyond was bound up for him with the loss of his wife. Human love had meant everything to him. Consequently, when death took her away, the centre of his being hung in the balance, and his inner life was ruled by hope and fear for nearly thirty years after she died.

It is clear that only a remarkable woman could have held and maintained this central place in a life of such splendid energy. She was as nearly his religion as one person can be to another. If their love had suffered shipwreck except by death, it would have been tragic for both of them. They possessed the experience as rare in fact as it is common in fiction. It survived every test. He was thirty-three before he became engaged;

he was a husband for fifteen years; he lived for twenty-eight years a widower. There was only one love in his life, and only one in hers. Despite all the conventions to the contrary, this is a strange and wonderful thing. Among love-stories it is a fairy-tale, and it is true.

That two human beings capable of this experience should realize it together is exceptional, that both should also be poets is doubly strange. In their life and in their work they were the complementary opposites of one another. She was feminine to the marrow, and only became a complete poet when she put her woman's response to his love into her verse. The very circumstances of her early years were the feminine counterpart of his. He had all the world before him, masculine energy and a free life. She had ill-health, a sofa and her books only. In her family she was a prisoner living at the whim of her autocratic father, whereas he was happy and untrammelled in his home. Both were scholars and widely read, but, unlike him, she preserved the innocence of childlike faith quite untroubled by her reading or the scepticism of her time. There can be little doubt that he reposed upon her certainties, and found in her the finest witness to the beliefs that he struggled to hold. When he lost her he lived, to take a phrase from his essay on Shelley, "in that depth of conviction which is so like despair." In her company the hopes that Shelley had assaulted in his youth, and that his generation continued to attack, almost became faith again, but a faith, like health, once lost, never recovers its simplicity. Her love and her death were the two crucial facts in his life, and both help to explain much of the work he wrote after he had lost her. Perhaps we may sum up their relation by saying that she was that which Shelley had promised, but failed to remain, to him: a lyric poet of love "showing the correspondency of the natural to the spiritual," a human being " tender and sincere " who, through her capacity for love, radiated something of divine power and influence.

Beyond the facts that both poets had their roots in the Romantic Movement, that love and hope were the bases of their creed, and that both refused to turn their backs on the world of men and women, little comparison is possible between them. Her best work confined itself to love in a personal relation. His imagination, not purer but much richer than hers, travelled over the world and delighted to study and analyse the individuals in it. In her Sonnets she left a beautiful portrait of herself. Rarely speaking in his own person, he created a great gallery of portraits, and he put also into verse discussions of the great questions that agitated him and his time. He was also a great teller of stories, for a portrait by Browning gives us the drama of a life. The vividness in which his work excels is heightened by his use of idiomatic English so that, at his best, he makes the whole tongue seem poetical, while his flatter passages, as William Sharp showed by quotation, if printed as prose would not look out of place. It is impossible to read him anywhere, however, without realising that he is a great master of English. Only one poet is estimated to have had a larger vocabulary, and the amount of his poetry is, I believe, the largest. Shakespeare did not leave so much.

Both poets were in the Puritan tradition, and both were individualists : she in a wayward feminine fashion, he in a vigorous masculine one. Both were keenly alive to the facts and ideas about them, but, whereas she took what she wanted and left the rest, and was interested in public movements, he grappled with all he observed and was less interested in movements than in men. The scientific tendencies of the day encouraged a few hopes in her but left her untroubled. In him they awoke an already restless intellect to life that he might defend by rational argument the rationalistic assault on cherished beliefs. Very many of his characters are presented to us in the moral dilemmas that engaged him and his time so that, though his range is very wide, there is a want of detachment in his treatment. His work arouses interest and curiosity because so much of it is related to a point of view, and it remains to be seen how far this will be fatal to its permanence. While there is no doubt that the core of his poetry will endure, there is little doubt that his longer and later poems, except *The Ring and the Book*, have failed to retain their readers.

With this great poem she is connected in more than the passages addressed to her. Pompilia is one of his very few idealized creations. The feeling that she had for Caponsacchi and for her child are quick with memories of Mrs. Browning as the poet remembered her at the time of her betrothal and her motherhood. But with this poem she does not vanish from his work. She is in the beautiful epilogue to *Fifine at the Fair*, in the reserve claimed for his private life by the poems " At the Mermaid " and " House " in the *Pacchiarotto* volume, and it is possible that " Fears and Scruples " would not have taken quite this poignant form had she been still alive. Anyway *La Saisiaz*, occasioned by the sudden death of Miss Egerton-Smith almost at his door, argues the hope of survival and re-meeting so intensely that the question, " Was ending ending once and always, when you died ? " is clearly a recurrence to the problem underlying all his thoughts since 1861. In *Jocoseria*, in the exquisite songs " Wanting is—What ? " where he calls the world a " framework which waits for a picture to frame," and in " Never the Time and the Place " even more plainly, the old desire appears :

> Do I hold the Past
> Thus firm and fast
> Yet doubt if the Future hold I can ?
> This path so soft to pace shall lead
> Thro' the magic of May to herself indeed !
> Or narrow if needs the house must be,
> Outside are the storms and strangers : we—
> Oh, close, safe, warm sleep I and she,
> —I and she !

She is in one or two of the songs that interleave
Ferishtah's Fancies, and the haunting epilogue even asks
if all his hopes of eternal life may not be the reflection
of what she had given to him :

> Only at heart's utmost joy and triumph, terror
>   Sudden turns the blood to ice : a chill wind disencharms
> All the late enchantment !   What if all be error—
>   If the halo irised round my head were, Love, thine arms ?

This, I think, is the only place in which Browning
carries his doubts to the point of asking if human love
may not be our highest reality, the promise and foundation of Nothing beyond. It would be tedious to
enumerate the several references to her in the little poems
that help to make *Asolando* a priceless volume. It is
better to quote two of the less well-known. First
" Speculative " and then the first and most terrible of
the " Bad Dreams " : they speak for themselves :

> Others may need new life in Heaven—
>   Man, Nature, Art—made new, assume !
> Man with new mind old sense to leaven,
>   Nature—new light to clear old gloom,
>   Art that breaks bounds, gets soaring-room.

> *I* shall pray : " Fugitive as precious—
>   Minutes which passed,—return, remain !
> Let earth's old life once more enmesh us,
>   You with old pleasure, me—old pain,
>   So we but meet nor part again ! "

> Bad Dreams.   I.
> Last night I saw you in my sleep :
>   And how your charm of face was changed !
> I asked " Some love, some faith you keep ? "
>   You answered " Faith gone, love estranged."
>
> Whereat I woke—a twofold bliss :
>   Waking was one, but next there came
> This other : " Though I felt, for this,
>   My heart break, I loved on the same."

The dead poet must pardon us for reading these references into his work.   What he has written he has written, be his protestations what they may.   In truth, he himself did not deny that he *was* speaking of himself in the fine third verse of the epilogue to *Asolando* :

> One who never turned his back but marched breast forward,
>   Never doubted clouds would break,
> Never dreamed, though right were worsted, wrong would triumph,
>   Held we fall to rise, are baffled to fight better,
>   Sleep to wake.

If his own voice can be heard in this passage, it can be overheard in the little poems quoted above.   He kept his courage, and, if baffled, trusted that this was in order that his courage might be proved.   It was tested severely during his long years of widowerhood, and his manner hardened.   What may be called ossification is apparent in his later work.

His loneliness tried three means of distraction : a short period of slightly morbid seclusion, a phase of active social life, and, to justify this last, a tendency to concentrate on long narrative poems and long philosophical discourses.   People may be excused for not attempting *Red Cotton Night-Cap Country* or *The Inn Album*, though a good critic has called the former " of all Browning's works perhaps the easiest to read."   This opinion is worth remembering.   The long poems of this period are often dismissed without trial because by the time people have read what everyone reads they have had enough of Browning *La Saisiaz* is only not too long. The parables in *Ferishtah's Fancies* are not, I think, completely successful, and, despite the splendid passages in the colloquy with Gerard de Lairesse, the *Parleyings* are essays in verse rather than fine poems, and inconclusive. Nothing can alter the fact that verse is the wrong medium for abstract argument, and Browning threw into verse matter that other poets would have put into essays. Had he written Wordsworth's prefaces and Shelley's pamphlets, he would have put them into verse. What is the appropriate term for writings which we feel that only a great poet could have written, but which we do not want to read ? *Aristophanes' Apology* is a masterly portrait, but it contains such a wealth of learned allusion that probably it can only be appreciated by readers who are also profound scholars. The considered opinion of Meredith upon this poem would have been worth having. The stories that compose the *Dramatic Idylls* vary in quantity, but even " Ivan Ivanovitch " is too long. With the short pieces in *Jocoseria*, and particularly in *Asolando*, there is a wonderful and welcome return to the freshness of youth. It is an astonishing record of productivity in which the quantity becomes an enemy to itself.

When these long poems are compared with the twelve parts of *The Ring and the Book*, a comparison that we are entitled to make, we feel a glory to have departed, the method to have survived the old magic, though a great poet is in the background all the time. The moment we descend from total to particular impressions a more favourable estimate reappears. But the best is the best notwithstanding, and, if we were forced to choose, we should sacrifice the poems that succeeded *The Ring and the Book* to the poetry that culminated there. The interest and excitement of this poetry are not only local

z

or temporary adjuncts which detract from it with the passage of time; they are often definitely part of the poetry itself. If it be still urged that the poetry of Browning loses for want of repose, the reply is that, in these poems, we do not miss it but are carried by the poet while we read into his own world of vigorous healthy imagination, a world so rich, vivid, and finely fashioned that it is one of the most original and dramatic possessions of our literature. In this legacy her letters are the framework and her *Sonnets from the Portuguese* the central point of rest. The poet and the lover are enshrined there by the woman best entitled to know and to describe the twofold being that he was.

SHORT BIBLIOGRAPHY

Elizabeth Barrett Browning. By John H. Ingram, 1888.
The Letters of Elizabeth Barrett Browning. Edited by F. G. Kenyon (2 vols., 1897).
The Letters of Robert Browning and Elizabeth Barrett Barrett (2 vols., 1899).
Records of Tennyson, Ruskin and the Brownings. By Anne Ritchie, 1892.
Elizabeth Barrett Browning in her Letters. By Percy Lubbock, 1906.
The Note-Books of Nathaniel Hawthorne.
Memories of Hawthorne. By Rose Hawthorne Lathrop, 1923.
La Vie et l'œuvre d'Elizabeth Browning. By Mlle. Germaine-Marie Merlette, 1906.
The Works of Edgar Allan Poe, Vol. IV. Criticisms. Edited by J. H. Ingram, 1899.

Life and Letters of Robert Browning. By Mrs. Sutherland Orr, 1891.
Robert Browning : Personalia. By Edmund Gosse, 1890.
Robert Browning. By Edward Dowden, 1904.
The Brownings : their Life and Art. By Lilian Whiting, 1911.
Robert Browning and Alfred Domett. Edited by F. G. Kenyon, 1906.
Browning. By G. K. Chesterton (*English Men of Letters*), 1908.
Handbook to the Works of Browning. By Mrs. Sutherland Orr.
An Introduction to the Study of Browning. By Arthur Symons, enlarged edition, 1916.
Essays on Browning's Poetry. By J. T. Nettleship, 1868.
The Poetry of Robert Browning. By Stopford Brooke, 1902.
George Chapman : A Critical Essay. By A. C. Swinburne.
The Browning Society's Papers.

INDEX